About the author

Robin Lee Riley is an assistant
professor in the Women's and
Gender Studies Department,
Syracuse University.

Depicting the veil

Transnational sexism and the war on terror

ROBIN LEE RILEY

Zed Books

LONDON | NEW YORK

Depicting the veil: transnational sexism and the war on terror was first published in 2013 by Zed Books Ltd, 7 Cynthia Street, London N1 9JF, UK and Room 400, 175 Fifth Avenue, New York, NY 10010, USA

www.zedbooks.co.uk

Set in OurType Arnhem and Monotype Futura by Ewan Smith, London
Index: ed.emery@thefreeuniversity.net
Cover design: www.alice-marwick.co.uk
Printed and bound by CPI Group (UK) Ltd, Croydon, CR0 4YY

FSC
www.fsc.org
MIX
Paper from
responsible sources
FSC® C013604

Distributed in the USA exclusively by Palgrave Macmillan, a division of St Martin's Press, LLC, 175 Fifth Avenue, New York, NY 10010, USA

A catalogue record for this book is available from the British Library
Library of Congress Cataloging in Publication Data available

ISBN 978 1 78032 129 5 hb
ISBN 978 1 78032 128 8 pb

Contents

Acknowledgments

This book is partly inspired by an Iraqi woman I met while walking at Green Lakes State Park near my home. We had a funny and, for me, haunting interaction, in part due to my lack of Arabic and her new English that had me thinking about her for a long time afterward.

I am grateful to the department of Women's and Gender Studies at Syracuse University for a leave and for support on this project. Gwen Pough's refusal to entertain my doubts about whether I could write this book meant more than I can say. I was reminded again and again while writing about the enduring importance of the work of Chandra Talpade Mohanty. Vivian May provided outstanding feminist solidarity. My love and gratitude go to my chosen family, Hannah Britton, Diane Fine, Nancy Cantor and Steve Brechin, Naeem Inayatullah and Sorayya Khan. Your love and support lift me again and again. Dana Olwan is an amazing person and a brilliant scholar whose friendship has been a gift and an inspiration. Given the nature of this work, happy distractions are critical. Thanks to my family for faith and patience and for getting and staying healthy. Deb Ford was a great cheerleader (in a good way). Matt Himley and Reecia Orzeck give great conversation and NBA stats. The unexpected but much-longed-for appearance in my life of Robyn and John, Griffin and Lewey Vincent has enriched it beyond description. Harvey Milk Riley-Himley and June Jordan Himley-Riley are such wonderful companions who make me laugh every day. Margaret, as always, I'm so lucky.

for Robyn

Introduction

> Three allegorical figures have come to dominate the social land-
> scape of the 'war on terror' and its ideological underpinning of a
> clash of civilizations: the dangerous Muslim man, the imperiled
> Muslim woman, and the civilized European, the latter a figure who
> is seldom explicitly named but who nevertheless anchors the first
> two figures. (Razack 2008: 5)

Aafia Siddiqui, Huda Saleh Ammash, Aesha Mohammadzai, Rihab
Taha, Amal Ahmed Abdel-Fateh al Sada Fattah. These are not household names in the West and yet they are all women whose lives have
been irrevocably altered by encounters with the West.[1] These are the
names of some of the faceless, disembodied women for whom the
'war on terror' has meant unwanted notoriety, loss of loved ones, false
accusations, displacement from home, and demonization. These are
their names. Contact with the West in the form of government and
media attention has meant that these few women who actually have
the attention of the Western media – most women don't – further
lose their identity as persons because, instead of being identified by
their names in the Western press, they are now called: the woman
without her nose on the *Time* magazine cover, Dr Germ, Mrs Anthrax,
the female al-Qaeda, and Osama bin Laden's wife. This lack of identification, misidentification, or renaming has its roots in the history
of colonialism, in Orientalism, in visibility/invisibility problems for
women in wartime (see Riley 2008), and in transnational sexism. The
war on terror, like any other war, has enormous impact on the lives
of women.

Since September 11th 2001,[2] media of various forms in the United
States and among English-speaking Western allies have been focused
on Osama bin Laden and 'terrorism.' The media creates and elaborates
ideas of who this 'terrorist' enemy is and how 'they' came to 'hate
us.' The concept of terrorism in this discourse is something that only
happens to the West. It is never perpetrated by the West. By way of
attempting to provide some explanation for the events of September
11th 2001, hundreds of stories were told on television, newspapers,
magazines, radio, etc., that included expositions on Islam, terror, jihad,

and shortly thereafter, war. In most of these stories, women are not mentioned at all.[3] In other versions, they are mentioned only as victims, coupled with children, as collateral damage from Western bombs, or as duped and oppressed by men with brown skin. Still others point to Afghan and later Iraqi women, indeed all Muslim women (even though not all women from Afghanistan and Iraq are Muslim[4]), as dangerous, as the mothers of baby jihadists, as creators of weapons of mass destruction, and as walking – veiled – threats to Western well-being. The story of women in the war on terror is told by a media preoccupied with drawing lines between 'us' and 'them' in order to shape an enemy. This enemy is gendered and raced yet is abstruse. In order to create and maintain it, then, a complicated endeavor must be engaged so that the enemy can become immediately recognizable. As part of this effort, people of various religions and nationalities are lumped under one rubric (Arab), one religion (Islam), and one practice (terror).

In the buildup to the war on Afghanistan, people in the US were told that invading Afghanistan was necessary not only because it was believed that Afghanistan was hiding Osama bin Laden and hordes of other 'terrorists,' but also because the situation for women in that country was terrible and needed to be rectified. In the words of Gayatri Spivak (1988), we in the West had to 'save brown women from brown men.' Similarly, in her work in mapping the geopolitical consequences of the war on terror on Muslim men and women, Sherene Razack writes: 'Globally, while Muslim men have been the target of an intense policing, Muslim women have been singled out as needing protection from their violent and hyper-patriarchal men' (Razack 2008: 4).

This pretense of concern for the rights of Afghan women is impor-tant to note because it marks the beginning of almost a decade of depictions of first Aghan and later Iraqi women (and indeed all women believed correctly or incorrectly by the Western media to be Muslim) as weak and in need of rescuing, and simultaneously as mysterious, dangerous, and evil.

Is this possible? Can these women simultaneously be oppressed and powerful, dangerous and vulnerable? In part, this depiction of Afghan and Iraqi women is accomplished by practicing transnational sexism[5] in presenting these women in contrast to the 'liberated' woman of the West.[6] Transnational sexism, as I use the concept in this instance, is the deployment, use, and propagation of ideas about Muslim women to Western audiences. It functions through popular culture, where it is spread by a multibillion-dollar industry of newspapers, magazines, the internet, and radio as 'news' and in film, TV shows, novels, etc., as 'art.' The logic of transnational sexism, while centralized around the assumption of Muslim women's oppression, is simultaneously contradictory: at times, it imagines Muslim women to be objects or victims in need of rescue and saving from local patriarchs while it also imagines these very same Muslim women to be subjects of terror and fear. These contrasts hinge on constructions of race, along with the practices of gender, and with participation in global capitalism as both workers and consumers. In these comparisons, Western women have freedoms – sexual, occupational, cultural – that Muslim women do not. Consequently, as the story from the Western perspective goes, women from those regions, those religions – over there – are under the control of primitive, brutal, fundamentalist men who would imprison women and brainwash them in order to have them under their sway. In this scenario, Western men are posited as liberal and free-thinking, and appreciative of every aspect of female liberation. They therefore pose no threat to the women of Afghanistan and Iraq. On the contrary, Western men are the potential saviors of these women.

In the West women continue to be used to promote or justify war in spite of the West's belief in itself as a bastion of forward think-ing about women's rights and gender expression. The perils imposed by Western military actions on women are ignored, and Iraqi and Afghan women associated in various ways with 'the enemy' are de-picted (along with Western women soldiers) in either stereotypical ways associated with the practice of femininity, that is as helpless victims, or alternatively as exceptional – suicide bombers or weapons creators.[7]

For people in Afghanistan and Iraq, it was not enough that col-onialism disrupted gender relations in those parts of the world under the control of the Western imperial powers. The occupation this time, the new imperialism, has meant that the West attempts to impose a second disruption of gender relations.

> Gender operates as a kind of technology of empire enabling the West to make the case for its own modernity and for its civilizational projects around the globe. Where gender is relied upon in this way, Muslim women find themselves stranded between the patriarchs of their own community and the empire's bombs. That is, either we accept the diag-nosis that our cultures and our men are barbaric and take the cure (the bombs on our heads and the camps), or we endure patriarchal violence. (Razack 2008: 18)

The situation that Sherene Razack describes above is key to

3

understanding the conundrum in which Iraqi and Afghan women find themselves. The current disruption of gender relations is more widespread as it is assisted by the power of Western media that is now available through various means – television, film, the web, etc. – around the world, and the persuasion is assisted by the expenditure of millions of dollars, euros, or British pounds by Western governments on public relations. Under the reordering of gender relations, a Westernized definition of liberation for women prevails. Dubious as this 'liberation' is, it is pointed to by Western governments and media as a sign that conditions are improving for women there, that Afghan and Iraqi men are being 'tamed' or 'civilized' by the presence of Western soldiers. Women in Afghanistan, then, can participate in *Afghan Idol*, they can play soccer, become police officers. Iraqi women can have unnecessary Caesarean sections (Associated Press 2010). Muslim women throw off traditional dress in favor of Western miniskirts. They pose for *Playboy*. This is liberation.

The study

Following the events of September 11th 2001 in the United States, I was struck by how race was invoked to both fashion the enemy and to shape a newly united American populace, how class became momentarily visible inside the US in the form of rescue workers, firefighters, and police, and how the reactions to the events of that day were so very gendered. I have argued elsewhere that the attacks on the World Trade Center and the Pentagon constituted an assault on the masculinity of the United States. Thus the status of the US as a world military and economic power was assailed. The penetration of the airplanes into those buildings in Manhattan could not be tolerated by a state so invested in flexing its military muscles around the world. Because the United States was and is so implicated in capitalist accumulation, so heavily reliant on military might, so invested in the production of weapons, a potent masculinized, militarized response was required. The invasion of Afghanistan and then Iraq and the accompanying governmental and media propaganda efforts that told the story of September 11th 2001 and the subsequent bombings and occupations are suffused with Western (read white) militarized masculinity (Kellner 2004: 145). The government and media created a narrative about who Osama bin Laden, Saddam Hussein, the Taliban, al-Qaeda, and ultimately Muslims were and are that is so misguided, so full of Orientalism, racism, justifications of Western imperialism, and gender assumptions, that, to me at least, it required urgent analytical intervention.

I was surprised to see so little attention paid to gender in the analysis of September 11th and the resulting war on terror. That surprise grew as I witnessed the parading of women members of the Bush administration – Mary Matalin, Paula Dobriansky, and Karen Hughes along with Laura Bush, wife of George Bush – to exhort women of the United States to articulate outrage over the treatment of women in Afghanistan by the Taliban (Stout 2001, Marks 2001, and others). This deployment of women exploiting the bonds of presumed 'sisterhood' to help legitimize imperialist wars was written about and commented on in Western media sources with some amusement but not much outrage. Some Western feminists agreed that the maltreatment of women by the Taliban in Afghanistan served as the justification for the bombings and subsequent invasion (Mahmood 2009, Russo 2006). This agreement helped silence dissent against the new imperialism. A few feminists raised voices in protest, and Fox News gleefully reported that the 'Iraq war may kill feminism as we know it,'[8] but we in the West still heard almost nothing from women in Afghanistan and Iraq.

When the full media assault began, only days after September 11th with a feature in the Sunday *New York Times Magazine* on Pakistani women (Addario 2001), I was struck by how women's lives and social roles and how ideas about the proper practice of gender were being combined with Orientalist ideas about who these women were/are along with the fantasy of white supremacist capitalist patriarchy (hooks 2005) to create a perception of danger. I realized that I had no idea who these women, in particular, really were beyond experiencing a vague sense of unease at the way they were raising their children (Addario 2001), being fantasized about as rewards for jihad (Raymond 2001; Heffernan 2005; Lister 2003; Dickey and Kovach 2002), or feared as the creators of Weapons of Mass Destruction (WMD) (Jelinek 2003b; Lowther 2003; Swanson 2003; Nasrawi 2003; Faris 2003). I imagined that the power of these interpellations was enormously persuasive to the majority of citizens untrained in media literacy, in analyzing popular culture, and in examining public discourse. I don't mean to suggest that the majority of people are not intellectually gifted; rather I am suggesting that many people only rarely ask questions about what they consume from the news, others don't ask enough questions. As Stuart Hall and others have suggested, we, all of us, would benefit from greater media literacy, especially in a time when tropes are rehearsed and repeated on endless loops. In this case, the public was manipulated into believing certain things about groups of people with whom they had little or no familiarity. I felt compelled, given white women's history of complicity and silence in matters of white men's imperialist desires, to speak out. I believe I am obligated, as a feminist, a white woman living in the US, an anti-racist, and an educator, to do something to interrupt the propagation of these racist and sexist depictions. It is after all white women's work to fight racism, to point to the ways we are implicated in racist practices and benefit from privilege, to refuse the veneration that comes about through nonsensical comparisons, and to interrupt patriarchal imperialist fantasies. White women need to point to the ways Western popular culture contributes to transnational sexism by dehumanizing all women, but particularly women of color, and by glorifying war and upholding harmful ideologies.

I started collecting pieces of 'news' about Afghan and Iraqi women as a way to make visible these oppressive practices and processes. Actually, this collection can be viewed as a way of making visible Afghan and Iraqi women generally, since they are so often absent in stories about the war or present as faceless, nameless victims of Afghan and Iraqi men and not of the occupying forces. Following in Cynthia Enloe's (2004) tradition of asking 'where are the women?'[9] in this study, I respond to that critical question by making Afghan and Iraqi women visible in ways that complicate and critique mainstream media representations. Not only do I want them to be visible here, but I also want to use their names, remove them from the abstract iconic figure of danger or innocence, and present them as *real* persons with complicated, multiple, and even contradictory histories, lives, narratives, and pursuits.

Over the last ten years, I have gathered hundreds of pieces of data from various sources that contain references to Afghan and Iraqi women, or that reference the wars in general. Mostly, the sources of these data are Western[10] newspapers, but there are also magazines and fictionalized television and feature film examples. In choosing which pieces of data to write about, I not only utilize the most startling examples of the argument I am trying to put forward, but I also recognize in my argument the preponderance of stories, images, or ideas. Doing content analysis, I attend to how issues or particular groups are generally talked about in order to place the stories in context. That is, I am not speaking from an argument about the exceptional but rather about the quotidian, for therein lies the power of these ideas and images. And these ideas circulate.

The materials were gathered using Lexis Nexis searches at first and then Google search alerts. Initially I also used newspaper alerts online from the *Washington Post* and the *New York Times* to gather materials before those services were suspended. The Google alerts were supplemented by periodic Lexis Nexis searches using search terms like 'Iraqi women,' 'Afghan women,' or particular names such as Aafia Siddiqui and Rihab Taha, as well as generalized terms such as 'Osama bin Laden's wife.' Given my screening of the results of all of these searches, I have looked at thousands of pieces of data and culled from that larger harvest hundreds of pieces from which to construct the book.

Secondarily, I have also amassed examples from popular culture of television programs, popular magazine articles, and feature films that deal with these topics. Again, overwhelmed with data, I carefully chose examples that were connected with each other and with similar examples from the 'news.' In this collection of data, one can observe the circulation of recurring tropes that become evidence of claims. For example, I had planned to write about the depiction of Muslim women that occurred in *Sex and the City 2* because it was so reminiscent of depictions of Muslim women in the news. *Law and Order* in its various iterations has run no fewer than seven episodes since September 11th 2001 that include a Muslim criminal, and the Showtime series *Homeland* places virtually all wartime atrocities in the hands of an amorphous Muslim enemy. Maureen Dowd writes about donning a burqa in Saudi Arabia which connects with Alissa Rubin's *New York Times* reporting from Afghanistan, and the internet and social media are full of 'jokes' about Osama bin Laden, Saddam Hussein, and George Bush and Tony Blair that have to do with ideas about masculinity and sexuality. Throughout history, jokes have been one means of circulating ideas about one's enemy.

Propaganda

> The enemy is a joint production. It is rarely a phenomenon achieved by any one person alone, but it is something done socially by all of us together. (Aho 1994: 6)

The conducting of war requires public support, and governments and the media have long gone hand in hand when it comes to the promotion of war and the creation of an enemy. Throughout US history, media-produced propaganda has assisted in this production (Bradley 1998; Finch 2000; Horten 2002; Koppes and Black 1990; Page 1996; McChesney 2008; Shaheen 2008). Generally, the public has little interest in or patience for exploration of international relations or global issues, and government leaders believe that citizens need to have complex international relations issues explained to them in simple, easily digested terms, hence, the emergence of propaganda as the primary means of understanding the state of the world (McChesney 2008).

Propaganda, as a means of information sharing, lends itself to various mediums. For example, ever since the creation of the film industry in the US, the proliferation of films glorifying war has helped us think of war as a noble enterprise, while showing men the most certain available route to the pinnacle of masculinity and heroism (Koppes and Black 1990).[11] In the five years prior to the first Persian Gulf War, and ever since, Hollywood has been busy creating for a US audience an Arab enemy[12] (Prince 1993: 239; Shaheen 2008). Contemporary propaganda sometimes takes the form of humor or play while utilizing Orientalism with its accompanying white heterosexist notions about masculinity to demasculinize and de-heterosexualize (Puar and Rai 2002: 1).

The creation of the enemy now consists of much more than simply Hollywood making films with Arab bad guys or newspapers printing political cartoons. The US government now hires public relations firms to 'manage' public information about the war. Some of these sources are quite traditional, as Hollywood has certainly done its best (or worst, as some have argued) to release several films that fit in the glorifying war category.[13] In the war on terror, however, other forms of media have joined the propaganda effort. We now rely mostly on television and the internet for information, and it is not only news shows that have highly politicized content. Television sitcoms and dramas, as disparate as, for example, *South Park* and *Law and Order*, have featured episodes on the war on terror.[14] Television 'news' talk shows have taken on the war on terror particularly enthusiastically, with Geraldo Rivera making himself a soldier with no country, or in this case no network, going to Afghanistan armed with a pistol ostensibly to search for Osama Bin Laden.[15] And late night host David Letterman has outdone actual news commentators in political content with his outrage at the attacks of September 11th 2001. Both Letterman and Jay Leno were relentless with their racist and homophobic 'jokes' about Osama bin Laden, al-Qaeda, and the Taliban:

> There is now a $5 million dollar bounty on Osama bin Laden. Which marks the first time in history there has ever been a bounty on a guy's head who wears Bounty on his head. (Jay Leno, politicalhumor.about. com/od/osamabinladen/a/Osama-Bin-Laden-Jokes.htm)

> Osama bin Laden has ten look-alikes to fool us Americans. Ten look-alikes, and he's married to five of them. (David Letterman, ibid.)

The late night jokes, then, as well as other forms of propaganda, serve to reinforce certain ideas about race, heterosexuality, and the proper practice of gender. Contributions to the enemy-creating discourse, however, are not happening only on television. Traditional print media are involved, as are the technologies available on the internet. It is important to acknowledge that much of what we in the West consume as popular culture, as entertainment, as news, is infused with propaganda. Recognizing the presence of propaganda is not always easy, though, as many of us have been taught to believe that 'the news' is free of such bias. A closer look, however, reveals the ways in which ideology combined with capitalist imperatives now structures what we think we know.

Learning war

> Media personnel depend on political leaders for information and are therefore vulnerable to manipulation by them. (Graber 2010: 83)

Popular culture is one of the primary means by which ideology in infused through a culture (Storey 2006: 2; Graber 2010: 163, 166[16]). The analysis of popular culture images – and news is certainly a part of popular culture – always raises questions about production and consumption. What constitutes news? How are decisions made about who and what to cover? Are deliberate decisions made about how to depict certain groups of people in particular ways? Are representations accidental? Unconscious? Who makes these decisions? How do we, as consumers of popular culture, as seekers of information, make sense of all this?

Ideas about male supremacy and white supremacy, along with militarism and imperialism, are pieces of ideology that guide news content. It is not that individual news producers or reporters set out to communicate racist ideas about Muslims or sexist ideas about Afghan women. Rather their choices of which stories to tell and how to tell them reflect who they are – mostly well-educated white men (Graber 2010: 82) – and the values that are already circulating in and around Western culture (ibid.).

Governments assist in this upholding of certain ideas, especially during wartime (ibid.: 80). There is a long history of media and government working hand in hand in the production and dissemination of propaganda. Contemporary propaganda efforts are a bit more sophisticated these days and are assisted by a media less interested in indulging or motivated to engage in critiques of government. Since September 11th 2001 in the United States, various government offices have been dedicated to the dissemination of information on 'who the terrorists are,' and there have been few investigations done independently by the media to either support the government descriptions and definitions or to provide an alternative idea. In mid-October 2001, only two weeks after the attacks of September 11th, a group of Hollywood actors, writers, and producers met with officials from the Bush administration to begin talks about how the government and media might work together to respond to the events of that day. So important was this collaboration deemed to be that by mid-November, Karl Rove, a key Bush advisor, had joined this group (Cooper 2001; Shaheen 2008). The Office of Strategic Influence in the US opened in October 2001 but was soon closed after a hue and cry was raised about its overt goals of propaganda and misinformation. The public was outraged to think that money would be spent in order to produce propaganda. Yet in July 2002 the Bush administration began a public relations effort aimed at justifying the war against Iraq by opening the Office of Global Communications to 'coordinate the administration's foreign policy message and supervise America's image abroad' (Miller et al. 2004a: 45). The more subtly named department was virtually ignored by the US media in spite of its cost in excess of $1 billion annually (Miller 2004b: 80). In Great Britain, where more attention has been paid by the media and academics to this issue, the Foreign Office spends £340 million annually on internal efforts to support public relations around the war (ibid.: 80).

Because news-producing entities are owned by multinational corporations whose primary goal is to make profit, capitalism of course enormously influences what stories are told and how they are told – how much time is allotted to each story, how many reporters are assigned, where those reporters are stationed, etc. (McChesney 2008: 10; Graber 2010: 84). Attention is focused on geographic areas of strategic interest – both corporate and military. As a primary motivation for sharing information, profit interferes with the actual gathering of news as advertisers and other multinational corporations – or sometimes the very corporation that owns the newspaper or television station – can influence content. In addition, the cost of producing news is now contained by limiting the number of reporters assigned around the world. As a consequence news organizations have access to less independently gathered information. Luckily for them, but not for the consumer of news, the product of all this government money, the public relations information produced by governments, is readily available at no cost. Government-produced information, then, is relied upon for explanations about world events as well as for descriptions of groups of people and individuals around the world. In addition, to keep costs down news organizations share sources to a greater degree than ever before, which narrows ideas about what is happening and who the groups and individuals are who are participating in these events (Graber 2010: 80, 90; Herman 2004: 176; McChesney 2008: 34).

The production of all this government information and sharing of sources means that the origins of stories or ideas about Muslims or people from Afghanistan or Iraq are obscured from the public. There are very few reporters on the ground, unaccompanied by Western troops, gathering information for news stories. Some other legitimate news sources that might provide information from on the ground, such as Al Jazeera, are discredited. Instead, our governments are almost the sole source of information about Iraqi and Afghan people. An unintended consequence of the narrowing of sources for news, though, is that we can observe and analyze the way that news – or what we have come to believe is news – circulates. Some stories appear numerous times, reworded only a bit differently in various outlets. The AP, for example, will put out a story that is then picked up by the *Los Angeles Times*, where the wording is only slightly different, and the *Guardian*, where a little more context is added, and Fox News, where a seemingly irrelevant aspect of a short story is made the center of the story. The stories about male same-sex desire in Afghanistan, described in Chapter 1, provide a good example of this practice. Other stories can be traced only to internet sources that, regardless of their overt political leanings, are relied upon as credible. News stories, then, become not so much a joint effort to report the facts but instead an agreed-upon fabrication that legitimizes the war by upholding certain ideas about the viciousness and inferiority of the enemy and the necessity of Western intervention. Do the producers of the nightly news, or *Newsweek*, or the *Washington Post* set out to create notions about Afghan women that legitimize war? Or images that depict Iraqi or Muslim men as brutes? As uncivilized? Probably not. The effect of ideology combined with the narrowing of access to information creates a situation in which notions of white supremacy and male dominance combine with Orientalized notions of the other to ensure that war can occur and be sustained.

Furthermore, how do audiences make meaning of those images? In the absence of any other paradigm, audiences, particularly in the US, where there is little or no education on media literacy, accept the images and representations, particularly those provided by 'news' personnel, as truth. In spite of frequent revelations of false reporting by numerous print reporters, the venerated *New York Times* notably among them (McChesney 2008: 112), as well as the clear political bias of television stations like Fox News, people in the US still seem to take as fact information provided for them under the guise of news. While it is really difficult to measure what people learn from the news (Graber 2010: 173), generally people in the US still believe that 'news' is somehow an accurate accounting of what goes on in the world. This does not mean that consumers have no agency to allow interpretation of what they see, hear, or read, only that many people are inclined not to question. People still believe that Saddam Hussein had WMDs because it was reported on the news, even though no such weapons were found (Begley 2005). Although many audiences may consume news stories as truth, others, including some feminists and anti-racists, know that the power of images cannot be overstated and that we need to have methods of understanding the messages contained in the narratives and images.

Reading the news

In their research about representations in *National Geographic* magazine, Catherine Lutz and Jane Collins outline the ways that consumers of the magazine might make sense of the images to which they are exposed (1993: 187). This explanation offers a useful way to think about consumers of both 'news' and the fictionalized accounts of Afghans, Iraqis, and Muslims that emerge from them. In talking about what they call 'looks and looking relations,' Lutz and Collins suggest that: 'the reader's gaze then has a history and a future, and it is structured by the mental work of inference and imagination ...' (ibid.: 196). Further, they provide a possible explanation for how members of multiracial societies, such as those in the US, Canada, and Great Britain, might share an experience of exposure to certain images or narratives. 'The reader's gaze is structured by a large number of cultural elements or models, many more than those used to reason about racial or cultural difference' (ibid.: 196). Sara Ahmed, feminist and post-colonial scholar, writing before the events of September 11th 2001, offers an extension of the analysis of Lutz and Collins by suggesting that boundaries between self and others in multiracial societies require policing that is assisted by representations.

> ... each time we are faced by an other whom we cannot recognize, we
> seek to find other ways of achieving recognition, not only by re-reading

the body of *this* other who is faced, but by telling the difference between this other and other others. The encounters we might yet have
with other others hence surprise the subject, but they also reopen the
prior histories of encounter that violate and fix others in regimes of
difference. (Ahmed 2000: 8).

Of course, Orientalism as defined by Edward Said (1979) plays a large
part in which stories appear in Western press accounts and how they
are told. Said points out: 'Covering Islam is a one sided activity that
obscures what "we" *do*, and highlights instead what Muslims and
Arabs by their very flawed nature *are*' (1981: xxii). He argues further
that encounters between the West and 'the Orient' are predetermined
by history and ideology. When the few reporters that remain in the
field engage an Afghan woman or an Iraqi citizen their stories are
always already known by the reporter regardless of the circumstance
(ibid.: 1981). Here, I am suggesting that the 'ways of looking' and of
making sense of the information presented to consumers of popular
culture – part of which is in the form of 'news'– even though not
presented to a uni-racial, uni-gendered, uni-ethnic populace, end up
communicating a message that upholds imperialist, white supremacist,
male supremacist ideology.

Transnational sexism

In *The Nation* in 2004, Arundhati Roy suggested that we are experiencing a 'new racism.' This new racism is about empire building.
It is intricately tied in to capitalism. It is centered in representation. It
utilizes certain people of color as tokens, or iconic figures, in order
to screen its sinister motives. The presence of these iconic figures
silences dissent. The new racism, I argue, is an important contributor
to what I am calling transnational sexism.

Because of the changes brought about by feminist movements
around the world, and the positioning of women in relation to war
as simultaneously *threat* and *victim*, *soldier* and *nurturer*, *bomber* and
bombed upon, we can now see that depictions of women are complicated and require a new and improved kind of sexism. This transnational sexism depends on what Zillah Eisenstein calls 'gender decoys'
(2007). She asks:

How does one attempt to live in a world when the ground beneath us
shifts? The shifting implicates those of us who live inside the U.S. in
new-old fashion. As the site we occupy becomes more singular and
defensive and aggressive we are given less information, less freedom,

less ability to see beyond ourselves. This imperial condition is both old – embedded in history – and new – openly defended by the imperial policing nation. (Eisenstein 2006: 241)

'The ground beneath us shifts' to reveal female-bodied women who act like men in order to perpetuate a 'fantasy of gender equality' (Eisenstein 2007: 37). The fantasy, though, exists only as a façade both inside and outside the West. It ensures that patriarchy remains unchallenged (ibid.: xii). Transnational sexism, as we shall see in Chapter 3, also has a visibility/invisibility problem for women (Riley 2008). Women are deployed mostly to further patriarchal goals. Of course, invisibility has its obvious drawbacks as women are not considered in decision-making and get no credit for the contributions that they make even when they further militarized patriarchal ends. Visibility, though, particularly when it occurs within male-dominated spaces, as we shall see, is perilous. In transnational sexism, all women's achievements are undermined while some new freedoms or inroads are granted to certain women while simultaneously certain other women are vilified or presented as victims. Transnational sexism has racism, classism, and homophobia as its foundation and uses them as a means to create divisions among women, but it also uses women, mostly women of color, but also lesbians and working-class and poor women, to create or reinscribe old divisions among people, between states, and within ethnicities.

Transnational sexism is most apparent in representations in the Western media. It utilizes certain women as tokens or as iconic figures who are meant to stand in for all women of a certain identity, position, or profession. In transnational sexism, Dr Germ, Mrs Anthrax, and Aafia Siddiqi represent all Iraqi and Pakistani women, and Bibi Aisha and the amorphous figure of the burqa-ed woman represent all Afghan women. While the bonds of the body – that is, shared sisterhood – are exploited as reason to go to war, gender, that is shared understandings about the proper practice of femininity, is utilized as a means of division between Western – read white – women and Iraqi and Afghan women.[17] Ideas about gender are extensively used in propaganda about the war mostly as a means to uphold a particular practice of militarized masculinity, but also to legitimize Western imperialism.

Transnational sexism is reflected in several aspects of the war on terror, including US military engagement both in Afghanistan and Iraq. In these configurations of gender, women assume multiple, sometimes conflicting, roles. Iraqi and Afghan women are demons and victims (not of the US in the Western narrative, of course, but of the Taliban, al-Qaeda, and 'brown-skinned men'). In this geography, Afghan women are the ultimate victims. They lack agency. They require rescue. Through the wearing of the burqa, though, their hidden bodies allow all sorts of Orientalist fantasies to be projected upon them. They shift, then, in the Western imagination from the perfect excuse for invasion, because of their helplessness, to the incarnation of danger. Who can know, the Western media seems to be saying, who or what actually is hiding under that burqa? Because they enjoyed relative freedom in terms of their access to jobs and ability to travel on the streets, Iraqi women, conversely, have been depicted in the Western media as dangerous. It was only after occupation, when Iraqi society began to deteriorate from the presence of the Western forces, that Iraqi women were seen as vulnerable. Transnational sexism is thus fraught with contradiction and requires constant policing and the production of an assortment of propaganda – news, email jokes, internet cartoons, characters in television shows, and feature film plots – in order to be maintained.

Depicting the veil

This is a book about Western media, about Western militarism, and Western imperial desires. Understanding the ways in which Orientalism, transnational sexism, and rescue narratives influence the depictions of Afghan and Iraqi women in Western media helps to uncover some of the workings of empire.

Chapter 1 explores media depictions of Afghan women. While women in Afghanistan live under horrible conditions with high maternal and infant mortality, and a lack of access to healthcare and education, the presence of Western militaries on Afghan soil has not alleviated their circumstances very much, and in some ways occupation has exacerbated their plight. Ironically, in Western media narratives Afghan women as victims are the focus of rescue narratives. They remain the ostensible reason for war in Afghanistan, and images of them and stories of their oppression continue to be used to legitimize occupation. In Chapter 2, the depiction of the wives of Osama bin Laden and Saddam Hussein and their families in Western media is examined. The story of Iraqi women's lives during the occupation is also explored. In fact, Iraqi women might have been seen as needing rescuing from other villainous Iraqi women. For example, the women who were related to Osama bin Laden, Saddam Hussein or Huda Ammash and Rihab Taha are portrayed in Western media as sinister, dangerous, and evil. The portrayal of certain Iraqi women as dangerous occurred at the same time that other Iraqi women, whose only crimes were marriage, family relations, or neighborhood proximity, were held without charge in US detention as a way to get information and to prompt the surrender of Iraqi men wanted by the US. Chapter 3 is about questions of visibility and invisibility of Muslim women in the war on terror. Aafia Siddiqui and Aesha Mohammadzai have become iconic figures in the West. Aafia Siddiqui represents the dangerous Muslim woman and Aesha Mohammadzai is the classic victim in need of rescue. The telling of the mysterious tale of Aafia Siddiqui, otherwise known as 'the female al-Qaeda' in the Western press, is analyzed. There is speculation that she was held in rendition for five years. She was arrested officially in 2008 and put on trial in New York City. The infamous *Time* magazine cover with the image of Aesha Mohammadzai's (as she is now known) face missing most of her nose is emblematic of thinking in the US about Afghan women. Reactions to the use of her image and her subsequent travel to the US where she is now living reveal how the US government and Western media work hand in hand to maintain ideas about the peril posed to women in Afghanistan. Chapter 4 is concerned with the deployment of Western women in the service of empire. Press accounts about members of the US and UK administrations and about US women soldiers who are assigned to special units that work to win the hearts and minds of Iraqi and Afghan women are examined. At the same time, Maureen Dowd donned a burqa in the pages of *Vanity Fair*, and Carrie, Charlotte, Miranda, and Samantha went to Abu Dhabi – joining in an effort to do their bit for the war on terror. Throughout, the reader can observe transnational sexism at work. Finally, in Chapter 5 the reader is urged to think about the meaning of liberation in the lives of women around the world and to ask questions about how these depictions of the veil keep us from coming together to interrupt imperialism and war.

1 | Rescuing Afghan women

War makes strange bedfellows. The body of the Muslim woman, a body fixed in the Western imaginary as confined, mutilated, and sometimes murdered in the name of culture, serves to reinforce the threat that the Muslim man is said to pose to the West, and is used to justify the extraordinary measures of violence and surveillance required to discipline him and Muslim communities. Against the hypervisibility of the Muslim woman's body (customs officers, shop clerks, and restaurant workers now all presume to know how Muslim women are oppressed by their terrible men), it is virtually impossible to name and confront the violence that Muslim women (like all groups of women) experience at the hands of their men and families without providing ideological fuel to 'the war on terror.'
(Razack 2008: 107)

Things are not good for women in Afghanistan. While much was made in the Western press of women throwing off their burqas[1] in joy at the removal of the Taliban,[2] sources on the ground in Afghanistan in 2001 reported that in fact very few women had given up the Muslim tradition of the veil in favor of Western garb or even a less extreme version of the veil (McCarthy 2001). Indeed, women in Afghanistan bear the brunt of the war more than ten years after Western troops most recently entered Afghanistan, now under the Bush administration's hand-picked leader Hamid Karzai.

Five years after the overthrow of the Taliban, Kabul has only 3 hours of electricity per day and unsanitary and inadequate drinking water. The healthcare system is nonexistent or run by foreign NGO's and primary schools lack teachers. The government undertakes almost no public works; there is no food safety system ... (Parenti 2006: 13)

The United Nations Human Development Index rated Afghanistan 173rd of 178 nations measured (Gall 2005). Even though the report was paid for by the World Bank and nations like Canada, which have played a role in the NATO-led invasion of Afghanistan and have a direct stake in having Afghanistan depicted as benefitting from, at that point, three years of war, they acknowledge that one in two Afghans live in poverty, the life expectancy of 44.5 years is twenty years lower than that of its neighbors, a woman dies from pregnancy-related causes every thirty minutes, and that Afghanistan has 'the worst educational system in the world' (ibid.).

More recently, according to their own accounting, Afghanistan, in spite of receiving some $36 billion in foreign aid in the form of grants and loans between 2001 and 2009, has been described in the Western media as 'a country in a persistent state of humanitarian crisis' (Turse 2010). The United Nations ranks Afghanistan last of 135 countries in its Human Poverty Index (ibid.). Thirty-six percent of the population live below the poverty level and another 30 percent are one incident away from not having enough food to eat (ibid.). Afghanistan is a place that is prone to incidents. There is no infrastructure to support the population or to protect them from catastrophe.

John Vidal of the *Guardian* reports that '80% of all Afghans are drinking contaminated water.' He goes on: 'More than 75% of the whole of the urban Afghan population live without water, electricity or secure ownership' (Vidal 2010). In addition, the rapid growth of Kabul in the form of expanding shantytowns presents a potentially huge environment problem. Around 80 percent of persons hospitalized in Kabul have diseases caused by overcrowding, that is, from the pollution of air or water (ibid.). There is woefully inadequate sanitation with no sewage system at all and 'only one in 10 or 20 households have access to clean water via the city water system, with everyone else sharing communal water pumps' (ibid.). This is what ten years of Western imperialism have wrought.

Thank you for the rescue

> Nine years after 11 September and the start of the operation 'Enduring Freedom,' which justified its commitment not only with the hunt for terrorists, but also with the fight for women's rights, the situation of women and girls in Afghanistan still is catastrophic. (Medica Mondiale 2010)

While the overall situation in Afghanistan is grim, as the quote above indicates, for women it is 'catastrophic.' Indeed, the war in Afghanistan is hardest on women. Contemporary methods of war-making with no established front lines, where fighting often occurs in urban settings, along with the United States' use of drones – that is, unmanned aircraft operated from within the United States that target certain individuals in Afghanistan, Iraq, or Pakistan (drones are advertised as being quite accurate to a target but, it turns out, frequently they are not[3]), but that frequently end up killing and harming civilians – have helped to create an atmosphere that is far more dangerous to women and far more disruptive to their lives than Taliban restrictions. One consequence of war for women in Afghanistan is loss of loved ones. For example, estimates show that there are 2 million widows in Afghanistan; one out of seven Afghan women is a widow (Partlow 2011; Obaid-Chinoy 2007b). Given the lack of education and limited options for women in Afghanistan, becoming a widow has significant economic implications on women's lives: 'These widows are not supported by the corrupt government and have no option except begging, prostitution and suicide – the most common means of escape. The recent imposed law banning beggary reduces this range of options still further' (Mansour 2009).

Yet there are not a lot of stories told in the West about widows in Afghanistan. It is almost as if to acknowledge their existence would be to implicate the West in their creation. In the few descriptions of the lives of women who are widows in Afghanistan, however, there is no direct correlation drawn between the presence of Western militaries and the creation of widows. That is, the 'problem' of widows, as told in the Western press, is talked about as one of lack of opportunity created by Afghan men and the long decades of war with unnamed amorphous enemies, not the current conflict that creates widows (Partlow 2011; Abawi 2009a). In a *Washington Post* story entitled 'Afghan widows form community on Kabul hill,' for example, the author, Josh Partlow, interviews four of the estimated one thousand widows in a particular area of Kabul noted for the concentration of widows living there. None of the husbands of the women interviewed was killed by Western forces. One woman's husband died in a car crash, another was killed by a suicide bomber, still another in a rocket attack during a pre-Taliban conflict. Both the decades of war and subsequent lack of opportunity in Afghan society afforded to women living alone, or alone with children, definitely contribute to the problem of widows. Yet, responsibility for at least one of those decades belongs to the West, and the proliferation of widows since occupation lies at the feet of Western governments, including that of the US. Commenting on the problem of widows in Afghanistan, Maria Akrami, a social worker for an NGO based in Kabul, said, 'If America invaded us to liberate our women, this is a clear sign that they are failing miserably' (Obaid-Chinoy 2007b).

The creation of widows and the subsequent erasure of Western responsibility in their creation is not the only way in which the presence of Western men, whose ostensible role was to rescue Afghan women from Afghan men, has impacted the lives of women in Afghanistan. How the world – and, for purposes of this study, the West – comes to know and understand who Afghan women are comes about as a result of the perceptions and ideas of Western men – more specifically Western white men. Indeed, as Doris Graber tells us, what we are exposed to, in the form of news, is racially determined: '… what becomes news depends in part on the demographics, training, personality, and professional socialization of news personnel. In the United States that means, by and large, upwardly mobile, well educated white males …' (Graber 2010: 82).

The 'upwardly mobile, well-educated white men' paint a particular picture of who the enemy, in this case Muslim men, is and the consequences of the actions of that enemy. In the case of Afghanistan, one of the consequences becomes the depiction of Afghan women as oppressed to the point of voicelessness by Afghan/Muslim men. The accompanying ideas about the potential for evil of Afghan men are reinforced again and again. Sherene Razack (2008: 5) suggests that:

> Three allegorical figures have come to dominate the social landscape of the 'war on terror' and its ideological underpinning of a clash of civilizations: the dangerous Muslim man, the imperiled Muslim woman, and the civilized European, the latter a figure who is seldom explicitly named but who nevertheless anchors the first two figures … The story is not just a story, of course, but is the narrative scaffold for the making of an empire dominated by the United States and the white nations who are its allies.

What we know about Afghan women, then, comes to us through a lens constructed by Western patriarchy colored by imperial desires.

Being widowed is not the only consequence of war on Afghan women's lives. Indeed, women themselves have died in large numbers, lost children and other loved ones, and suffered horrendous injuries. In 2004 Sonali Kolhatkar, director of the Afghan Women's Mission, quoted figures from the BBC in reporting that:

> There has been a continuous steady trickle of a few deaths here, a few there, in Afghanistan – not enough to warrant news headlines. In early December, six Afghan children died during a U.S. assault … The next day, nine more died in a field in Ghazni province after a U.S. air attack. More than two years after 'Operation Enduring Freedom' began in

Afghanistan, Afghan women and children are still enduring death by U.S. style freedom.

Sonali Kolhatkar is suggesting that transnational sexism changes the meaning of the word freedom in the Afghan context. Here notions of 'freedom' have very different meanings depending upon whether it is Western women's freedom or that of women of color, specifically Afghan or Muslim women. Apparently, in Afghanistan freedom might mean freedom from one's life, one's loved ones, one's home, one's right to self-determination. In 2010, RAWA (Revolutionary Association of the Women of Afghanistan) News claimed that 8,832 Afghan civilians have been killed in a combination of drone strikes, exposure to IEDs (improvised explosive devices), combat deaths and suicide bombings since 2007.

Is this what 'rescue' means? Are Afghan women now liberated? Responsibility for the increasing death toll cannot be solely that of Afghan men. It is the presence and activities of Western militaries that is to blame (Kandiyote, in Khaleeli 2011).

Victims or villains?

The Orientalized body becomes a projection of all that the West finds alien and abhorrent, but simultaneously exotic and alluring. In short, the Orientalized body essentializes otherness. (Jiwani 2006: 181)

Even though conditions for women in Afghanistan were not much improved by Western bombs or the subsequent and ongoing occupation, and some would argue that they have actually worsened, in his 2002 State of the Union address, George Bush declared that: 'The mothers and daughters of Afghanistan were captives in their own homes. Today women are free' (cited in Lamb 2011b). Currently, under the Obama administration, media coverage of the war continues to make the argument that Afghan women have to some degree been rescued. The media coverage focuses not on the supposed imperialist intentions of the Taliban, as Laura Bush articulated, but rather, as I will demonstrate, on rescuing Afghan women from brown men (Spivak 1988; Fanon 1965; Cooke 2002). We have already seen the machinations involved in creating this idea, but it is also important to recognize the Orientalist underpinnings of these stories as well as Afghan women's visibility/invisibility problem in news coverage (see Chapter 3).

Of course, media coverage of the war in Afghanistan waxes and wanes depending on how involved the US is at the time, how the news of certain US activities can be spun, and what other distractions may occur. During the most intense parts of the US attack on Iraq and subsequent occupation, but also during less warlike events like Michael Jackson's death or Hurricane Katrina, Afghanistan faded from the view of most Americans in spite of the presence of American troops there and casualties inflicted on both those troops and Afghan civilians. Watching network news in the US during those times might have provoked one to question the newscaster, 'Are we at war?'

Even when stories about the war in Afghanistan are told, women are often totally absent. Though women constitute almost one half of the population, they are almost never mentioned in news stories. In news photos about the war, women are rarely depicted except as victims or as recipients of Western largesse in the form of food or medical assistance, or as veiled, vaguely threatening figures. The depiction of Afghan women from the start of the war on terror has been conflicted. On the one hand, there is the veiled victim of the Taliban and, on the other, the hidden, al-Qaeda perpetrator of terror. In her study of stories on Muslim people that appeared in the Canadian *Montreal Gazette* post-September 11th 2001, Yasmin Jiwani argues that 'Of all the stories referencing Muslim women, Orientalist themes were especially apparent in those that focused on Muslim women living directly under Islamic rule' (Jiwani 2006: 186).

Those Orientalist themes and the perception of religious education and the religious practice of Islam as dangerous were very apparent in a photo essay that appeared in the *New York Times* soon after September 11th 2001. On 21 October 2001, the *New York Times Magazine* ran a *National Geographic*-like photo spread of Pakistani women who study or work in madrassahs for women. This marks the beginning of the loop of circulation of certain ideas about the Orientalized Muslim woman. The photos are terrific examples of Orientalism and the exoticization of women of color – the women are all veiled, for example, dressed in flowing robes, and looking sideways at the camera. It is not clear whether the lens is obscured or the women are in motion, but one photo of several women in burqas is somewhat blurry, making it seem as though the women are mysterious, secretive. In one photo, a ten-year-old girl named Munaza Kanwam is pictured at 'her Koran ceremony.' She wears a headpiece of brightly colored flowers. The quote underneath her photo reads: 'I am very happy. I feel like a bride ... I think Osama is a great man, and he is fighting America.' Other text that surrounds the pictures works to create the idea that these women are war-thirsty fanatics. One woman named Shafia Salaam was quoted as saying:

I have seen images in the newspapers of what happened in America, and I feel it was not good. But perhaps God punished America for the wrongs she is doing in other countries like Palestine and Kashmir. If America attacks us, we will fight. Non-Muslims are our enemy according to the Koran, so Americans are our enemy. We hate America. I believe in Jihad. I will do whatever I can do. *If I am provided the opportunity to get weapons, I will use them.* (p. 40)

The last sentence was reproduced in large, italicized text to emphasize and create fear, and yet the reader is expected to differentiate between what this woman said and the words of US women serving in the military, or for that matter, in a time when the thirst for war had reached fever pitch, among US women who support the war. This emphasis supports the Bush administration's claim that these women are militarized, as a result of Islam, taught to hate the West and the US so much that they are willing to do anything to harm Westerners.

Another woman in the *New York Times* piece named Rehima has named one of her six sons Osama:

I named my son Osama because I want to make him a mujahid. Right now there is war but he is a child. When he is a young man, there might be war again, and I will prepare him for that war. In the name of God, I will sacrifice my son, and I don't care if he is my most beloved thing. For all of my six sons I wanted them to be mujahadeen. If they get killed it is nothing. This world is very short. I myself want to be a mujahid. What will I do in this world? I could be in heaven, have a weekly meeting with God. Jihad is when you are attacked, you attack back. This is God's wish. We are not afraid. I am already asking my husband if I can go to Kashmir and train to fight. I will suicide bomb. If there are 20–30 non-Muslims there I will commit martyrdom. If America attacks, we will put our hands on the throats of the Americans and kill them. (p. 39)

Again, the representation of Rehima's words is meant to foment fear, to construct her as a fanatic, but her narrative is not very different from that of an American woman who is exercising her surest route to the status of patriot by enlisting in the military, sending a child off to military service, or teaching American children to believe that the enemies are the 'evil ones.' The primary difference in Rehima's life is the presence of Islam as a motivator. Her religion, the newspaper tells us, makes her more bloodthirsty, more determined to sacrifice herself and her sons. For readers who have missed all the other signs, the fact that she has a child named Osama puts Rehima clearly among the most menacing of all – the mother of *the* terrorist. These representations were and are effective; they fomented fear and helped pave the way for the invasion of Afghanistan and then Iraq.

Burqa, hijab, chador, niqab: veiling Orientalism

In part, the visibility/invisibility problem for Afghan women in the Western press is assisted by the wearing of the burqa. Women get dehumanized in Western eyes when they wear them. The burqa then provides a convenient excuse for the media to ignore women, to not show the peril caused to them by Western imperialism. Their facelessness in representations enables their objectification, allows them to be named as collateral damage, and facilitates their use as justification for the war without any real concern for Afghan women or providing any understanding about what the war means in their lives. Of course, women are routinely ignored in accounts of war regardless of whether they are wearing the burqa. In spite of increased participation in militaries around the world by women, an understanding of the real numbers of civilian casualties incurred in today's kind of warfare – many of them women – and increasing numbers of women in positions as world leaders, war is still believed to be the purview of men. Anatomy continues to be seen as a guarantee of tendency towards war or peace, thus justifying the exclusion of women from considerations around war. The burqa becomes the repository for all of Orientalist thinking. Meaning gets heaped onto and inside of it and it is almost impossible to unpack it all. Orientalism is at work here too, though in the sense that this particular war – the war on terror – has a mysterious, particularly troublesome enemy. Orientalism includes ideas about the practice of gender that has to do, in part, with the wearing of the burqa. Initially at least, the burqa[4] marked, in the Western press, subservience and oppression (Zeiger 2008: 266; Garcia 2003):

> International Human Rights advocates have long been focused on the burqa as the symbol of oppression for Afghan women, a simplistic association argued Soraya Rahim, deputy minister in the Ministry of Women. 'The west equates removal of the burqa with progress for women.' She said, 'Burqas are not the issue. Why women wear them is. Their husbands make them. Some are afraid the Taliban will come back. Others don't have jobs and wear burqas to conceal their tattered clothes. Others are sick and use the burqa to conceal their pain. Real issues lie beneath the burqa.' (Garcia 2003)

Soraya Rahim's quote above shows how the burqa is worn for many reasons, but the primary ones have to do with fear of husbands and the Taliban, or if they are hiding pain or sickness. This quote feeds into the West's obsession with the burqa as a symbol of men's power and women's subservience. Still, Soraya Rahim is attempting to present some complexity around the wearing of the burqa by showing that the burqa cannot be worn freely or in good health under current conditions. Malcolm Garcia of Knight Ridder, however, reduces all that complexity around gender relations, poverty, and alienation to: 'Burqa no longer law, but women remain oppressed in Afghanistan.'

One part of the complexity of the wearing of the burqa that Soraya Rahim misses is that it also provides an opportunity to demonize men of color, in this case Afghan men, and to reinforce the rescue narrative.

Real criticisms of the burqa are that it inhibits movement, that it is an instrument of isolation, that it shames the face, and that it closes off the sensory realm. But the criticism is seriously compromised – and its motives suspect – when the burqa is used as it has been in the Western media; as a tool of imperial domination, justification for warfare, disguise for violence, erasure of history, and method of reifying hierarchies of class and race. (McLarney 2009: 20)

The real damage wearing the burqa does, McLarney claims, is giving ammunition to the West to demonize Afghan men. If Afghan men require Afghan women to wear this terrible thing, they might as well be saying, Western men are defenders of women's liberation by default. By not requiring this particular sign of adherence to the cultural constructs of femininity, Western men's superiority is confirmed, and their desire to intervene on Afghan women's behalf is legitimized.

The burqa or niqab does attract the eye of the Westerner. And it does make for dramatic photographs. Western media sources are nothing less than obsessed with veils and love the use of them for titillating headlines. Some have to do with freedom from the veil, which is, of course, presented as a Western male accomplishment: 'Springtime may liberate some Afghan women from their burqas' (Salome 2002), 'Afghan women: burqa-free is still only for the brave' (Coker 2002). Other headlines, while still upholding Western male rescue narratives, serve a double purpose in demonizing Afghan men but also associating Afghan women with danger: 'Veiled threat: to fully grasp the dangers of the post-September 11 world we have to examine the Taliban's hatred of women' (Ehrenreich 2001), 'The rifle and the veil' (Goodwin and Neuwirth 2001: 19A), 'The fear beneath the burqa' (Amiri 2002: 19A),

25

'Afghanistan's veil of oppression' (Rather 2009). In the second paragraph, the latter article explains: 'It is a strange, perhaps disturbing sight: anonymous, mysterious figures hiding behind a full-body veil called a burqa.' 'Strange' and 'disturbing'? The women are 'hiding'? Is that why after ten years of war Westerners still have almost no idea who Afghan women are other than a vague sense that they are oppressed by Afghan men? Perhaps that is why we know almost no Afghan women by name. It is not the fault of Western xenophobia or transnational sexism, this author suggests, Afghan women are hiding.

As unusual as the sight may have been to some Westerners before 2001, the insistence that the burqa represented all that was wrong and dangerous about this culture about which we knew (and some would argue continue to know) almost nothing, and that the wearing of it should be abolished, is not new. There is a long history of the wearing of the veil waxing and waning and of prohibition of the veil by governments, in various states, not only in the West, but surely due to Western influence or coercion (Kahf 2008). The Western press hardly ever distinguishes between varieties of veil worn. They use the words veil and burqa interchangeably. The word veil is used more frequently in headlines, but they are often referring to burqas. Joan Wallach Scott points out that in the debates about headscarves that occurred in France in the 1990s, the term headscarves was used 'interchangeably' with the word 'veil' (2007: 16). This melding together of all styles of veil paints all women wearing any version of the veil – and there are several – as simultaneously religious extremists and oppressed, both without care for ethnicity, cultural practice, or the agency of the wearer.

In a strangely troubling but also kind of amusing article written by the *Vancouver Sun*'s[5] Tiffany Crawford entitled 'Afghan women face health risks wearing burqas, activist says,' Crawford reports that a woman named Sima Simar,[6] in a speech about Afghan women that she gave to high school students in the United States, claimed that: 'Burqas are causing health problems for women in Afghanistan because their bodies are not absorbing enough vitamin D from sunlight.' '"The problem is when they are forced to wear them," Samar said. "When they choose to wear them, then this is something different."' The absorption of vitamin D is influenced by one's reasons for wearing a veil? But not by the presence of war, the dropping of missiles, the threat of drones, the necessity to stay indoors to avoid the scrutiny of imperial troops? The health risk that Samar is describing is not depression, which one might imagine could come from being required to wear clothing that makes one 'an anonymous, mysterious figure' (Rather 2009), or a 'blue ghost' (Rubin 2011d), but a bone disease that afflicts only those wearing the burqa involuntarily. This claim seems incredible – and, I would suggest, defies science.

The burqa does not just provide for provocative and implausible titles and articles, though. It also provides tantalizing images. A photo essay or what Reuters calls a 'Slideshow' is available for viewing on their website. It features twenty-five photos of Afghan women and is entitled 'Lifting the veil in Afghanistan.' The slideshow may have been more aptly named 'Lifting the burqa in Afghanistan' as there are no photos of women who wear no veil at all except for young children. In fact, most of the photos include women wearing burqas either singly or in groups. Twelve of the photos are of women completely covered by burqas. In some of the group photos, there are mixed groups of women; some are wearing burqas, other women having either thrown the burqa back to reveal their faces – sometimes the camera catches these faces, sometimes it does not – or wearing some other variety of head covering. It becomes apparent, as one views the slideshow, that most of the women not wearing burqas are young girls, children. There is a photo of an Afghan woman police officer. She wears a veil over her hair under her police cap. There is another of an election worker at a polling place completely covered by her burqa. Two of the images are remarkable in that they further dehumanize already covered bodies. In one photo of women at a food distribution site, the photographer shoots the image from above so he is looking down at the top of the heads of these women. Even if these women were not wearing burqas, their faces would not be visible. In another, women stand in line at a food distribution center; we are told in the caption only that it is in Kabul so it is not clear whether this is the same distribution center or another. This image of daily life in Afghanistan without specificity tells a story of gender segregation, of women's hunger, of meshing together women and children into one infanticized unit, of Western largesse. The photographer is focused on the face of a young girl child standing at her mother's side, so all we see of the mother and the other women in line is the billowing blue fabric of their burqas. The woman is dehumanized by the Western media this time, instead of, as the overarching narrative suggests, by their own husbands, brothers, fathers. The final photo in the slideshow features a young girl with no head covering or burqa turning her face away to the wall behind her. The caption reads: 'A girl turns her head as U.S. and Afghan soldiers walk past in Jelawar in the Arghandab Valley north of Kandahar.' What causes her to cringe in this way? Is the girl reacting to being seen by these men to whom she is not related? Why, then, is she not veiled in some fashion? Is it the presence of American troops that makes her feel vulnerable? Has she had some experience that would make visible her femininity? The viewer is left to speculate about that, but it is very clear that no actual 'lifting' of the veil has been done. Veils, including burqas, are abundantly present.

Meyda Yegenoglu describes the Orientalism involved in Western thinking about veiling.

> The veil attracts the eye, and forces one to think, to speculate about what is behind it. It is often represented as some kind of a mask, hiding the woman. With the help of this opaque veil, the Oriental woman is considered as not yielding herself to the Western gaze and therefore imagined as hiding something behind the veil. It is through the inscription of the veil as a mask that the Oriental woman is turned into an enigma. Such a discursive construction incites the presumption that the real nature of these women is concealed, their truth is disguised and they appear in a false deceptive manner. They are therefore other than what they appear to be. (Yegenoglu 1998: 44)

The belief is that these women are hiding, they are dangerous, they are the tools of their oppressive fathers, husbands, brothers (Fanon 1965: 165). Frantz Fanon explicitly describes Western frustration when he writes: 'This woman who sees without being seen frustrates the colonizer. There is no reciprocity. She does not yield herself, does not give herself, does not offer herself' (ibid.: 169). Fanon and Yegenoglu provide great understanding for how women are Orientalized in the Western imagination because of wearing the veil. But it also prepares us for current fears about the blurring of gender lines that currently incite such fear in Western militaries on the ground in Afghanistan. The burqa has come to be seen as dangerous as it might hide a potential attacker, male or female, and it signals the presence of Islam, which has come to be regarded as a threat to Western well-being.[7] Certainly no news source examined for this project attempts a clear and thorough explanation of the very complicated meaning of wearing the veil. What would motivate such an explanation? It would lack the mystery that Orientalism requires, it would not titillate, or offer self-congratulation to the Western reader.

Even news stories that attempt to do the right thing by pointing to the difficult situation that occupation has created for Afghan women end up using language that positions Afghanistan as primitive, hopeless. Jessica

Leeder (2009), of the *Canadian Globe and Mail*, produced and reported in a six-part series on the state of Afghan women in Kandahar, where women are, as Leeder says: 'sold like livestock.' She describes Kandahar as an 'Almost prehistoric slice of Afghan society.' Really? Prehistoric? Do cavemen live there? She does admit, though, unlike most US news sources, that the situation for women, in Kandahar at least, has indeed deteriorated since the US/Canadian/Western invasion. She says that on her last visit to Kandahar, prior to the series being released in 2009, the situation for women was 'more precarious than it had been 5 months earlier.' She goes on to say that women are 'further from shedding their burqas, instead, they are scrambling to put them back on.'

In contrast, Alissa Rubin of the *New York Times* recently wrote about her experience wearing a burqa. She tells of purchasing one in order to be safer as she travelled 'unembedded' into Taliban territory. 'I had always thought of the women wearing them as blue ghosts or as invisible – because a woman without a face in a sense does not exist' (Rubin 2011d). Rubin is setting out to interview women who are ghosts, who do not exist? This is revelatory of the process in which Afghan women's stories are always already known before the interview. What can a non-existent woman or a ghost possibly tell you that you don't already know? Anne Cubilié tells us that calling Afghan women in burqas 'ghosts' predisposes us to hear only certain parts of their stories and ensures that we will never really know who they are:

... we privilege voice and individuality in the face of death and repression, but only in the stories that we are prepared to hear, not necessarily the stories survivors would tell if we listened differently. To name a woman a 'ghost' because we cannot see her face not only removes her (again) from the human but privileges her speech as that which comes from the realm of the dead or the uncanny. (Cubilié 2005: xii)

Alissa Rubin, however, continues to imagine that she can put herself in the position of the Afghan woman merely by putting the burqa on:

I felt rejected with my burqa down, as if I were not good enough to be seen in public. I leaned back in the seat and felt a wash of passivity come over me. Nothing was demanded of me except silence. I could sleep through life in this veiled state or, if I were someone who readily got angry, I would probably feel moved to tear it off. But I am not someone who readily gets angry, and I knew how much the trip depended on my being invisible until I absolutely had to show my face in order to do interviews. (Rubin 2011d)

She describes 'passivity' coming over her, which of course adheres to the idea of veiled women in the Western imagination. Yet the Western media is also always anxious to laud women throwing off their veils and acting outside of culturally accepted roles. How does this happen if the veil confers 'passivity'? Alissa Rubin displays how deeply she believes in the suffocation caused by the burqa as she indicates that she cannot or will not conduct her interviews with veil in place. She insists on unveiling the women she interviews, violating their decency codes in order to produce her story – which will benefit her career – that will represent Afghan women only in the always already known, over-determined way. The burqa is only for hiding for her, for guaranteeing safe passage. She goes on:

> The burqa here is a complicated item of clothing. Wearing one is seen by a number of women in Kabul – Afghan women as well as Westerners who live here – as a political statement; as acquiescence in or even endorsement of a hierarchy in which women have little power outside the home, and where their status is dependent on their being for all intents and purposes unseen. Some see it simply as a throwback to Taliban times, which they want to banish forever. When I told an Afghan friend here that I had worn a burqa for the trip, she shook her head and said, 'Oh no,' I could tell that she worried that next I might stop caring about women's rights. (Ibid.)

Maybe her 'Afghan friend' was appalled at Rubin's use of the burqa as disguise, as a means of safe passage. Maybe she was worried that Rubin would write something like this about wearing the burqa that seems to deliberately misunderstand or misrepresent how Afghan women see or experience it:

> For the woman wearing the burqa, however, the experience can be quite a bit more routine. In many parts of Afghanistan, for a woman's face and neck to be seen is to be considered cheap. And to be cheap is to be at the risk of death. A woman who is seen as a prostitute, or as someone with the intent of seducing men, is a candidate for an honor killing. Although it reflects the culture's restrictive views about women, wearing one is a ticket to getting out of the house, to going to the market or to a friend's house or to visit your mother or to work, because if you are wearing one you are unlikely to be accused of being a seductress. (Ibid.)

Is this what the West is attempting to achieve in Afghanistan? Giving women the right to appear 'cheap'? Available? Here Rubin invokes the specter of honor killings to be sure the reader does not forget how dangerous Afghan men can be, how oppressed Afghan women are, and how necessary Western rescue is. Even though, as she enumerates later, wearing the veil bestows various freedoms on women – they can see family, socialize, and, more importantly, shop – their liberation, their ability to seem to be a prostitute, relies on Western men. So the aim of Western involvement in Afghanistan is to rescue women from their virtue. In writing about the history of the wearing of the veil and Western interpretations of the practice, Mohja Kahf argues that Western influence has meant prohibitions on wearing the veil from time to time that are always resisted. She, like Denise Kandiyoti (Khaleeli 2011) and others, argues that it is not the veil itself that oppresses and that the West would not be 'freeing' Afghan women from it (Kahf 2008: 38):

> It is possible that power is not given or taken away from Muslim women by the absence or presence of the veil, but by the presence or absence of economic, political, and family rights. It is possible that women who want to veil have their own reasons, stemming from their own priorities and not those of patriarchal authorities. (Ibid.: 39)

A woman named Aziuta Rafaat told a reporter from the *New York Times* that she was 'ready to stay veiled forever if necessary: "They think it's all about the burqa," she said. "I'm ready to wear two burqas if my government can provide security and rule of law. That's O.K. with me. If that's the only freedom I have to give up, I'm ready"' (Nordberg 2010). Here Aziuta Rafaat seems to both critique Western obsession with the burqa and the failures of the occupation and acknowledge that the wearing of it oppresses her. She says that not wearing the veil would be a 'freedom I have to give up,' but then indicates her willingness to do so in order to live a life safe from violence, from occupation.

Joan Wallach Scott quotes former French President Jacques Chirac as saying 'Wearing the veil, whether it is intended or not, is a kind of aggression' (2007: 158). She goes on, 'In this comment, Chirac was conflating terrorism and the veil with an oblique reference to the hidden danger of women's repressed sexuality. Out there to see, women's sexuality was manageable; unseen, it might wreak havoc' (ibid.: 159). She suggests that all of this focus on unveiling is more about Western men's freedom and desire than about rescue:

> The aggression he [Chirac] referred to was twofold: that of the veiled woman but also of the (Western) man trying to look at her. The

aggression of the woman consisted in denying (French) men the pleasure – understood as a natural right (a male prerogative) – to see behind the veil. This was taken to be an assault on male sexuality, a kind of castration. Depriving men of an object of desire undermined the sense of their own masculinity. Sexual identity (in the Western or 'open' model) works both ways: men confirm their sexuality not only by being able to look at – to openly desire – women but also by receiving a 'look' from women in return. The exchange of desirous looks, the availability of faces for reading, is a crucial aspect of gender dynamics in 'open' systems. (Ibid.: 159)

Once again, here is liberation, being stripped of one's culture, one's material history, one's religious practices in order to be seen by, to flirt with, Western men. It is the aggression of the Western male whose message is that women *should* be available to be seen and to see.

Orientalizing Afghan masculinity

Of course, it seems that to the West, the greatest fear about the burqa is not that evil women – or ghosts – hide beneath them; it is that brown men do. In 2009, the *Independent on Sunday* wrote about an attack on government offices in several cities that featured men disguised by burqas (Sengupta 2009). More recently, according to various Western news sources, including Voice of America (28 June 2011), 'More and more male militants are dressing as women to escape capture from security forces in Afghanistan.' The *Washington Post* reports that the men who attacked a compound in Kabul in September 2011 with intentions to attack the US embassy and NATO headquarters were 'dressed as women' and burqas were found among the weapons they possessed (Londoño and Hamdard 2011). *The Australian* published a photo from the Associated Press in July 2011 that featured seven men, four of whom had burqas draped over their heads and shoulders with their faces revealed. One of them is bearded. Some of the rest of their clothes seem to be printed with 'feminine' designs. They are handcuffed. Phyllis Chesler, former radical feminist and renowned anti-Islam writer, seized upon this image as she blogged in *Front Page Magazine*:[8] 'There they all stand, guilty as sin, Afghan Taliban terrorists disguised in women's burqas but exposed ...' She includes additional photos that look like they might be staged or faked. The same men appear in one of the photos, but even though they are outdoors, in front of them is a table that clearly belongs indoors with lots of guns piled on it within easy reach of these supposed prisoners.[9] The third photo is of a figure in a burqa being searched by soldiers. It is not clear whether this is one of the men from the story or a woman. Chesler cites Daniel Pipes in enumerating supposed crimes men disguised in burqas have committed, including: 'peeped into women's bathrooms.' So along with resisting the occupation, Chesler seems to be suggesting, these men are perverts – cross-dressing and being voyeurs. Daniel Pipes, founder and director of the Middle East Forum and Campus Watch, was appointed by George Bush to sit on the board of the United States Institute of Peace. He is virulently anti-Islam and claims to have '60 million page viewers' for his blog.[10] In arguing for a ban on burqas, Pipes relates various crimes that were committed by burqa-clad criminals. The first is a robbery that occurred in 1998, where the proprietor of a liquor store claimed to be hypnotized by burqa-wearing thieves. He includes the Elizabeth Smart kidnapping in this list, as he claims she was shrouded in a 'niqab-like garment' in order to obscure her identity. He seems a bit confused here at who the actual victim is – Elizabeth Smart, who wore the 'niqab-like' garment, or the kidnapper, who, interestingly enough, was not Muslim. Pipes includes crimes in various locations such as Pakistan, Somalia, Philadelphia, Toronto, and Great Britain among other places. The variety of locations and types of crimes included defy the imagination and seem rather undisciplined in their composition. Chesler too makes an argument to ban burqas based only in part on fear of males masquerading as women. She goes on to ask: 'Why are burqas allowed in public? Or rather, why don't we view them as potentially suspicious as opposed to a religious custom which we infidels are obligated to honor and revere? For reasons of safety, the West, and for that matter the entire Muslim world, should immediately ban the burqa as a security threat.' Finally, she makes an outrageous claim in which she conflates adherence to gender norms, religion, or cultural custom with terrorism: 'And, as I have said before, wherever burqas, chadris, or the extreme Saudi or Iranian versions of female head, face and body covering exist, you will probably find fundamentalist Islam and potentially infidel-hating, Jew-hating terrorists. Burqas and jihad go hand in hand.'[11] While neither Pipes nor Chesler is a journalist, they are both well-known public figures in the US and both have followings and influence journalists and academic writings. The ideas they articulate on their websites that play on fears circulate. So they quote and support each other and pieces of their arguments get taken up and made into news – or truth – by journalists as their arguments feed right into the logic of war.

'Strange sex' and 'dancing boys'

A good example of the way these ideas circulate, sometimes with little or no foundation, to be made into facts, has to do with questions of sexuality in relation to the Afghan people, particularly Afghan men. A connection gets made between Afghan men's supposed willingness to hide under a burqa and their sexuality. On his website, Daniel Pipes has an entry entitled 'Strange sex stories from the Muslim world.' He claims that: 'The deepest differences between Muslims and Westerners concern not politics but sexuality.' Some of the headings he has created for articles that he includes are revelatory in their heterosexist and gender-normative biases: 'Muslim men desiring Jewish women on Israeli beaches,' 'Iranian authorities endorse gang rapes,' 'Camp for "effeminate" schoolboys in Malaysia,' 'Sexually aggressive Saudi females,' 'Afghan girls dressed as boys to attend school,' 'Homosexuality rampant in Afghanistan but denied.' The last few stories from Afghanistan are interesting in that they demonstrate this circulation issue and the ways that these ideas move around the world to create notions about who Afghans are. Jenny Nordberg of the *New York Times* wrote a story in September of 2010 describing how some families dress their little girls as boys in order to create opportunity for them to attend school, work outside the home, and so that they can be more respected in their communities. From the story, it appears that pragmatic concerns drive this practice rather than any desire on the family's or children's parts to gender-bend or change gender. There is only one person, Zahra, in the story who refuses to change back in the way most young women do around the time of puberty. '"People use bad words for girls," she said, "they scream at them on the street. When I see that I don't want to be a girl. When I am a boy they don't speak to me like that."' Zahra's refusal, however, at least according to what she tells the reporter, is based too on practical concerns such as safe passage through the streets. Pipes, however, uses this story in order to make it appear that there are unusual sexual or gender practices taking place in Afghanistan. Zahra gets lumped in with 'sexually aggressive Saudi females' and '"effeminate" schoolboys in Malaysia.' Even these Afghan families' ingenuity in avoiding oppression for their girl children gets named as perversity or strangeness, revealing how thin the ostensible Western concern for Afghan women actually is.

Of greater concern, though, is the way stories about sexuality that have suspicious origins get taken up and circulated. Pipes, like other right-wing bloggers and publishers, has repeated a story reported first on Fox News (2010) about same-sex practices among Pashtun men.

As Pipes quotes Fox: 'an entire region in the country [Afghanistan] is coping with a sexual identity crisis.' They quote a woman named Anna Maria Cardinalli[12] (another woman deployed to screen colonial desires or create them), who reportedly works for a 'Human Terrain Team' research unit of the military. These Human Terrain Teams are groups of social scientists who are charged with conducting research that facilitates military missions. These units are quite controversial, with disciplines such as anthropology in the US taking a strong stance against participation. Nonetheless, they do continue to exist under low visibility. Fox News is the originator of this story in the US about Afghan men's sexual practices, and they claim that they are quoting from an unclassified HTT report, but Fox News and the *Washington Times* (Gertz 2010) are the only conventional news organizations to run the story.[13] In the UK, though, the *Telegraph* ran the same story in January 2011 but claimed that the research was done at the request of British military officers who were concerned that their troops were being approached by Afghan men in the region for sex (Farmer 2010). The Fox story claims, and Pipes repeats, that 'Pashtun men commonly have sex with other men, admire other men physically, have sexual relationships with boys, and shun women both socially and sexually – yet they completely reject the label of homosexual ...' Here same-sex relationships make these men perverts, and yet their refusal of the category of homosexual is also proof of their perversion. Jasbir Puar and Amit Rai (2002: 124) point to the ways that the men Chesler and Pipes and now others would name as terrorists are always already sexually suspect in that they are assumed to practice a kind of 'failed heterosexuality' and they are likened to 'monsters' whose history can be traced to 'racial and sexual monsters of the eighteenth and nineteenth centuries' (ibid.: 117).

All of these stories repeat the following: 'The report also detailed a disturbing practice in which "older men of status" keep young boys on hand for sexual relationships. One of the country's favorite sayings, the report said, is "women are for children, boys are for pleasure."' Not coincidentally, this story appeared in January 2010 at exactly the time the initial airing of PBS's *Frontline* film, *The Dancing Boys of Afghanistan*, was supposed to occur. The airing was delayed owing to the producer's wish to secure safety for one of the boys profiled in the film, and it was eventually aired in April 2010. Since this film had to be in production long before the initial air-date, one wonders how much the film informed the HTT report and subsequent news stories. The *Guardian* had previously published an identically titled story on this practice in September 2009, as had CNN, and BBC News. CNN is the only news entity that made specific reference to the marginality of these practices: 'It's pretty much unappreciated by [the] society, unaccepted and illegal' (Abawi 2009b). In the other stories, it was made to sound as if the practice was widespread, including, in the *Frontline* film, among members of President Karzai's government. One critic, John Doyle of the *Globe and Mail*, wrote about the *Frontline* film: 'The program ... really makes you wonder about the country, and the post-Taliban Afghanistan we have sent our soldiers to help create and to protect ...' This, it seems, is the point of all this. Accusations of widespread non-normative gender practices and same-sex sex fit in very nicely with Orientalized ideas about Muslim men. Phyllis Chesler weighs in on this story with more invective, claiming that: 'Homosexual pederasty is epidemic in the Muslim world.' And, of course, she blames it on the burqa!

> Look: Wherever women are forced to wear chadors, burqas, niqab, be sure that in addition to woman-abuse and woman-hatred, children are also being abused. For men, especially warriors who are brought up apart from women, taught to fear and despise women, their major erotic and social drives will be male-centric, not female-centric. Homosexual pederasty accompanies extreme gender apartheid in an extreme way. (Chesler 2010b)

While Chesler's comments are stomach-churning in their overt racism and hatred of Muslims and queer people, she is only really articulating a stronger distaste for those groups than is probably present but more carefully obscured in the other pieces. The publication of these stories in certain politically right-leaning sites is evidence that there is sufficient homophobia in the West to prompt not only legitimization of Western imperialism, but a wholesale condemnation of entire states, regions, or religions. While the practices made visible in *The Dancing Boys of Afghanistan* where young boys are exploited by older men need to be condemned in the strongest possible terms, one must also recognize that these practices occur with alarming regularity in other cultures as well. One need only consider the Catholic priest scandal in the US and elsewhere in the last several years or the more recent allegation against a certain high-profile sports coach at a major university in the US to begin to grasp the enormity of the problem of pedophilia. Given its prevalence, one has to assume that it is not accidental that *Frontline* and the *Guardian* both chose to focus on Afghanistan in order to conduct an exposé on this practice. Exposure to these stories helps the West to focus disgust and hatred on Afghanistan, on these 'monsters,' thereby legitimizing war and imperialism.[14]

Elections, immolation, safe(r) spaces

Even with visibility/invisibility problems, the lives of Afghan women are made visible by the Western media at key times in order to uphold the rescue narrative. The Western media helps create, authorize, and buttress the guise of concern for women. Lest we forget the reason we are in Afghanistan, women, and women's concerns, become temporarily visible. Afghan elections constitute one of those times. In September of 2010, while parliamentary elections were being held there, the Sunday *New York Times* ran a photo of Afghan women election officials. Nine women covered by burqas are seated at tables outside a polling place. There is what appears to be a male child standing on one of the tables. There are two figures in the background who appear to be draped in black. They may be women as well, although it is difficult to tell. The caption under the photo reads: 'Polling agents in Kabul waited Saturday during Afghan parliamentary elections; many voters were deterred by attacks.' Of course, there is no reference to how these women may be endangered by the 'democratic' process put in place by the occupiers, a process ostensibly intended to liberate them. The accompanying story by Elizabeth Bumiller and Rod Norland, both longtime correspondents in the area, does not mention women at all, or these particular women and their safety or lack thereof. There is someone called Shafiqa who I assume is female. Shafiqa is quoted on the last page of the story, after descriptions of shootings and grenade attacks at various polling places. She talks of her determination to vote in spite of these circumstances and warnings from her family. 'My family insisted I not come but I have to because this is my country and I want to use my vote for someone I like' (Bumiller and Norland 2010: 14). We are left believing that it is worth it for Afghan women to take their lives in their hands to participate in elections known to be corrupt. It is the guise of democracy that counts, the façade, the snappy quote. In 2005 in the *Washington Times*, five Republican members of Congress submitted an op-ed that described the changes in Afghanistan in glowing terms that include: 'The astounding numbers of men and women who put their names on the ballot is quite an achievement and a testament to their belief in representative government.' They continue: '... millions of Afghans emphatically demonstrated their rejection of Taliban violence and asserted their desire to have a representative and democratically elected government.' They go on to describe all the beneficial changes our occupation has meant to the Afghan people, particularly Afghan women, citing things like improvement in maternal mortality rates, which all other sources suggest have not occurred. The *Toronto Star*, reporting on the same elections, included information on both women candidates and women voters. They quote a woman as saying: "'I am so happy, so happy." Said Khatereh Mushafiq, 18, her black veil decorated with white flowers pulled back from her face as she went to vote in a girls' school in Kandahar. "We are also now taking part in the government and in society. People must take part; people must have a say."' The other persons interviewed for the story are male and they do acknowledge, in the second- and third-to-last sentences in the article, that the turnout among women was quite varied: 'Women voters participated heavily in some locations such as the southern city of Kandahar, where reports said women outnumbered men in some places. In other provinces, female turnout was expected to be in the single digits.'

On the eve of the 2004 elections, Robert Charles, an assistant Secretary of State who oversees the training of Afghan police, judges and prosecutors, is quoted as saying: 'I think a year from now, Americans are going to look back and they are going to be prouder than proud' (Zoroya 2004). The story goes on to say: 'Politics as a form of expression, has been rapidly embraced. The candidates have been counseled by U.N. communication specialists about selling themselves to the voters. "Convince him that he needs you, that you will make his life easier or better," teaches one of the specialists ... Forty percent of the registrants are women, surpassing all expectations. And yet, 87% of Afghans responding to a survey say women should be guided by husbands and fathers in choosing a candidate, according to a survey conducted early this year by the Asia Foundation.'

The BBC Online, on the eve of the 2010 elections where a record number of women stood for parliament, included photos of two women candidates, Robina Jalali and Hawa Nooristani, with their faces visible. The third woman pictured, Shaima Shafaq Sadat, is described as a business owner who was asked for a comment on the women running for office (Somerville 2010). During the same election, the *Guardian* ran a story on the killing of campaign workers who worked for one of the female candidates. This story featured a photo of four women completely covered by burqas (Boone 2010a).

Overall, in spite of the intermittent visibility in times of elections in the Western media that signals women's apparent rescue by Western ideas, the war must still be justified. Thus Afghan women's liberation, despite their having the right to vote, cannot be seen as a completed project. In the *New York Times*, Elizabeth Rubin reports that Afghan men remain unconvinced: 'Because the men are saying: "Don't vote for women. It's not Koranic. It's only on the order of Bush's wife Laura that women are candidates"' (Rubin 2005). Female candidates have been the victims of assassination attempts and several high-profile Afghan women have been assassinated. Western news sources confirmed that, for Afghan women, running for office was dangerous when many of them reported in 2010 that women were getting death threats (Boone 2010a; Hunter 2010; Somerville 2010; King 2010). Unfortunately, there are questions as to the motivation of some of these female candidates, and there is speculation that they may be running at the behest of powerful men in Afghanistan, who, once the women are elected, will be calling the shots (Cavendish 2010; Starkey 2010; Douglas 2010). This is a regrettable situation, whether the story about women running is simply rumor or conjecture or true.

Under the terms of Afghanistan's hybrid constitution with its mixture of Islam and Western-style democracy, there was initially great hope among Afghan women and some international feminists that there would be improvements in the lives of women there. The accompanying debate over women's role and treatment within the Loya Jirga, however, along with the continuing controversy over women's roles within the society itself (for example, the question of whether women are full citizens under the law), is not a hopeful sign that things will be resolved positively for Afghan women (Heyzer 2003; Suncer 2004). Afghan women do have an important role to play in the new imperialism. Not only did they serve as a handy excuse for the invasion of Afghanistan, but under the contradictions inherent in transnational sexism, certain of them were also utilized to represent all women from that part of the world as dangerous, the creators of baby terrorists – or as screens for male bloodthirsty terrorists. The same Western press that willingly creates and promotes these images, that repeats the Bush and Obama administration's ostensible concern for Afghan women without question, and that frequently portrays Islam as primitive and archaic, is silent on the subject of women's lives being governed by Islamic sharia laws under the new constitution. This 'now you see and care about women, now you don't' trick in the policies of the US and in press reports is a manifestation of transnational sexism. Empire-building and concerns for women's rights do not easily go hand in hand. Cynthia Enloe tells us that '... A government that invades another country in the name of women's liberation shows

39

its true colors when it passively accepts its local allies' patriarchal policies' (2004: 23). In fact, the Western states have done worse than this; the invasion has created a situation in which local patriarchy is exacerbated and facilitated and then layered with Western patriarchy and transnational sexism, creating a new super-oppression.

In the ongoing media practice of the now you see them, now you don't approach to Afghan women, while Western audiences do not see images of women harmed as a direct result of war, there are multiple stories, sometimes including photos, of harm that befalls women as a result of oppressive patriarchal practices inside Afghanistan. For example, the disfigured face of Bibi Aisha appeared on the cover of *Time* magazine under the caption 'What happens when we leave Afghanistan.'[15] Rob Nordland of the *New York Times* calls Kabul a 'misogynist desert' in an article about the restored 'Women's Garden' in that city. Ivan Simonovic of the *Guardian* suggests that all Afghan men are dangerous to Afghan women – even the police: 'The only safe haven for victims of domestic violence are NGO-run shelters for women and girls, yet Afghan authorities have recently threatened their continued operation' (Simonovic 2011). Most damning is this passage:

> 'Violence in the lives of Afghanistan's women comes from everywhere: from her father or brother, from her husband, from her father-in-law, from her mother-in-law, and sister-in-law,' said Dr. Shafiqa Eanin, a plastic surgeon at the burn hospital which usually has at least 10 female self-immolation cases at any one time. (Rubin 2010b)

Accompanying this story in the *New York Times* is a photo of an Afghan woman named Farzana who allegedly burned herself because 'her father-in-law belittled her.' The online version of the story includes a slide show of fifteen photos of several different women who are being treated for burns. It is horrifying. Accompanying the last photo is the legend 'The most sinister cases are actually murders masquerading as suicides said doctors, nurses, and human rights workers.' Alissa Rubin's blog piece has a video accompaniment that begins with a woman in the hospital screaming in pain. It is too horrible to watch.

In case Western readers and viewers remain unconvinced about the danger posed to Afghan women by their relationships to Afghan men, there are an abundance of stories about Afghan women's self-immolation. In these stories, while the oppression of innocent Afghan women is obvious, often other Afghan women, usually those related to husbands but sometimes the woman's own mother, are depicted as quite evil in their own right. It is tricky to portray these kinds of women simultaneously. Nic Robertson of CNN reports: 'Afghan society is closed to outsiders even to neighbors, but if you are a woman here you risk entrapment sealed off more completely inside the home than out. No one will know your pain, few will hear your screams, and if they did, its unlikely they'd dare care.' *Time* magazine's headline read: 'When women set themselves on fire' (Hauslohner 2010). The *New York Times*' Alissa Rubin has written extensively on this issue. In one piece she suggests that the women are discouraged from admitting that they burned themselves for fear they will be murdered by doctors (Rubin 2010b). She succinctly describes the situation for women in Afghanistan in 2010, after seven years of occupation:

> 'The choices for Afghan women are extraordinarily restricted: Their family is their fate. There is little chance for education, little choice about whom a woman marries, no choice at all about her role in their own house. Her primary job is to serve the husband's family. Outside that world, she is an outcast. You run away from home, you may be raped or put in jail and then sent home and then what happens to you?' asked Rachel Reid, a researcher for Human Rights Watch who tracks violence against women. Runaways are often shot or stabbed in honor killings because families fear they have spent time unchaperoned with a man. (Ibid.)

Why this focus on presenting women and women's bodies around this issue and no other? Women being burned or burning themselves in domestic situations is the Western media in general's equivalent to the *Time* magazine cover. It serves as both justification for continued presence in Afghanistan and warning to those who would advocate the troops leaving. Afghan men are still dangerous to women. They are dangerous both directly – through the faking of suicides for those they have murdered – and indirectly when their family's actions or their neglect cause women to become so depressed as to set themselves on fire.

In a similar vein are the numerous stories about girls being attacked when going to school and the coverage of the acid attacks on girls going to school. There seems to be no hesitancy in showing photos of these young women. Accompanying Dexter Filkins's front-page story in the *New York Times* (Filkins 2009) is a photo of two girls in school. One of them, a victim of such an incident, has her face turned to the camera so that her scar is visible. There is also a slideshow of Afghan girls who are suddenly visible now that they have been attacked by Afghan men. There are numerous stories written about women in the newly constructed shelters in Kabul (Sidner and Moshaberat 2012; Rubin 2011a; Lawrence 2011). All of these stories include photos. The MSNBC story (Sidner and Moshaberat 2012) features a woman whose face is scarred from an acid attack from a scorned suitor; the *New York Times* story (Rubin 2011a) has a picture of a woman feeding her baby inside the shelter. The third (Lawrence 2011) features the usual photo of two women in burqas. Afghan women's visibility in Western popular culture depends on their vulnerability to Afghan men.

It feels redundant, depressing, and useless to keep enumerating the horror that constitutes Afghan women's lives, and yet it may never be enough to offset the power of the rescue narratives that are enumerated in the Western press. It is only the threat of Western withdrawal that prompts many news sources to begin to report on women's lives, and then only to suggest that they have improved greatly but are vastly at risk if the West leaves.

2 | 'Real housewives': married to the enemy

Only one wife had a face. A blurred image from her passport was sole proof that the three remaining wives of Osama bin Laden existed. In the days after the killing of Osama bin Laden, the story about Amal Ahmed Abdul Fatah, his youngest wife, referred to mostly as simply 'his Yemeni wife,' kept changing in the Western press. First she had been used as a human shield by bin Laden. Later, she had tried to defend him against the Navy Seals who killed him. In these stories she is at the same time a nameless object so without worth or agency that she can be used for male protection and a fierce defender of her husband. The Western news coverage of Amal Ahmed Abdul Fatah illustrates the conundrum of visibility/invisibility and the problem of representation when Muslim women are depicted in the war on terror. In this chapter the press coverage following the assassination of Osama bin Laden that focused on his wives is examined alongside news accounts from various Western popular press sources about the family of Saddam Hussein in order to examine how transnational sexism is enacted in public discourse about Muslim women. When women are included in these narratives, they are deployed not only to support the Bush and Obama administrations' foreign policy and aggression in the region, but also to reinforce Western male supremacy and white supremacy.

Perhaps because, according to Western standards, Iraqi women were less oppressed than Afghan women prior to the West's invasion, in Western news stories about Iraqi women, they are depicted as menacing, the creators of the WMDs, supporters of Saddam Hussein, creators of peril. Unlike Afghan women, they were not, initially at least, characterized as victims. Both Iraqi women and men needed only to be 'rescued' from Saddam Hussein. The rescuing Iraqi women required was from a particular brown man, Saddam Hussein, rather than brown-skinned men in general. Iraqi women are depicted in Western media as much more villains than victims. Other women are similarly characterized as dangerous, such as bin Laden's wives, Saddam Hussein's daughters, or the figure of the female suicide bomber.

These news stories further reveal how gender relations are thrown into flux by the presence of Western militaries whose influence remains long after troop withdrawal.

Married to bin Laden

The killing of Osama bin Laden in May 2011 occasioned a plethora of news stories about the manner of his killing, about joy in the US about his death, and about the manner in which he was living, with a particular focus on his three wives. Some of the headlines were as follows: 'Talk of who betrayed Osama bin Laden sparks a harem scuffle' (Lamb 2011a), 'I want to be martyred with you; Bin Laden's young wife's suicide pledge to terror mastermind' (Daily Mail 2011), 'Slut and traitor. Otherwise known as Osama's widows' (Skoch 2012), 'Osama Bin Laden's matchmaker: real housewives of Abbottabad' (Ross 2011), and 'Osama Bin Laden: keeping up with the Kardashians?' (Ross 2012). These headlines and the accompanying stories position the women in bin Laden's life as suicidal victims, squabbling harridans, Orientalized objects of male desire, and finally fame-seeking reality stars. Transnational sexism is rampant in these depictions. Bin Laden's wives are always placed in opposition to the Western liberated model of femininity, but here they are also depicted as practicing femininity in a manner reminiscent of the least admirable Western women, such as the Kardashians.

Maybe because Western news reporters can't seem to get the women's names right, the narrative of what happened the day bin Laden was killed and the history of their relationships with him and what has happened since to these women is quite muddled. Masood (2012) identifies the three women as Kharia Hussain Sabir, Siham Sharif, and Amal Ahmad Abdul Fateh. In the *Washington Post*, as in several other publications, the two older women are identified as sharing the same surname: Siahm Saber and Khairiah Saber. Here, bin Laden's Yemeni wife is identified as Amal Ahmed al-Sadah (Leiby 2012). In a CNN story (Todd and Lister 2011), she is identified as Amal Ahmed al Sadah. In Jean Sasson et al.'s book *Growing up bin Laden* (2009: 305) and in the *Daily Mail* the woman from Yemen is referred to as Amal al sada (G. Smith 2012). A Reuters report from the same day as the CNN story doesn't name the three women at all. The practice of not naming these women, but instead referring to them as bin Laden's wives, is a common practice in Western news stories. The irony of their lack of proper identification by news sources located within states purportedly interested in their liberation seems not to have occurred to the writers of these stories.

The news stories are rife with misogyny and transnational sexism. Early news reports had Amal either being the only wife present in the compound (Todd and Lister 2011) or coming most recently to join bin Laden in Pakistan and betraying him. Others blame the betrayal on Khairiah. It is important to note that many of these stories position one of the women as being the betrayer of bin Laden. This is contrary to early and enduring reports that bin Laden's courier was the means to the US locating him. The implication of these accusations is that women cannot be trusted in spite of the fact that two of bin Laden's wives were with him in hiding for years. Stories about the raid on the compound had bin Laden using Amal as a shield to guard himself against the Americans, and then reports were that she had flung herself in front of her husband, though subsequently those stories were disproved (Yasin 2011). An extraordinary number of stories describing the raid and the compound and what happened when the US Navy Seals arrived quickly emerged.[1] This was surprising given that so much secrecy surrounded the mission. Then, when that topic had been debated and numerous false accounts had been floated and invalidated, stories began to appear about whether the wives were giving information to US and Pakistani authorities. Other stories were focused on how much the women supposedly disliked each other.

It seems that the Western media did not know quite how to depict these women. None of the roles transnational sexism had carved out for them through these long years of war seemed to fit. Were they loyal to an extreme – Amal throwing herself in front of a bullet for bin Laden? Or were they dangerous to bin Laden and consequently friends of the West when either Khairiah or Amal betrayed him? In either case, they did not require rescue and they did not seem to be immediately dangerous. One reporter dared to say: 'The bin Laden wives have never been involved with al Qaeda' (Shah 2012). Still, a CNN report hints that the women had the potential to be deadly: 'He said bin Laden's three wives lived in harmony in the same house. They would go on family outings – bin Laden in a car followed by the family bus. On such outings, Abu Jandal said, the al Qaeda leader would teach his wives how to use firearms' (Todd and Lister 2011).

Here, unlike in other reports, the household seem harmonious, but the women's shooting lessons seem ominous. In spite of bin Laden's spending his entire working life in male-only spaces and his articulation of rage at the presence of women soldiers in Kuwait and Saudi Arabia during the Gulf War, this report has him seeing his daughter by Amal, Safiyah, as a warrior in the making: 'But in the weeks after

9/11, bin Laden told Pakistani journalist Hamid Mir that he had plans for his youngest daughter, Safiyah. "I became a father of a girl after September 11," he said. "I named her after Safiyah who killed a Jewish spy at the time of the Prophet. [My daughter] will kill enemies of Islam like Safiyah'" (ibid.).

This story suggests that, like the US military leaders who are resigned to having to work with women soldiers, bin Laden too is relying on women as warriors of the future.

The Western press would have you believe, though, that the women are fit only for fighting among themselves. Western media sources report with glee that the wives of bin Laden were not always living in harmony as suggested above. While in custody in Pakistan, the women were accused of having a 'vicious catfight' (Skoch 2012):

> The youngest of the late Al-Qaeda leader's five widows, Amal, 29, had to be pulled apart from his eldest bride Khairiah, 61, after the pair began brawling in a Pakistan prison ... Guards have now been ordered to make sure their paths never again cross. (G. Smith 2012).

> The three widows of Osama bin Laden are turning on each other in custody, with two older Saudi women blaming a much younger Yemeni wife for leading US intelligence to their hideout. 'It's vicious,' said a Pakistani official briefed on the interrogation of the widows. (Lamb 2011a)

The likening of the women to animals – the allegation about a 'catfight' – raises old ideas about women of color being closer to nature. These ideas are reinforced by the notion that the women were fighting over who had betrayed bin Laden or who had more of his attention. It is inconceivable to the makers of these stories that three women could live in harmony and be supportive of each other and their husband. Other news sources argue that it was the conditions in the compound that created strife between the women:

> Phil Mudd, who helped lead the CIA's search for bin Laden, says the life described by the terror leader's youngest wife, particularly the six years of close confinement in an Abbottabad compound stuffed with spouses and offspring, sounds uncomfortably familiar. Mudd said the living situation guaranteed strife. 'If you look at the size of the compound, it's not huge,' he said. 'You've got wives who range from fairly young, right now his Yemeni wife is still only 30 years old, to wives who range much older. You have sons involved in moving the family around. You have newborn kids coming in during the time he was on the run.

You certainly can't go out go to the market place or go to a movie. It's hard to imagine over the course of years that that didn't become a very difficult environment. I can only begin to imagine that that looked like American reality TV,' said Mudd, 'that he was living in some version of the Kardashians in Abbottabad'. (Ross 2012).

It seems that Phil Mudd is confusing the Kardashians with the Brown family from Lifetime's *Sister Wives*, an American television show about a Christian polygamous family. The Brown family's houses are stuffed with children and uproar. The Kardashians live separately and their money insulates them from the kind of chaos that Mudd suggests might be stressing out Amal and Khairiah. Perhaps he is not confused at all and simply is looking for a way to demean the women and their lifestyle since the Kardashians are often ridiculed in US popular culture. The Kardashians' interest in fame, their dedication to fashion, a particular performance of femininity, and monogamous heterosexuality make comparisons with the bin Ladens impossible.

In fact, numerous reports emphasized the poor living conditions of the bin Laden family in Abbottabad. On CNN, Peter Bergen describes a visit to the compound in Abbottabad after the assassination, and he declares the family to be living in 'squalor' (Bergen 2012). Another reporter adds about the house: 'Pictures of the home showed modest furnishings, cheap foam mattresses, no air conditioning, and old televisions though there was a large, seemingly well-tended, vegetable garden' (Burke 2011). The implication here is that it is remarkable that anyone could be living without air conditioning and with only 'old televisions' and believe it important to have a 'well-tended' vegetable garden. This reads as yet another manifestation of transnational sexism where women who live modestly within the confines of their culture and their religion are likened to the worst examples of Western excess.

Remarkably, bin Laden's widows have also been likened to other American reality television characters: 'Although the compound where bin Laden hid for five years was large, the three wives were all cooped up in the same house. Pakistani officials who have been debriefing the women portray life in the compound as an Islamic version of *Desperate Housewives*' (Lamb 2011a).

Desperate Housewives is a fictional, intended to be camp, portrayal of women who live in an upper-middle-class neighborhood in the US. The show aired for several seasons on ABC. There was a lot of sex, at least one murder, and some infidelity. The connection with women living together in a modest house, or 'squalor,' with one husband in a city in Pakistan is elusive. Perhaps the 'desperation' is projected on to them by Westerners who cannot conceive of living in that kind of situation in such conditions. Brian Ross of ABC News did a story entitled 'Real housewives of Abbottabad' in which questions about bin Laden's arranged marriage come up. Here, Amal is said to have entered into the marriage with bin Laden of her own will. In the Kardashian version of the story, the claim is that Amal was given to bin Laden as 'a gift' (Ross 2011). There are photos of Khairiah and Siham, but their faces are blacked out. The contrasts with any of the reality shows in the *Real Housewives* series that takes place in various US cities could not be stronger. In the opening of the show each woman from that cast is photographed preening in front of the camera while she is heard in voice-over describing how much she loves luxury, enjoys pampering herself, or is turned on by earning money. No matter the city, they all spend inordinate amounts of time shopping and dining in beautiful restaurants. They go on lavish trips and live in luxurious accommodations. Not so Khairiah, Siham, and Amal.

In the midst of all these stories, headlines like 'Osama bin Lothario: terror chief "was a sex machine who would vanish into the bedroom with his wife for days"' (Bates 2011) were circulated among various news producers. Especially on television, photos of bin Laden's bed often accompanied the stories about his assassination, indicating the enormous interest in his sex life and apparently his (im)potency. One story that seems to have originated at NBC News speculated that he used 'herbal Viagra' (Aleccia 2011; Kennedy 2011). It was also reported that investigators found pornography on computers that were seized in the raid on the compound (Shane 2011; Hosenball and Zakaria 2011; Saletan 2011). It was not clear whether the pornography was owned by bin Laden or whether it had been put on the computer by a previous owner, or whether in fact he had viewed any of it. The reporters were quick to note that his possession of it might tarnish his reputation as a good Muslim (Shane 2011). Reuters reports that there was no internet service at the compound, which could lead one to speculate that there was no pornography at all and that the claim was made simply to discredit bin Laden (Saletan 2011). In Jean Sasson et al.'s book, she quotes Najwa bin Laden, his first wife, as saying that they spent a lot of time in bed and then Sasson quotes Omar, one of bin Laden's sons with Najwa, as saying: 'Omar said that when he was a child, Osama would come home from Afghanistan and take Najwa into the bedroom and they wouldn't come out for days' (Sasson et al. 2009: 41). Indeed, some of the conflict between the wives in Pakistan was said to have to do with sexual jealousy. Numerous reporters said that the older wives were jealous that he spent most or all of his nights with Amal. Reporters said things like: 'Brainy Khairiah was said to be jealous about Amal getting to sleep with Osama all the time' (Skoch 2012). Khairiah is often designated as 'brainy.' So smart women aren't sexy? Or is Khairiah being compared with Najwa, his first wife, who had eleven children? Would she be designated as motherly? Are reporters simply surprised that he had smart wives? Or are they indicating a basic sexist assumption that most women are not smart? Below, the competition between the women for bin Laden's attention is elaborated: 'Khairiah accused Amal of sticking to Osama like a prostitute who wanted sex 24 hours a day. The two women did not get on when they lived together with Bin Laden, and a third wife, in his hideout in Abbottabod Pakistan' (G. Smith 2012).

Are we to believe that these were Khairiah's exact words and that she likened her sister wife to a prostitute? Iva Skoch makes a similar claim when she writes that in the midst of their fighting, the women were influenced by Western culture enough to call each other slut: 'Slut this slut that. And you know the slut PR machine is working well when even Osama bin Laden's widows in Pakistan are slut-calling each other' (Skoch 2012).

In the *Real Housewives* story, Brian Ross includes the opinion of a veiled 'expert on the role of women in Islam,' who suggests that Khairiah, Siham, and Amal 'would be called to do almost anything bin Laden wanted.' The expert's claims about the women's role in the family constructs these women as having no ability to choose a mate or to act upon their own desires. She suggests that they have no agency and they will enact their husband's wishes without question. The use of an expert here is revelatory of Westerners' inability to conceptualize what the lives of these women are like. Many reporters also seemed to obsess over the sexual arrangements in the family. The stories about sex, as usual in the Western imagination, put the women in competition for male – in this case bin Laden's – attention. There seems to be no question that the women would be acting out of their own desires. After all, Amal had been given to bin Laden as 'a gift.'

Finally, the notion that these women are simply motivated by or acting upon duty to the exclusion of their own well-being or desires is rampant in Western news accounts. Even the supposed betrayal of bin Laden is framed in terms of duty:

I have one final duty to perform for my husband. (Ross 2012)

At one point when pressed by Siham's adult son Khalid about why she had come, Khairiah said it was because she had 'one final duty' to perform for Bin Laden. It seems that even Bin Laden feared that she would turn him in, and he 'kept telling' the other two wives to leave but they refused, Qadir said. (Shah 2012)

Would Khairiah have betrayed her husband out of duty? Was leading the American forces to him part of her duty to her husband? Or was this duty instead to the state and to Westerners who promised rescue? Was bin Laden finally captured as a result of misguided loyalty to a man, an ideal, or a state? In any case, here Khairiah is depicted as having no will of her own. She is simply performing a duty regardless of whether that duty might put her, the other women, and all of their children in danger. Heedless of her own well-being, Khairiah does her duty. The lives of Khairiah, Siham, and Amal are difficult for most Westerners to understand. Whether they were directly working for al-Qaeda or not, their devotion to bin Laden carries with it a sense that these women are dangerous.

Another kind of rescue tale

On 15 December 2011, the US formally withdrew troops from Iraq. The troop stand-down was staggered, but the ceremony marking the US leaving was held on that day. It had been almost nine years since the US invaded Iraq, in spite of the protests of many US citizens and the objections of people and governments around the world. A few government leaders went along with George W. Bush's fictions about the connection between Saddam Hussein and the events of September 11th 2001 in the US, and others were persuaded by the never-discovered 'weapons of mass destruction' (WMDs). Of course, Iraqi women paid a heavy price for the actions of the Bush administration, both before the invasion – as a result of sanctions – and particularly after, as the invasion disrupted gender relations and curtailed women's freedoms.

During the US occupation of Iraq, women, who constitute 65 per cent of the population of Iraq (Sandler 2003a: 14), lived in a kind of 'de-facto house arrest' (ibid.: 11). Under Saddam Hussein's rule, women had enjoyed safety on the streets. Following the US occupation of Iraq, however, the rate of rapes and kidnapping within Iraq skyrocketed. This is particularly notable given the great social and legal discouragement of rape-reporting (Bjorken et al. 2003: 10). Iraqi women, already afraid to leave their homes, were being pressured, sometimes through open harassment on the street, to cover their heads (Colson 2003).

Stories about so-called 'honor killings' were quite abundant in the West. These stories are about crimes committed by a woman's family reportedly as the result of women being harassed or raped (Sandler 2003a: 23). That is, women who were abducted or raped are believed to bring shame upon the family and can be killed for being the victim of such an attack. Of course, these stories support the rescue narrative by confirming Western male superiority in the Western imagination and so are presented without question.

The real threat to Iraqi women, however, did not come from within families, or from Iraqi men. It came from the occupying forces. The US occupying force, eager to placate Iraqi men now in power, did not want to appear in word or deed too concerned about the status of women in Iraq (ibid.: 14). Nadje Al-Ali and Nicola Pratt (2009: 81) argue that US carelessness during the invasion and subsequent early occupation, when little was done in the form of providing security for the people or towards reconstruction, is responsible for the emergence of what they call a 'hyperpatriarchy' practiced by Iraqi men against Iraqi women.

> ... the post-invasion situation has created new and even more devas-
> tating forms of oppression for women by a range of social and politi-
> cal actors. The deterioration in the provision of basic services and
> infrastructure has not only increased women's burden with regard to
> domestic duties but helped to fuel the violence and criminality that is
> preventing women from participating in public life. Simultaneously,
> the negative situation for women is being rationalized in the form of
> new conservative social attitudes propagated by Islamic parties. (Ibid.)

The 'new conservative social attitudes' of which Al-Ali speaks are being promoted and bolstered by the occupation. In spite the pledge of L. Paul Bremer III, the US 'chief administrator' in Iraq, that 'We in the coalition are committed to continuing to promote women's rights in Iraq' (Filkins 2004a), reporter Lauren Sandler (2003a: 14) was told by one American official, 'We don't do women.' This statement is in direct contradiction to what Bremer said above, and more saliently it is inconsistent with the blatant deployment of women to justify the invasion and occupation of Afghanistan.

Of course the US does 'do women,' but only when it suits the goals of empire-building. The US military felt free to break conventions of warfare and alarm human rights groups when they seized civilians and family members of Iraqi officials' 'Most Wanted List' to question them or utilize the families as bargaining chips (Raghavan 2003). Izzat

Ibrahim al-Douri was a high-ranking official in Saddam Hussein's government. As a means to try to force him out of hiding, his wife and daughter, along with other family members, were arrested by coalition forces. While the case of Izzat Ibrahim al-Douri's family being taken into custody received only a little attention in the Western media, this practice of arresting family members was apparently quite widespread. The AP reports that 'American forces have frequently arrested relatives of fugitives to interrogate them on their family members' whereabouts and as a way of putting pressure on the wanted men to surrender' (AP, 27 November 2003). Colonel James Hickey, commander of the Army's 4th Infantry Division, explains, 'The upshot is, if you want to know what's going on with these guys, you've got to get inside their families' (Hendren 2003: 2).

Amnesty International has condemned these arrests (Bazzi 2003) and it is impossible to explain the arrests in the context of the 'freeing of the Iraqi people' that became the justification for the war since no weapons of mass destruction were found. Of course, feminists have long argued that use of the generic 'people' or 'citizens' erases the presence of gender and women in particular, so here we find the same old sexism women have objected to for many years. It is the new transnational sexism, however, which combines Orientalism and racism with gender oppression, that allowed the US military to arrest women and children in the name of fighting 'terror.' The terror imposed on these Iraqi families did not seem to matter. This version of transnational sexism enabled a US administration that was supposedly interested in the 'sanctity of families' to interfere with Iraqi families in this fashion. These same US government officials who claimed to want to protect women, to 'free' them from oppressive rule, arrested Iraqi women and held them responsible for the alleged actions of their fathers, husbands, brothers, sons.

All in the family

While much was written in the US about the role of American women in the torture of Iraqi men at Abu Ghraib, the presence of Iraqi women in that prison and others like it was scarcely acknowledged. It is reported that ninety Iraqi women and sixty children were being held in Abu Ghraib at the time of the torture incidents in 2003. All were arrested because of their relationship with particular men who were of interest to the occupying force (McKelvey 2005). Even Major General Taguba, in his report on the US military's investigation into the events and practices at Abu Ghraib, acknowledged that images of women were present in the masses of photographs taken there. He confirms, for example, that there is a photo of an Iraqi woman 'having sex with an American soldier' and others of women 'being forced to bare their breasts' (Harding 2004). Taguba's misnaming of rape or sexual assault as 'having sex' is revelatory of the ways in which US soldiers are tacitly given permission to take part in these atrocities. The women detained were not accused of any crime but rather were referred to as 'security detainees,' who were 'held without charge or legal access' (ibid.). The story above was printed in the British paper the *Guardian* in 2004 and was not widely available in the US. We will probably never know how many women were actually arrested in the long years of occupation. Still, as late as 2010, the *Christian Science Monitor* reported that these practices of unlawful detention of family members continued: 'Four days ago when one of the men wouldn't confess they said, "Bring in his wife." They put her in a separate room nearby and beat her so he could hear her screaming,' says the witness. 'They went back to the man and said, "We will rape her if you don't confess."'

Tara McKelvey has another horrible story:

> Four months after her husband was arrested, a woman named Selwa was seized from her home. She was asked such probing questions as: 'Do you know any insurgents?' The next day, a stocky American officer in boots and a T-shirt told Selwa she was responsible for the disposal of waste ... Human waste is dumped in metal containers, mixed with lighter fluid, and set on fire. Detainees are force to stir the mixture to speed its dissipation. That afternoon, the American officer lit a mixture of human feces and urine in a metal container and gave Selwa a heavy club to stir it. She recalls, 'The fire from the pot felt very strong on my face.' 'I became very tired,' she says. 'I told the sergeant I could not do it.' 'There was another man close to us. The sergeant came up to me and whispered in my ear, "If you don't, I will tell one of the soldiers to fuck you."' (McKelvey 2005)

It seems the women supposedly in need of protection from brown men instead need protection from the protectors. It bears repeating that these women were not accused of any crimes. Not that their actual guilt of any crime would warrant the threat of, or actual, rape. Imprisonment by the occupying force carries with it the implicit threat of rape. Here the soldier is explicit in his threat but the prevalence of rape or the threat of rape figures prominently in these accounts, revealing so much more about the detainers, about Western masculinity, than the supposed threat to these women from family members. Hegemonic masculinity in the West values violence and includes it as a means of controlling women (Pharr 1988).

There is also actual rape. In 2005, MADRE, an international women's rights group, reported that '... no one knows how many Iraqi women have been raped since the war began in 2003. Most crimes against women are not reported because of stigma, fear of retaliation, or lack of confidence in the police' (Badkhen 2008). The Iraqi National Association for Human Rights reported that 'women held in Interior Ministry detention centers endure "systematic rape by the investigators"' (ibid.). Of course, it is not just Iraqi men who commit rape. A briefing paper written by Kristen McNutt for the United Nations Commission on Human Rights begins, 'Iraqi female detainees have been illegally detained, raped, and sexually violated by United States military personnel' (McNutt 2005: 1). Amal Kadham Swadi, an attorney who represented women detainees at Abu Ghraib, said: 'Began to piece together a picture of systemic abuse and torture by US guards against Iraqi women held in detention without charge.' This was not only true of Abu Ghraib, she discovered, but was, as she put it, 'happening all across Iraq.' Amal Kadham Swadi states that 'sexualized violence and abuse committed by US troops goes far beyond a few isolated cases' (ibid.: 3).

McNutt goes on to suggest that 'these and other incidents are being covered up for US domestic consumption.' Democracy comes at quite a price for women in Iraq.

In one case that was made public (there may very well be others), a woman named Mithal was detained and questioned for three months about the activities of a neighbor thought to be hostile to the occupation (McKelvey 2005). A neighbor! These women are not officials themselves, merely associated by marriage or family or neighborhood to the missing person of interest. The persons in question, like Izzat Ibrahim al-Douri, often remained at large. The tactic apparently was unsuccessful, but can we imagine Lynn Cheney or Joyce Rumsfeld being arrested and held by an invading force? American (read white) women are regarded under the codes of militarized masculinity and transnational sexism operating here as sacred, sacrosanct, and yet Iraqi women under this same code of militarized masculinity were fair game for persecution. What is it that allows this practice to occur without widespread condemnation in the West? How must the Bush administration and military leaders have been thinking about Iraqis generally and Iraqi women in particular to order these arrests, and subsequently remain silent about the treatment of the wives and children of Iraqi government employees? Is this a new form of transnational sexism at work? Or is it just the same old sexism?

In contrast to the family of al-Douri, long before his capture by US troops, the wife and family of Saddam Hussein, although denied asylum in Britain, were apparently provided protection by the British (Lee 2003). His two daughters, Raghad and Rana, have since been granted asylum in Jordan. Saddam's wife, Sajida, is very seldom discussed in the Western press but the little that is said of her describes her as 'Saddam's 1st cousin' (Basu 2003: 5A), a 'bottle blonde' (ibid.: 5A) who was 'famous for her shopping sprees' (Lee 2003). Although she had been separated from Saddam Hussein for quite some time prior to the occupation, and he reportedly has had a child, Ali, with another woman, Samira Shabandar, Sajida is still regarded as 'important to the family complex' (Mackey 2002: 58). Even though it was said in 2003 that 'the women in Saddam's family kept a low profile and played no significant role in the regime' (Basu 2003: 5A), their low profile did not protect them from a racist and class-based attack in the press, as one reporter asserted that their 'tribal roots' were showing as 'No matter how much money they spent on their palaces, they were still incredibly tacky. The décor was a reflection of what their social status really was' (ibid.: 5A). Indeed, references in the US press to Sajida's dyed hair and prior family relationship to Saddam Hussein all serve to call her taste and virtue into question. She is a slut, they seem to be suggesting, she alters her appearance and engages in incest. The reference to her shopping again indicates a looseness of virtue – materialist greed. Here, transnational sexism shows us how distant Sajida is from US women who are naturally blonde, who do not marry their cousins, and have HGTV to help with the decorating. The same old sexism can be observed, however, in the questioning of her 'virtue.'

Soon enough, however, Sadddam Hussein's family underwent a makeover of the journalistic kind. By 2007, the Western press seemed to have forgotten that the family was not really involved in Saddam Hussein's policies and full-scale demonization, in particular of his oldest daughter Raghad, began. Saddam Hussein's sons had been killed during the invasion. His two daughters, Raghad and Rana, both living in exile in Jordan, became the subjects of transnational sexism writ large in the media. No longer portrayed as not involved, they are instead depicted as evil masterminds of the Iraqi insurgency (Farrell 2007; Sengupta 2007), responsible for orchestrating the legal defense of Saddam Hussein on trial (Farrell 2007; Gallagher 2007), and at other times as superficial, plastic-surgery-obsessed shopping addicts.

No matter the depiction, though, evil or feckless, the renderings are always gendered and Raghad is most often demeaned when physical resemblance to her father is featured: 'With her blonde highlights, designer jeans and gold jewelry, Raghad could be any suburban mum. Only the distinctive dark, piercing eyes she shares with her father hint at her identity – she is the eldest daughter of Saddam Hussein, the Butcher of Baghdad' (Harvey 2006). 'If Raghad took on Saddam's persona, as she grew up she also developed an unfortunate physical resemblance to him. Less attractive than her younger sisters, she has her father's heavy eyebrows and cruel upper lip' (Jones 2007).

So Raghad has her father's eyes, eyebrows and 'cruel upper lip.' Other authors focus intently on her devotion to spa treatments and plastic surgery. Wouldn't you think the first thing corrected might be a 'cruel upper lip'? Surely on one of those spa visits she would have had laser hair removal or even waxing to take care of that eyebrow problem. Perhaps Raghad, living most of her life in Iraq, missed the lessons about which physical issues are most important. Unfortunately, transnational sexism means that she can on the one hand be ridiculed for resembling her father, while on the other hand her attempts to improve her appearance are met with derision: 'Remembering her obsession with designer clothes, beauty treatment, and preserving her eight-and-a-half-stone figure (she is rumored to have had her breasts enlarged, a tummy tuck, and a nose job) she is more Imelda Marcos than Mother Teresa' (ibid.).

> Raghad's svelte figure is impressive for a woman who bore her first children when she was 16 and had four more by the time she was 26. The look is, however, not all down to visits to the gym – it also owes something to surgery … It is not the first time that Raghad has taken advantage of exile in Amman to improve her appearance. During her last stay there, she also had operations to reduce the width of her nose and reduce the bags under her eyes. (Sherwell 2004)

> While the streets of Iraq run with blood, Raghad and her family live like royalty across the border in Amman. Her trim figure and elegant looks are not just the result of regular gym sessions. While Iraqis struggle to find cash for their next meal, Raghad has splashed out 7,200 pounds on plastic surgery. (Harvey 2006)

Women in the West who have had similar procedures are widely respected for 'taking care of themselves,' for staving off signs of aging, for adhering to Western standards of beauty. Perhaps it is just that –

Raghad's possible aspiration to those Western standards, the 'blonde highlights,' enlarged breasts, nose job, tummy tuck, etc. – which opens her to ridicule and scorn. Of course, the multibillion-dollar plastic surgery industry around the world capitalizes on just this wish among women of color to adhere to white standards of beauty. Influenced by images seen on satellite television and the internet, Iraqi women still living in Iraq are reportedly having plastic surgery in increasing numbers (Ahmed 2009; Jamjoom 2010). Perhaps Raghad would be better served staying as she is – that is, physically unsatisfactory in comparison to Western white women, looking like Saddam Hussein so she can more easily be made sense of, be known, be marked as inferior.

Raghad is also condemned for participating in her father's defense, or accused of being responsible for the deaths of many Iraqi citizens by organizing the insurgency: 'These people [Raghad and Sajida] are responsible for most of the bombings and indiscriminate killings aimed at hurting the Iraqi people, and starting a sectarian war between Sunnis and Shiites,' declared Iraq's national security advisor, Muwaffa al-Rubiac (Jones 2007). While ordinary Iraqi women have been detained quietly in order to obtain information or flush out a former Iraqi official in hiding, Raghad has been the subject of an Interpol warrant (Sengupta 2007). 'An Interpol warrant issued at the instigation of the Iraqi government, accuses the 38 year old woman of "crimes against life, incitement, and terrorism." If extradited from Jordan, and convicted, she faces life imprisonment and possible execution' (ibid.).

In Western media accounts, Raghad is either totally involved in the insurgency or callous about it, as in the quote by Harvey where she is busy worrying about her appearance while Iraqis starve. In the *Sunday Telegraph*, Phillip Sherwell joins in on her demonization by suggesting she was unmoved by the US killing of her brothers, as well as the deaths or injuries of other Iraqis:

> ... Raghad had undergone cosmetic surgery on her breasts, and possibly also a tummy tuck last August, shortly after her brothers Uday and Qusay were killed in a shoot-out with US forces in Iraq. At the same time, survivors of the bomb attack on the United Nations headquarters in Baghdad were being treated in nearby wards. (Sherwell 2004: 28)

Even though Uday and Qusay were depicted in the Western press as important members of Saddam Hussein's administration who carried out his often brutal policies, and, in Uday's case, being mentally ill, Raghad is expected to postpone surgery to properly mourn. Her failure to do so makes her more monstrous than them. Here the same Western media that considered these men so evil that their bodies could be shown after death condemns their sister's appearance of callousness.

Among Raghad's many character deficiencies cited in the Western press, most discussed is her interest in shopping. While participation in capitalism through the consumption of particular gendered products including clothes, shoes, make-up, etc., is required for Western women so that they can fulfill their place in the proper practice of femininity, for Raghad, her interest in such goods and practices marks her as evil:

> Driven wherever she pleases by bodyguards, she has an almost comical appetite for designer clothes and accessories and shops with a gusto that would earn approval from the high-spending wives and girlfriends of England's footballers. 'She buys shoes by the sack-load,' said a woman close to Raghad's circle of friends. 'But the store-owners are wary of her because she can be a difficult customer and nothing is ever good enough for her. There's a shop in Amman called Boutique de Francais that she goes to frequently where the staff are terrified of her.' Raghad is said to have a penchant for Gucci handbags and Sergio Rossie boots and pays for them – or rather her personal assistant pays for them – with a thick wad of crisp US dollars. It is perhaps not surprising then that Raghad was pampering herself in a beauty salon rather than engaging in, say, a humanitarian act on behalf of her troubled people, when she learned of her father's fate last week. If not out shopping, she can be found in Dazzle or in the Iraqi owned ladies gym above it, Body Design, where she works out most mornings. Raghad is an avid Hello! magazine reader, also has her hair styled three times a week and is said to have received cosmetic surgery – nose, breasts, bags under the eyes – at the Amman surgical hospital. It is a life straight out of Footballers' Wives and a far cry from that of her father, who languished in Camp Cropper in his last years [sic] on earth. (Gallagher 2007)

Here there is actually almost pity for Saddam Hussein in order to demonize or make a monster of his daughter.

> While not engaged in Émigré politics, Raghad has the lifestyle of others in the diaspora of rich Iraqis in Jordan. For a long time, her favorite designer store was a place where she was said to have had a particular penchant for boots and bags. A member of the crew for the Channel 4 film [Saddam's Tribe] remembers Raghad and Rana spending $9,000 in 20 minutes at duty-free shops in Qatar. (Sengupta 2007)

Her spending on clothes would be approved of by 'high-spending wives and girlfriends of England's footballers,' but it is clearly not approved of by the Western press. She should be honoring her father's memory, perhaps mourning him, these reporters suggest, and yet her work on behalf of the Iraqi people has earned her an Interpol warrant! Here she dishonors not only the Iraqi people but also her father by her interest in shopping and the maintenance of her body. Yet should she let up on either of these practices, her failure to participate in the proper practice of femininity would also leave her open to a different kind of ridicule. Here transnational sexism demands a kind of femininity that only certain women are allowed to practice. Others cannot be feminine, cannot be human no matter what they do. The author mentions her 'almost comical' appetite for designer clothes. Do we laugh at Western women's interest in clothes? Actually interest in fashion in the West lands one on the Vanity Fair Best Dressed list – not an occasion for ridicule at all. On the contrary, interest in fashion and the purchase of lots of expensive designer clothes lends Westerners legitimacy, entrance to the upper classes. For Raghad, though, it is depicted as a character flaw. It is clownish.[2]

In the Western imagination, the connection between Iraqi women and the men in their lives is something that warrants attention and concern. In Raghad's case, this means that identification with her father does not stop at her appearance. She is known as 'Little Saddam.' She is described as having a 'volcanic temper' (Gallagher 2007).

> Raghad fled Baghdad at night in the aftermath of the 2003 invasion and settled in Amman. For a while, she spent her time being photographed for magazines and visiting hospitals. Then US troops killed Uday and Qusay ... and their sister became the unlikely holder of the Hussein mantle. Her nickname, 'Little Saddam' was coined about this time and not, as sometimes reported, because of her haughty behavior while growing up in Baghdad. (Sengupta 2007)

> Until this week, Raghad was known as 'Little Saddam' for all the wrong reasons. She was given her nickname because she bears a remarkable resemblance to her father, and possesses his quick temper, capriciousness, and misplaced superiority complex. (Jones 2007)

This connection with her father is not accidental. The relative freedom of Iraqi women prior to the occupation meant that their depiction in the Western press focused on them being dangerous, inscrutable, as we shall see in the next section. Even though Saddam Hussein is now gone, the consumers of Western media coverage are left with a little fear in their minds about the potential for violence inherited by Raghad.

She is noted as having 'an air of defiance behind her favoured Gucci sunglasses' (ibid.). She is prone to fits of temper: 'There was much arm waving, cursing and shrieking but as a member of the staff noted when recounting the story, this behavior is hardly unusual' (Gallagher 2007). The woman has lost her husband, father, brothers, home, country, and untold numbers of other relatives and friends. It seems she's entitled to a little anger. So she cannot mourn or express anger? Maybe she is less than human. More worrisome to the West, though, are her possible political aspirations. 'With her father gone she will no longer have a legal team to manage and will find herself with time on her hands. How will she ever fill it?' (ibid.). Finally, in one perfect package of transnational sexism, Raghad is described as a female version of her father and as the quintessential threat to the West: 'Despite her repeated insistence that she has no political ambitions, informed observers believe that this pampered, surgically-enhanced chip off the old Baghdad block might one day assume her father's mantle' (Jones 2007).

Should Raghad run for office, though, she will not be the only, or perhaps the most, dangerous woman in Iraq. According to the Western press, others have preceded her.

Dr Germ and Mrs Anthrax

Sajida Hussein remains in exile in Qatar as of this writing (Farrell 2007). Of course, the family members of Saddam Hussein and other members of his regime are not representative of all Iraqi women. Actually, the amount of press coverage received by the women associated by family with the regime was very little in contrast to the myriad of news stories that appeared in early spring 2003 about two other Iraqi women who also are not representative of all Iraqi women and yet have been treated by the press as if they were. Rihab Taha and Huda Salih Mahdi Ammash were referred to in Western popular press accounts as Dr Germ and Mrs Anthrax.[3]

Huda Salih Mahdi Ammash, also known as Mrs Anthrax, is a US-educated microbiologist. She was the only woman in the US military's 'most-wanted' deck of cards. She was designated as the five of hearts. Although her father was reportedly assassinated by Saddam Hussein in 1983 (Jelinek 2003b; Seper 2003; Roberts 2003, and others), and her actual position within the Saddam Hussein government was that of overseeing Iraq's youth activities and the trade bureau, she was believed to be one of Iraq's top chemical weapons experts, said to be responsible for amassing large stores of biological weapons since the first Gulf War (Jelinek 2003b; Lowther 2003; Swanson 2003; Nasrawi

2003).[4] It remains unclear how these various positions connected. Unfortunately for Huda Ammash, in the build-up to Gulf War II, she was pictured in a photograph on Iraqi television as the only woman present at what was purported by US officials to be an Iraqi government cabinet meeting (Roberts 2003; Lowther 2003, and others). US intelligence officials believed that her presence there was a signal that Saddam Hussein was planning to use biological weapons against the invading forces. It is unclear from these accounts whether it was at this same meeting or at another that she was seated next to Qusay Hussein. On the basis of that proximity, popular news accounts of her arrest assert that US intelligence officials believed that she had a particularly close relationship with Qusay Hussein.[5]

Rihab Taha, also known as 'Dr Germ,' another microbiologist, who was trained in Britain, was also reputed to be responsible for the production of large amounts of biological weapons. None of the news accounts examined for this work includes her actual government position or title. She too is guilty by association, at least in part, as she is married to General Amer Rashid,[6] a member of Saddam Hussein's government who once acted as liaison with the UN's weapons inspection team (Rose 2003), and is said to have held a number of important positions in the government, including oil minister (Leinwand and Parker 2003), in charge of missile programs (Borger 2003), 'point man on weapons delivery systems' (AP, 27 November 2003), or head of Iraq's 'military industries' (Kelley and Soriano 2003: 11A).

Western news accounts also conflict as to whether Rihab Taha was actually in charge of the missing chemical and biological weapons stockpiles or was posing as such in order to protect someone else (Borger 2003; Dickey and Soloway 2002). One month prior to her arrest on 18 April 2003, the Associated Press said of her: 'The Iraqis presented her as the head of the biological program, but inspectors suspect she might have been fronting for someone more senior.' The *Guardian* reported that Stephen Prior, an American bio-defense expert, said that 'She seems to have been on the periphery rather than someone at the center of things' (Borger 2003). Richard Spertzel, a former UN bio-weapons inspector, stated in *USA Today* that 'She may or may not know about weaponization. We believe she does but she may not.' Again we must ask whether these questions arose out of the old sexism, whereby it is impossible to believe that women were/are responsible for bio-weapons, or any weapons for that matter. Of course, these stories seem to say, she is only a front for a man who is the real brains, the real power here.

The ambiguity around her actual position, along with the absence of the weapons she supposedly created, might have inhibited another war propaganda machine but not this one. Stories in the American press allege that she is evil personified. The *New York Daily News* calls her 'The most dangerous woman in the world' (Faris 2003: 8). In the set-up to an interview, Diane Sawyer claims that Taha was the 'architect of Iraq's biological weapons program' and that she made 'enough bio-weapons to kill everyone on earth two times over.' She is described as 'The mother of all Iraqi biological weapons' (Hoffman 2002a) and supposedly has 'overseen the production of at least 130,000 gallons of anthrax and botulinum toxin' (ibid.).[7] Transnational sexism here imagines women as maternal figures with a twist. Taha does not give birth to children, the story suggests (although many of the stories do mention that she has a daughter), she produces anthrax.

All of this highly charged rhetoric is then juxtaposed with a depiction of Rihab Taha as 'housewife.' Several of the stories suggest that Taha retired after marrying her husband – 'tamed' by the love of a powerful man (Dickey and Soloway 2002; Osborn 2003: 1; Leinwand and Parker 2003; Rose 2003). *Newsweek* goes so far as to say:

As for Taha herself, Spertzel [former weapons inspector] believes she's a full-time housewife these days. Or is she? 'You wouldn't want to make her mad,' says Ekeus, the former inspection chief. 'With this wife you would want to be cautious with your morning coffee, she has all the poisons at her disposal.' (Dickey and Soloway 2002: 40)

It is as if the creators of these stories cannot resist reverting to traditional Western representations of women – a mother, housewife – even while they construct these two Iraqi women as the most evil of the 'evil ones.' Taha is described as 'demure' (Faris 2003), 'unassuming' (Hoffman 2002a), and 'plain looking and normally mild mannered' (ibid.). The transnational sexism of the Associated Press is fully apparent in their description of her as 'difficult and dour.' In their construction of her, she could not be 'demure' – a characteristic associated with Western femininity[8] – and still be responsible for the creation of bio-weapons, so the press creates a personality for her that fits with their conception of her as evil. Transnational sexism demands that the women are demeaned even as the story of their power is being told.

The stories go on to suggest that Taha was spying for Iraq while she studied in the UK at the University of East Anglia (Rose 2003): 'She arrived here in a first class seat on Iraqi Airlines from Baghdad during the autumn of 1979; a slight anonymous 24 year old, already vetted by

Saddam Hussein's Iraqi intelligence services and with a secret plan that has transformed her into one of the most dangerous people on earth.'

Rose goes on to assert that Rihab Taha pretended to be a poor (i.e. failing) student in order to stay in the country longer so she could steal secrets of the UK's biological weapons program (ibid.). Other media take up the idea of her poor classroom performance without the spying bit to suggest that she is intellectually inferior (Hoffman 2002a; Dickey and Soloway 2002). The actual quote from one of her professors on which these reports of her poor intellectual ability are based does not suggest stupidity, however, but rather lauds her diligence.

Dr John Turner, the biology department's head, used to invite her to his family home: he remembers that she always came with presents for his children, sometimes dates bought on her regular trips to Iraq. 'She was an introverted, pleasant, extremely polite girl,' says Dr Turner. 'She was not a gifted student but was very hardworking. It's a great shock, like finding your daughter has gone and done something dreadful.'

These suggestions about her ability as a student are also contradicted by assertions that that she is a brilliant scientist: 'She was very, very smart,' Ekeus, the former inspection chief, recalls (Dickey and Soloway 2002). Here transnational sexism allows her to be both brilliant scientist and terrible student, hardworking and inept, 'demure' and 'dour' and 'one of the most dangerous people on earth.' These contradictions keep us from seeing her as a person. The reader gets only a vague sense of her while reading how dangerous she is, while she's simultaneously described by a few characteristics associated with femininity in the West. The Orientalized woman of mystery remains intact.

Unlike Huda Salih Mahdi Ammash, Rihab Taha had a much more public persona before the war. In interacting with UN weapons inspectors and in interviews with the press, she says several times that she has destroyed all the weapons, but of course, they don't believe her. 'We spent a lot, hundreds of hours with them [the UN inspectors], clarifying things to them. If they are fair, they should close this matter,' she said (ABC News 2003). In her frustration with their skepticism, Taha began to express strong emotions which were read by the inspectors as a sign of mental illness or feminine histrionics (Hoffman 2002a; Rose 2003): 'She made a big scene, crying, and slamming down her fists and running out the door and slamming it,' the courtly Swedish ambassador recalls. 'The other Iraqis looked at us like we were not gentlemen' (Dickey and Soloway 2002: 40).

The 'look' from the Iraqis in the room was enough to impugn the masculinity of the UN inspectors. This encounter, along with sexist and Orientalist ideas about women generally and Arab women in particular, may have obscured the truth of Taha's assertions from the inspectors. We also see here, though, the contradictions in the press's creation of Taha. She is both demure and dour, calculating and hysterical. She is a mystery, unknowable.

Huda Salih Mahdi Ammash is not similarly accused of emotional imbalance. Her crime is much more serious as she too is both accused of being the brains behind the bio-weapons program and a dupe sitting in for someone else (Hemmer and Boettcher 2003). She is also accused of ignoring the assassination of her father at the hands of Saddam Hussein in favor of her personal ambition (Nasrawi 2003; Swanson 2003; Roberts 2003, and others).[9] More importantly, though, by not refusing a career, by sitting near Saddam Hussein at a meeting, by not staying home and raising children, she is implicitly accused of failing the femininity test. Perhaps Western journalists are so steeped in old sexist patriarchal notions of who women are and what they are capable of that they cannot grasp the possibility that women could produce or provide the means of mass destruction. (Not that this is a role to which women should aspire!) Of course, all this analysis is complicated by the fact that no weapons of mass destruction in fact existed in Iraq at the time of the recent inspections, so this schizo-phrenic portrayal of these women might simply be a result of a lack of concrete information about the weapons programs.

Nonetheless, the descriptions of Ammash are rife with Oriental-ist references about Arab women. She is described as: 'mysterious' (Swanson 2003), and a 'ruthless zealot who directly ordered the torture of her fellow scientists' (Lowther 2003). Of course, in the construction of femininity operating in these Western journalists' minds, she can't be a real woman if she is involved or alleged to be involved in the production of weapons: 'She doesn't have a feminine side. Since she was young she has acted like a man' (ibid.). Despite the fact that women in the US are involved in the production of weapons every day, and their femininity is never called into question, Ammash's occu-pation in this Orientalist narrative sets her apart from other women. Indeed, because she is a woman of color and, therefore, not like a white woman, and because in the construction of gender operating here she 'does not have a feminine side,' she can be likened to an animal: 'Ammash, who used to wear an Islamic scarf over her military uniform, was nicknamed the "Fox" by many Iraqis because of her witty style of appeasing Saddam and her quick ascent to the party's hierarchy' (Nasrawi 2003).

She is 'the Fox,' close to nature, hard to read, dangerous. Finally, in spite of her lack of accepted practices of femininity, gender does prevail and she is reduced to identification with articles of clothing. 'She also represented Iraq in women's conferences in Egypt, Jordan, Lebanon and Yemen, where she was dubbed Saddam's velvet glove' (ibid.).

These narratives play out old ideas that associate whiteness with purity and depict women of color as closer to nature and dangerous. They also provoke questions about the intentions of US military officials in first declaring Ammash as one of the most wanted Iraqi officials and then arresting both her and Rihab Taha. Of course, we can imagine that the press would seize upon the story of mysterious, potion-concocting women of color given their Orientalist inclinations, but what is the government's excuse? Were these two women destined to be blamed for the weapons program? Did authorities hope to put extreme pressure on them to reveal something? Were the women truly intended to be dupes for the West by representing a bio-weapons program that did not exist? Did US intelligence believe that they could manufacture lies and these women would admit to them? Or is it simply that Orientalist ideas about who Muslim or Arab women are allowed the government and the press to imagine these women as the creators of destruction? Can women be both the reason to go to war and the perpetrators of it? Is this what we can expect from transnational sexism, a kind of backlash directed at women for daring to participate in war no matter how indirectly in the case of the arrested Iraqi families or on very flimsy evidence in the case of the missing WMDs and Huda Ammash and Rihab Taha?

These news stories point to how confused the US intelligence on Iraq really was, how little the government and the military as well as the media did know and how willing these same institutions were to make things up, to take very little evidence and manufacture whole stories in order to put the blame on women. This examination of Western news stories, then, is not only about the press but also appears to be about how sensitive intelligence information is gendered and how it gets created and told.

Questions of representation in the stories of these two women and indeed all the press coverage – or lack thereof – of Iraqi women are not only about the creation or demonization of an enemy that one expects while war is being waged or in anticipation of war. These representations are complicated by Orientalism, and by the same old sexism which, through objectification, destabilizes ideas about who women are and how they should act and requires enormous effort on the part of the creators of these stories to put the gender order back together again. Huda Ammash is 'the Fox' and a 'velvet glove,' Rihab Taha is dangerous but she is also demure. They have children and do housework. These women can be deployed to legitimize the war, to scare Westerners, but because they are 'demure' and 'velvet,' because they are capable of being mothers, they can be recuperated into traditional Western roles associated with femininity. For all the West's pride at the liberation of Western women, we are most comfortable with women who perform the roles Western patriarchy allows and approves – mother, housekeeper, seductress. These are the roles the West intends as part of our liberation of Muslim women.

According to the *Guardian*, Rihab Taha and Huda Salih Ammash were released from prison in Iraq in 2005 (Borger 2005). Almost a year earlier, however, only a couple of weeks before the search for WMDs was officially abandoned (ibid.), the BBC had reported that Ammash was 'dying' and had requested release owing to her illness. *Stars and Stripes* in 2008 reported that 'high-value detainees who were former members of the regime of Saddam Hussein,' including ten women, had been transferred to an 'Iraqi controlled women's prison in Baghdad.' Wikipedia too claims that the women were released in 2005. Indeed, Rihab Taha even has a Facebook page. The contents of the page, though, are almost exactly the same as those that appear in her biography on Wikipedia. I was unable to find any reference in a major US newspaper to their being released, only calls for their release by Iraqi hostage takers. It is difficult to determine exactly what happened to them. Has Ammash recovered from her illness? Does Taha know she has a Facebook page? It seems the Western media either doesn't know or refuses to tell us. The depiction of these women as deadly and the seeming inability to present them as anything more than signifiers of danger, empty of any human characteristics, are mirrored by representations of another group of women who are similarly depicted in the Western press as unduly influenced by brown-skinned men and as dangerous. Women suicide bombers mostly remain unnamed and unseen but much speculated about.

More dangerous women: suicide bombers

The most terrifying and inscrutable figure to Westerners is the woman suicide bomber. Like the bin Laden widows, women suicide bombers are represented in the Western press as having no agency. So steeped are Westerners in thinking of women as uninterested and uninvolved in war, it is incomprehensible to the West that women would commit an act of war of their own volition. In spite of what we have already seen with increasing numbers of women in Western militaries performing a diversity of tasks that actually prosecute or support the war, in spite of how women are deployed to justify the war and to prop up colonial missions, masculinity gets associated with war and femininity means avoiding it. So the prospect of a woman willingly choosing to participate in so violent an act as a suicide mission is almost inconceivable and ignites dark fantasies about the inscrutable, dangerous Arab or Muslim woman. Dorit Namaan, in writing about Palestinian suicide bombers, argues that in the press women suicide bombers' lives are examined to a much greater degree than are men's lives. 'As a result, women fighters have often been represented – especially in mass media – as deviant from prescribed forms of femininity, forms that emphasize a woman's delicacy and fragility but also her generosity, caring nature, motherliness, and sensitivity to others' needs' (Naaman 2007: 935).

Patriarchal confusion about the existence of the female suicide bomber evokes horror, but it never risks disturbing the gender order because suicide bombers are seen as abnormal or damaged. The practice of reporters delving into the lives of these women in order to find the cause behind their actions is readily apparent in a cursory reading of articles appearing in the Western press on the topic of women suicide missions. What is also apparent is the inability of reporters to conceptualize women performing these missions of their own volition. Instead, these women are depicted as being crazy with grief, tricked into doing it, or forced by sinister male figures in their lives. In this fashion, the women remain helpless, weak, potentially rescueable even in the face of their often deadly actions:

U.S. and Iraqi officials say Sunni insurgent groups, especially al-Qaeda in Iraq, are using religion, money, and empty promises to persuade sometimes vulnerable women to conduct suicide attacks, highlighting the movement's desperation at a time when its influence and ranks have declined ... 'These women become broken,' Rubaie [an Iraqi military official] said. 'Nobody will marry her. No one respects her. She commits a suicide bombing to get rid of the criticism in her society and the isolation. The pressure comes from relatives, not friends.' Some bombers have been tricked into committing bombings. In

March, two women with Down's syndrome were used in an attack on a crowded market in Baghdad; and in May a 14-year-old girl in Baqubaah was strapped with an explosives vest that was detonated by remote control. In some instances, impoverished women have been promised assistance for their families if they become bombers. 'There has been a lot of pressure from al Qaeda leadership on women,' Maw [US Army Intelligence] said. 'There have been promises of money to the family, although we have not seen one incident where that has played out.' (Raghavan 2008: A01)

Many have lost close male relatives. Many of the women live in isolated communities dominated by extremists, where radical understandings of Islam are the norm. In such places, women are often powerless to control much about their lives; they cannot choose who they marry, how many children to have or whether they can go to school past primary years. Becoming a suicide bomber is a choice of sorts that gives some women a sense of being special with a distinguished destiny. Some are just criminal. Many of the women who became bombers were from families immersed in jihadist culture. (Batal al-Shishani 2010)

... the woman gave her name as Um Islam ... an Iraqi who said her husband was killed by U.S. forces last year. As fighters died in increasing numbers she said, 'hatred and a sense of revenge' drove their widows to rise up against the Americans. (Raghavan 2008: A01)

These quotes are rich with stereotype and assumptions. The women described here by commentators, reporters, or military officials, both US and Iraqi, are represented as dupes, they are weak, they are gullible. They have been widowed. They have been abandoned. They have been 'tricked.' They are poor, they are developmentally disabled, they are not attractive to men. They are from religious families. When all stereotypes are exhausted, assumptions of their criminality dominate their representations in the Western press: 'Some are just criminal' (Bata al-Shishani 2010). In other quotes they might be religious zealots. What they are never portrayed as is thoughtful agents or resistance fighters acting of their own volition.

In the *New York Times* Stephen Myers (2009b) wrote about the arrest of a woman named Samira Ahmed Jassim al-Azzawi, who was accused of recruiting women for suicide missions in Iraq. Myers was quite matter-of-fact in his explanation of her case: 'In the parts of her confession shown, Ms. Jassim did not explain what drove her to join the insurgency, whether ideology or despair.' Dorit Naaman explains:

The media treatment of the phenomenon both in the Arab world and in the West relies on convenient stereotypes and conventional narrative frames. Those representations deny women agency and instead represent them as monsters or brides in a hegemonic framework that enables readers and viewers to maintain both the comfortable gender status quo and their preconceived notions about the Palestinian–Israeli conflict. In this respect, the case of the female suicide bomber is not that different from other news events as they are covered by media. That is, while the phenomenon of female suicide bombers is relatively new, its media coverage is organized as news stories packaged to reassert old beliefs. As such, news coverage of the phenomenon is in the end rather old news insofar as gender, terrorism, and the Palestinian–Israeli conflict go. (Naaman 2007: 951–2)

Naaman suggests that the figure of the female suicide bomber is always already determined as damaged, deranged, or deluded. In other words, female suicide bombers are not understood as agents, committed to fighting oppression and participating in armed struggle. Rather, through Orientalist and transnational sexist narratives, they are firmly established as lacking both in identity and character. While the situation in Iraq and Afghanistan is not exactly like that of women in Palestine, similar aspects in the representations of women suicide bombers across state borders can be observed. In 2009, Samira Ahmed Jassim al-Azzawi was accused of being a recruiter of between twenty-eight (her estimate) and eighty (Iraqi government estimate) women suicide bombers (Myers 2009b). She was tied by Iraqi authorities to one suicide bombing, but no others, and it is not clear what happened to the (twenty-seven or seventy-nine) women she had recruited and was grooming for new missions. In the press's description of Jassim's activities, over-determined ideas about gender and violence are upheld: 'She also appeared to confirm what many military and intelligence officials had asserted: that insurgents prey on women in dire social and economic situations who are often suffering from emotional or psychological problems, or abuse' (ibid.).

Increasingly in the reporting on suicide missions, there is an implication that the person carrying out the mission – male or female – might not be entirely acting of their own volition. While stories about women suicide bombers have long held suggestions of brainwashing,[10] there are now sometimes claims of more physical manifestations of coercion. Raghavan (2008) describes above a fourteen-year-old girl whose suicide apparatus was 'detonated by remote control.' In a story about a bombing in central Baghdad in the *New York Times*, a witness explained:

> People on the street tried to get him to stop because they feared what would happen to him from guards at the Sadeer Hotel entrance: 'The bomber looked at them and nodded slightly. Moments later he detonated his payload. The man's hands were handcuffed to the steering wheel, said a hotel guard who saw them.' (Tavernise et al. 2005)

In another story, Alissa Rubin describes what happened to a woman suicide bomber who could not change her mind:

> Her choice of suicide was not entirely hers to make. The suicide vests the cell gave to participants were outfitted with remote detonators so that someone else could explode the would-be bomber if she failed to detonate herself. This was a relatively new aspect of suicide bombing in Iraq. A second person with a second detonator would go on the mission to ensure against changes of heart. (Rubin 2009: 60)

I find these stories chilling because they take the assumption of lack of agency into the realm of coercion. Here, suicide bombers are not even in control of their own acts of resistance. Emptied of any free will, the suicide bomber is a robot, a tool in the hands of violent, controlling and manipulative men. Is this depiction of suicide bombings another way of undermining these efforts? Is it simply a way to make it seem that the women are tricked into performing these acts? Or depicting the men as crazed religious zealots? Is this an attempt to make Westerners believe that this organization called al-Qaeda is so evil that it would use people as human bombs against their will, thus proving a justification for continued endless war on terror?

In the same article, Rubin claims that suicide bombing is a business: 'For Baida (who lost 5 of her 7 brothers and sisters) as for many suicide bombers violent insurgency was the family business' (ibid.: 59). This troubling connection of religion and politics and business is deceptively reductive. It situates the actions of the suicide bombers in biology, in family relations, and in economic decisions, and it excludes any external causes such as oppression and occupation. In addition to Orientalism and Islamophobia, the stories may be told in this fashion as a way to halt the glorification of the suicide bomber in certain communities. If women suicide bombers are tricked or forced into doing this, these reporters might as well be saying, then such acts are not so brave, not a sign of one's devotion. While suicide bombings are deplorable and must be condemned strongly, for ordinary women attempting to live their lives in the tumult these occupations occasion, the option of accompanied or unaccompanied suicide must sometimes seem like a desirable option.

'Survival sex'

Grief, loss, and financial necessity contribute to an environment in which relationships between men and women throughout the occupied regions have been thrown into tumult owing to the occupation. The situation in Iraq today is precarious. There is intermittent violence and the constant threat of civil war (Smith 2012; Rosen 2010: 18). The damage done by the war and occupation is both physical and cultural. Iraq has been so disrupted by occupation, as Al-Ali suggested earlier, that the hyperpatriarchy she suggests has been created does not provide much protection for men either. The tensions between Sunni and Shiite are acted out all over the country with former neighbors turning on each other and certain streets being purged of Sunni or Shia so that people lose their homes (Tavernise 2008). This sectarian hostility has been exacerbated by the occupation (Smith 2012; Rosen 2010). One author in the *New York Times* suggests that: 'Perhaps two million people have fled Iraq' (Healy 2011). In addition, the wars, sanctions, and sectarian violence have meant enormous loss of life for Iraqis:

> The numbers of people missing in Iraq is astounding. Since 2003, under the West's occupation, estimates suggest that well over 100,000 people have gone missing, many during the violent insurgency and sectarian killings between Sunni and Shia Iraqis that paralyzed the country between 2005 and 2007. (Williams 2011)

Of the women that remain, many find themselves living alone and trying to find work. Approximately two million women inside Iraq are responsible for the entire household income (Kami 2011).

Most estimates suggest that there are around 1.5 million widows in Iraq after the last thirty years of conflict (Ashton 2011). Widows are eligible for a small social-security-like payment, but the system that distributes such payments is vast and corrupt, with agents demanding bribes along the way and much confusion surrounding the process (Kami 2011). Many women simply give up. When Saddam Hussein was in power, widows were given homes and automobiles and encouraged to marry soldiers (ibid.). Of course, these efforts were aimed less at benefitting women and more at using women to bolster the military. Still, it was some support. Recently in Baghdad, 150 mobile homes with no water, sanitation system or electricity were provided for widows

(Bruce 2008). One widow, Hameedya Ayed, is quoted: "'Our life has been turned into misery and desperation," she said. "This is what we got from occupation and the dreams of democracy: orphans, widows, homeless, displaced, and fugitives.'"

> For thousands of Iraqi women and girls, the conflict that began in 2003 was only the start of their ordeals. In the chaos of war and the confusion, lawlessness and poverty that followed, an untold number have become victims of sexual traffickers, some within Iraq and others sold over the borders. (Smith-Spark 2011)

What other women get from 'occupation and the dreams of democracy' is the freedom/necessity to work in the sex industry either by choice or deception.

Iraqi women, both those who remain inside Iraq and those who have fled the fighting and occupation, are in large numbers participating in what one woman called 'survival sex' (Bahadur 2008). 'One Iraqi non-governmental organization, The Organization for Women's Freedom in Iraq, estimates that about 4,000 women, one fifth of them under 18, disappeared in the first seven years after the war' (Smith-Spark 2011).

Some of the disappeared women are refugees. Women refugees, particularly in places like Syria where many Iraqis have fled, are forced to turn to prostitution in order to feed their families and provide shelter, a way to support themselves in a culture and an economy that are unrecognizable to them. There are estimates that there are more than one million Iraqi refugees in Syria (Hassan 2007). Unable to work legally, many women (maybe as many as 50,000) complain of being sexually harassed or attacked by landlords or landlords' family and friends (McNamara 2009; Hassan 2007; Soquel 2010). Others are tricked into taking jobs as sex workers by family members (Hassan 2007). Refugee Tahira al Sayed survived domestic violence at the hands of her husband while in Iraq. Nonetheless, when his life was endangered in Iraq, she fled to Jordan with him. When he disappeared a year later, she was left with four children. The Maktab Al Khomeini office known for assisting Shia war widows advised her to get a *mut'ah* or 'pleasure marriage' in order for her to have a male guardian. Her desperation is apparent when she is quoted as saying: 'Maybe if I lit myself up the world would see there are Iraqi women and children living in darkness' (Soquel 2010). Other women have remained inside Iraq but are separated from their families because of the shame involved in this kind of work.

Of course, the presence of all those Western military personnel has created a need for sex workers, a need Iraqi women and others reluctantly fulfill in order to stay alive and provide for their children. Yanar Mohammed estimates that there are thousands of women working in the sex trade in Iraq (Jamjoom 2009). Transnational sexism means that these women are disposable. Some families, though, make their children available for the sex industry as well, and they too find willing customers.

> The former guard, who asked that his name not be used out of concern for his safety, said that in 2005, he watched older boys collect dollar bills while Iraqi girls, some as young as 12 or 13, performed sex acts. The former guard said that he reported what he saw to his Blackwater superiors but that no action was taken. 'It sickens me to talk about it even now,' he said. (Schwellenbach and Leonnig 2010)

The practice of militaries utilizing the bodies of local women for their rest and relaxation goes back, at least in the case of the US, for a long time (Enloe 2000: 52, and others). What is notable here, though, is the complete disregard for cultural prohibitions against these practices, the consequences for women in terms of their relations to families and communities, the way this practice seems to have been extended to include the private contractors the US has been using in Iraq and Afghanistan, in this case Blackwater (now called Xe Services), and that these men are sexually abusing children.

Blackwater, or Xe Services,[11] is also implicated in the trafficking of women from other countries into Iraq to work in the sex industry:

> 'The women were recruited from their home nations with promises of well-paying beautician jobs in Dubai,' said an Army summary, 'but were instead forced to surrender their passports, transported against their will to Iraq, and told they could only leave by paying a termination fee of $1,100.' (Schwellenbach and Leonnig 2010)

A spokeswoman for Blackwater said the firm 'vehemently denies these anonymous and baseless allegations.' She said Xe policies forbid human trafficking (Schwellenbach and Leonnig 2010). In the US, there is legislation pending in Congress prohibiting such actions. As the law currently stands, human trafficking, as well the sexual abuse of women and children by Blackwater employees, is subsidized through US taxpayer dollars. In part what marks transnational sexism is the enactment of oppression against women around the world, not just by traditional militaries but also in the way in which violence is meted out by these private companies. As a consequence, transnational sexism is perpetrated by broader economic and military networks than in the past.

Westerners, though, hear very little about this through the Western media. Neither the thirst of Western militaries for local bodies for recreation, the tumult in gender roles caused by the presence of Western troops, or the role of Western corporations in sex trafficking is mentioned by mainstream media sources. In fact, quite the contrary. In a CBS news story about Iraqi refugee women working as sex workers in Damascus, Syria, the blame is placed solely on the shoulders of the Middle Eastern men who are the consumers of these women's labors: 'There is no one to help, but a growing stream of men from all over the Middle East is eager to prey on the most desperate refugees from the war' (McNamara 2009).

While sex work clearly poses many dangers to women, both physical and psychological, other kinds of work that are available for women in Iraq are dangerous in different ways. On 23 January 2004, four Iraqi women who worked as cleaners and cooks at a US military base near Baghdad were killed as they traveled to work on the base (Chisea 2004). In Western terms, gendered relations have returned to normal. These women were doing what comes 'naturally' in white supremacist capitalist patriarchy – cooking and cleaning for white folks. They became targets because they were working for the occupiers. But they were not the only women who have been killed since the occupation.

Enjoy your freedom. Goodbye

Even though conditions for women in Iraq have been terrible since the Western occupation, the war on Iraqi women in the press has not abated. In a photo accompanying an AP article that appeared in the *Syracuse Post-Standard* on 15 May 2010, Iraqi women are depicted all dressed in black, faces covered, wearing white shawls, carrying a banner written in Arabic which reads 'coming for martyrdom.' The legend under the photo reads: 'Iraqi women, followers of radical Shiite cleric Muqtada al-Sadr, walk to attend Friday prayers in the Shiite stronghold of Sadr City in Baghdad. On the same day, al-Qaida in Iraq warned Shiites it plans a new campaign of violence.' The accompanying article is entitled 'Dark days soaked in blood: Iraqi citizens fear more violence as al-Qaida attacks increase.' While the article claims that Iraqis are frightened about sectarian warfare, the impression the reader is left with is that these women are frighten*ing*, not frightened. In the wake of the total destruction of Iraq, what is the point of continuing to demonize Iraqi women? Are we preparing for an eventual reinvasion of Iraq?

We still know very little about the lives of ordinary Iraqi women either before or during or in the aftermath of this most recent war. Instead, the Iraqi women Westerners were made familiar with were the Saddam Hussein family and the ominously nicknamed Dr Germ and Mrs Anthrax. The suffering of Iraqi women due to sanctions, obscured by Dr Germ and Mrs Anthrax and the Saddam Hussein family saga, was not a part of Western consciousness in the build-up to the war. Women were not the focus of the Western press, which was obsessed with the detailing of Osama bin Laden's and Saddam Hussein's sins and predictions of their future actions, and the oppression of Afghan women. Even as the war commenced, citizens in the US were rarely treated to images of ordinary Iraqi or Afghan women who attempted to go about their lives while the bombs dropped around, and sometimes on, them. Today, we still have little knowledge about how many ordinary Iraqi women were imprisoned by US or British troops as they swept across Iraq, and how many Iraqi women were killed as a result of American aggression.

While Paul Bremer asserted that he was willing to fight for women's rights to be written into the new Iraqi constitution (Sisk 2004), the presence of US troops actually had the opposite effect to that of granting rights to women. Visibility of Iraqi and Afghan women might for a moment have felt like a good thing to women so long ignored by the West, but these women soon discovered, as US women already have, that this visibility comes at an enormous price.

3 | 'Where are the women?' Muslim women's visibility and invisibility

> Women's bodies have long been the ground on which national difference is constructed. When the Muslim woman's body is constituted as simply a marker of a community's place in modernity and an indicator of who belongs and who does not, the pervasiveness of violence against women in the West is eclipsed. Saving Muslim women from the excesses of their society marks Western women as emancipated. (Razack 2008: 86)

We all saw her. She stared out at us from the cover of *Time* magazine. Her shiny hair and colorful hijab attracted our interest. We were pleased to see, at last, an Afghan woman's face – until we noticed the hole where we expected to see her nose. Accompanying her image, the chilling words: 'What happens if we leave Afghanistan,' not a question, but rather a warning. At first, she was called Bibi Aisha.[1] Later we were told that her name is Aesha Mohammadzai. She was the most visible woman in the war on terror. After all, she actually required rescue from a Taliban-influenced husband and in-laws. Her image perfectly justifies continued US presence in Afghanistan. She is iconic.

The images of Aesha Mohammadzai, and indeed all Muslim women, are utilized in the US and in other Western nations such as Canada and Great Britain in a variety of ways that dehumanize, stoke imperialist fantasies, and justify imperialism. In general, Muslim women have trouble in terms of their depictions in US media, not only in news accounts but also in film and television. In this chapter, the hyper-visibility of Aesha Mohammadzai is juxtaposed with a puzzling cycle of the invisibility and then sudden visibility of Aafia Siddiqui, the woman known in the US press as 'the female al-Qaeda.' Studying the appearance of Muslim women in mainstream media, and their disappearance from it, alongside fictional representations of Muslim women in US popular culture, this chapter shows how transnational sexism is at work in their depictions.

Aesha Mohammadzai's visibility is unusual. Other than Hamid Karzai, and the occasional male Afghan civilian, Westerners see very few

Afghans. Westerners almost never see Afghan women – unless they are fully covered by burqas – depicted in news sources. When their images are shown in the Western press, they are mostly veiled. Their faces are not seen. As I have suggested elsewhere (Riley 2008: 1193), women in war have visibility/invisibility problems. The depiction or non-depiction of Afghan women in the Western media provides an illustration of this problem. Visibility and invisibility problems for women are particularly pronounced in the war on terror.

> Visibility, invisibility, and hyper-visibility all have consequences not only for women but for all of us as we struggle to make sense of how war happens as a result of particular ideas about men and women and masculinity and femininity. Women are sometimes seen and sometimes not; sometimes as bodies to be moved, manipulated, and militarized; and at other times, their bodies are ignored as practices of femininity are used to emphasize weakness, vulnerability, and helplessness. These configurations are multiply deployed in relation to other axes of difference and processes of racialization. They are motivated by the demands of nationalism and the imperatives of global capitalism and often occur simultaneously. (Ibid.)

Whether they are seen or not, women suffer the consequences of wars that are most often not of their making or their choice. This presents a paradox. While the problems of invisibility are numerous, little consideration is given to the dangers women face during war. Women lack voice in decision-making about war, they are dehumanized, and visibility carries special peril for women in war. In the war on terror, visibility/invisibility is joined by hyper-visibility. Women in Afghanistan and in Iraq and now increasingly in Pakistan are not seen by the West except in the specific cases already mentioned. They become then a disembodied mass of non-humanness, insignificant except to be trotted out as proof of Western male supremacy.[2] Depending upon political and military contingencies, occasionally specificity is required. In those circumstances, immediate and intense visibility, or hyper-visibility, occurs, and suddenly Aesha Mohammadzai appears. Less effective for upholding the rescue narrative, but most salient for the propagation of war as we have seen, is the emergence from invisibility of the dangerous Dr Germ, Mrs Anthrax and, more recently, Aafia Siddiqui.

Bibi Aisha, Bibi Ayesha, Aesha Mohammadzai, or the Afghan girl without a nose

> She cannot read or write and had never heard of *TIME* Magazine until a visitor brought her a copy of this week's issue, the one with the cover picture of her face, the face with no nose. (Nordland 2010a)

The cover of *Time* magazine on Monday, 9 August 2010 had the soon-to-be-iconic image of a young woman whose name we did not yet know. The image was reminiscent, as many pointed out, of the *National Geographic* cover of another Afghan girl, Sharbat Gula, whose name we also did not know until years later. Sharbat Gula's image appeared in 1985, when Afghanistan was embroiled in a war with the Soviet Union. Aesha's pose in her cover image is a very similar pose to that of Sharbat Gula in hers. The photographers took the shots from the side, both of their heads draped by a brightly colored hijab, their hair revealed. Aesha's cover differs only in that her face is missing a nose, leaving what has been variously described as 'a yawning hole, a hideous second mouth in the very centre of her face' (Anthony 2010) or 'the heart shaped hole where 18 year old Aisha's nose should be' (Peltz 2010). Indeed, the similarities between the covers are noted by several commentators (Anthony 2010; Nordland 2010a). Perhaps the similar poses are not accidental. Two photographers, consciously or unconsciously, trying to capture a moment, an image, or editors similarly communicating the necessity of what bell hooks calls 'white capitalist patriarchy' to rescue Sharbat Gul in 1985 and Aesha Mohammadzai in 2010. Both women conform to a particular standard of white beauty, with Sharbut Gul's green eyes haunting the viewer. Their images uphold white colonialist fantasies of Western male superiority as they require rescue. Finally, their beauty and Orientalized allure help sell magazines. Aesha's image, this cover, appears nine years after the West has occupied Afghanistan, while ostensibly freeing the women there. It also appears in the wake of the WikiLeaks scandals in which the US military is revealed to be floundering in Afghanistan. Nonetheless, the photographer, South African Jodi Bieber, won the World Press Photo award for 2010 for this image. The prize was ten thousand euros, none of which seems to have been shared with Aesha Mohammadzai (Blackburn 2010).

Many of the commentators who wrote about the image of Aesha mentioned that she was beautiful.

> She was so beautiful that the first time I saw Bibi Aisha on the cover of *Time* magazine, it took me a moment to realize she didn't have a nose.

Her husband and his family had hacked it off when she'd tried to escape being abused in her home. The magazine said she was the graphically horrifying illustration for the fate that awaits many women if the U.S. withdraws from Afghanistan too soon. (Grigsby Bates 2010)

By constantly commenting on her beauty, it is as if they are saying that the crime committed against her was greater because she was so good looking. The comments perhaps unwittingly uphold ideas about women's primary value under patriarchy – to look good, to be decorative. Are there less beautiful women in the shelters in Afghanistan who have suffered similar fates whose faces we will never see? Is it because she is beautiful that her nose must be repaired? Can we not still see her as beautiful without her nose? Would the violence she experienced be less egregious if it had not marred her beauty?

The other women pictured inside the *Time* issue, save one, all have visible faces. Only one other photo is acknowledged to have been taken at the shelter where the photographer shot Aesha's photo. This woman, Sakina, is shown (pp. 24–5) in a three-quarter image across the fold. She is seated on the side of a bed. A child who has an injured leg that is bandaged and immobilized lies alongside her. Her lack of familial relationship with the child with whom she is pictured is puzzling. Are they to be seen by the viewer as one and the same, both requiring rescue from the brutality of Afghan men? The caption reads: 'The child bride. Sakina, seen with the daughter of a staff member at a woman's refuge, ran way from an abusive husband.' Because Sakina remains whole, seems physically intact, the child's injury provides emphasis to the message about the dangers Afghan men pose. There is no mention of Sakina in the accompanying story – none. She is there because she is physically pleasing. Her image does not cause the viewer to flinch, she looks innocent, and she invokes the maternal. Here visibility is useful for the women in the shelter as it calls attention to their plight. These shelters are completely funded from outside Afghanistan and such visibility lends urgency to fund-raising in the US and elsewhere. But surely a thoughtful reader might also ask whether the child was injured in the war rather than at the hands of an abusive father. And when was the last time a major news source in the US ran a story on abusive husbands or on a woman's shelter?

The images, as well as the accompanying article, are rife with Orientalism and transnational sexism. There is a photo of a woman wearing a blue burqa with a child by her side and another in her arms with the caption: 'The veiled wife, many women still find security in the burqa'

(p. 27). The caption prompts the question: Do women find 'security in the burqa' from dangerous brown men? Alternative captions for this photo might have read: Many women find tradition in the burqa, Many women find adherence to religion in the burqa, Many women find resistance to Western imperialism in the burqa. Instead of using the image and the caption to further demonize Afghan men, one might argue that women seek security in the burqa from Western occupiers whose presence has so profoundly altered their lives (Fanon 1965).

Signs of Afghan women's successes attributed to the Western presence there are also included in the story. These include a photo of a woman athlete, Robina Muqimyar Jalali. She is running with a hijab on in the company of three young men (p. 26). Also included is an image of Mozhdah Jamalzadah, a television host, who is seated in an ultramodern room, part of the set of her 'Oprah-style' TV show in Afghanistan (p. 23). Fawzia Koofi, a woman member of the Afghan parliament, is also depicted here seated under a photo of herself with Hamid Karzai. In the photo they stand stiffly beside each other (p. 22). In the accompanying article, Aryn Baker sets the scene for the reader to be relieved at Afghan women's liberation:

> Kabul 40 years ago was considered the playground of Central Asia, a city where girls wore jeans to the university and fashionable women went to parties sporting Chanel miniskirts. These days the streets of Kabul once again echo with the laughter of girls on their way to school dressed in uniforms of black coat and white headscarves. Women have re-joined the workforce and can sign up for the police and the army.
> (p. 24)

Here, women's liberation seems to have a lot to do with fashion – jeans and Chanel miniskirts versus burqas. It is, of course, wonderful that girls in the city can go to school. It is not without danger, though, as many other publications are delighted to report. Gender integration of the police and the military is also fraught with danger in the super-patriarchy that occupation has wrought, and the absorption of women into state apparatuses, as women in the West know well, is not a sign of liberation. Work for women is still quite hard to come by and for many sex work is the only option. These more complicated aspects of Afghan women's 'liberation,' however, are not the focus of reporting by Western media.

The minute the *Time* cover hit the newsstands, other media sources picked it up and ran their own stories about both the cover itself and Aesha. Diane Sawyer of ABC News did a number of stories on Aesha

Mohammadzai, including one from the shelter where she lived in Afghanistan as well as a follow-up story when she came to the US for treatment. Diane Sawyer described the woman who was then called Bibi Aisha as 'an emblem of brutality.' In the shelter in Afghanistan, while she was being filmed, Aesha held her hijab over her face. She was clearly being cajoled by someone off-screen to show her face. She occasionally aimed pained glances at the cajoler. So apparent is Aesha's discomfort at being displayed in this way on camera, her performance of reluctance and coercion makes the viewer wince.[3] Aesha finally shows her face and then her ears in turn. While Diane Sawyer warns the viewer at the beginning of the story that the video will be hard to watch, and Aesha's facial wound may cause one to flinch, the truly difficult thing to view is her discomfort at this exposure.

Did Jodi Bieber or the ABC news producer or crew, or anyone else, explain to Aesha what it meant for her photograph to be taken for *Time*, for her image to appear on the news in the West? How about her protectors, the Women for Afghan Women, who ran the shelter where she stayed? Instead, was she offered up by them as a publicity bonanza? A fund-raising gold mine? Was Aesha given any information about how many people would see her face sans hijab? What would her reaction have been had she understood? Grateful to the organization that helped her, offered her sanctuary, she might have agreed, or *Time* may have had to search for another cover girl who embodies the rescue narrative. Alternatively, is Aesha herself responsible for the propagation of these images? Did she see participation in this publicity as a way out of Afghanistan? Was she seeking a way to get medical treatment?

The Revolutionary Association of the Women of Afghanistan (RAWA), an Afghan women's rights organization established in the 1970s and which through the web has an active international presence, has three stories on their website that all claim that Bibi Aisha's (as they call her) story is not true (Iltis 2010; Hairan 2010; Khpalwak 2010). Abdulhadi Hairan claims that she is a woman named Nazia that he met in a shelter prior to either the CNN story or the *Time* cover, who told him that her elderly husband had maimed her. Khpalwak, also denying that the Taliban was responsible, places the blame on Aesha's husband and father-in-law (who was subsequently found not responsible), and her father Mohammadzai, whom her father-in-law claims asked him to kill Aesha. Once she got to the US, Aesha claimed her father's name as her surname. There is no mention of Taliban involvement until the story hits Western news sources. Rather, all three authors suggest that

Aesha's husband committed these acts in an exercise of ordinary, for Afghanistan, domestic violence. In the Iltis story, Malalai Joya suggests that the presence of Western troops has worsened the situation for women in such instances of domestic violence. She is quoted as saying: 'During the Taliban's regime such atrocities weren't as rife as [they are] now and the graph is hiking every day.' She says about the *Time* cover: 'Once again it is molding the oppression of women into a propaganda tool to gain support and staining their hands with ever-deepening treason against Afghan women.' Ordinary or extraordinary, this violence against women is horrific. In some ways, it would be comforting to blame the Taliban because, if they are responsible, one might help fix this problem by eliminating the Taliban. Even if what happened to Aesha was ordinary, the familiar problem of domestic violence amped up in a different context, then masculinity in Afghanistan might indeed be in crisis and maybe brown women do need rescue. Either way, occupation is not helping. We might also ask where and how the story acquired the part about Taliban involvement and how to balance these three stories with the barrage of media attention generated by the *Time* cover that makes that version seem like truth.

On the topic of Taliban involvement and US rescue of Aesha, there are several short videos available online at ABC.com. This video montage of Aesha stories includes one that begins with Diane Sawyer indulging in a little transnational sexism when she tells the viewer how lucky women are to live in the US. In describing the shelters and the support they get from the US, Sawyer says, 'Women who get to live in places like America reach out.' In the scenario that Diane Sawyer gestures to, fully liberated American women share their good fortune with less fortunate women around the world. The idea here is that American women have no complicity in creating and maintaining the super-patriarchy under which Afghan women must live. In another video, Aesha is arriving in the United States for treatment. The camera scans her new surroundings in California as if to remind the reader of the stark contrast between the beauty of California and the desolation of Afghanistan. Of course, the US contribution to that desolation remains hidden, while the implication that simply being in the US will heal her is repeatedly emphasized. Aesha is given something called the Enduring Heart Award by Maria Shriver in another video and then appears at a fund-raiser, perhaps benefitting Women for Afghan Women, where she is photographed with Marla Maples, formerly married to Donald Trump – a woman who knows a thing or two about a bad marriage. Aesha wears her prosthetic nose for these events. She is filmed in a room with Laura Bush, who can be heard saying, 'She looks so great.'

In an earlier video shot inside the shelter in Afghanistan, Diane Sawyer asks the assembled women, 'How many were physically beaten?' She seems reassured in her assumptions when all the women respond that they have been. Of course, asking that question inside a US shelter would get a similar response. She then asks the women from Women for Afghan Women, 'How many thousands do you think need your help?' They respond that millions do. Lest she be accused of doing feminist work by focusing solely on women, Diane Sawyer then begins talking about the work that the shelter does, including education for the men, and then says that the staff tell her, 'We'd be surprised how many Afghan men do react, do learn and need our help.' Esther Hyndman from Women for Afghan Women appears here to tell the viewer how many Afghan men realize the price of ignorance and have requested schools for girls and daughters. Diane Sawyer ends this story by talking about the care given to Aesha by the American military unit to which she was delivered by her family. She uses an expression here that gets repeated by numerous news-persons in talking about Aesha. She says that for Aesha, the personnel at the military unit in Afghanistan 'gave her something completely new, kindness.' This assertion serves to venerate the military unit which is there as a force of occupation, while simultaneously denigrating all Afghans. What happened to Aesha at the hands of her husband and in-laws was horrible beyond description. About that there is no question. Yet Aesha has known no kindness? Ever? Not from one single person in her family, no friends, no neighbors, not a teacher, a shopkeeper, no one?

Even though this abhorrent crime perpetrated on Aesha by Afghan men is depicted in this narrative as brutal beyond precedent, it is not. As Loewen reports on Christopher Columbus in Haiti: 'After Columbus's arrival in Haiti, when a native Arawak committed a minor offense, he/the Spanish "cut off his ears and nose." Disfigured, the person was sent back to his village as living evidence of the brutality the Spanish were capable of' (Loewen 2012 [1995]: 61).

Western men, proud of the brutality of which they were capable, had used these very tactics against indigenous people when engaging in earlier imperial adventures (Smith 2005). And apparently a crime as serious as adultery is deemed to be was not necessary to provoke such an atrocity. Here nose and ears were cut off for 'a minor offense.'

In another example of the blurring of the lines between government and media and the origination of 'news' stories, Gayle Tzemack

Lemmon, who works for the Council on Foreign Relations, a think tank that claims non-partisanship but that employs both Richard Haas (who served in both the George H. W. Bush and George W. Bush administrations) and Elliot Abrams (who worked for the Ronald Reagan and G. W. Bush administrations) among others, and who is an advisor for Women for Afghan Women, elaborates on Aesha's experiences at the hands of Western troops: 'The US military cleaned this young woman's wounds, offered her a haven for weeks and got her to a shelter. The young woman's father brought her to the local US military Forward Operating Base because he trusted them to provide his daughter with the care she needed.'

In contrast to the author on the RAWA website who claimed that Aesha's father wanted her killed (Khplawak 2010), Lemmon is the only writer to claim that it was Aesha's father who delivered her to the Americans. Others say it was another relative who did so after Aesha's uncle refused her any assistance. Here, her father not only assisted his daughter, he brought her to the true saviors, the American military. Indeed, in case the reader does not immediately get the point about the benevolent occupiers, Lemmon goes on to say: 'Aisha is only the most arresting example of the many women who have benefitted from the international community's presence in Afghanistan.' Finally, perhaps in response to the controversy the *Time* cover engendered, Lemmon elaborates her defense of the Western occupation:

> I have interviewed dozens of women over the past several years who, with government help, found their way to shelters and family crisis centers that did not exist before 2001. These women, many of whom have endured burnings, beatings and electrocutions at the hands of their spouses, now find safe haven in homes created by women for women and funded by the international community. Their stories are not props to be used by either the right or the left. They are simply their stories, paid for with a great deal of suffering. (Lemmon 2010)

The women's stories may not be 'props to be used for the right or the left,' but they certainly seem to be used by the organization she advises, Women for Afghan Women, to 'prove' the rescue role assumed by Western troops and to legitimize the occupation. Indeed, Lemmon's piece on the CNN site is an occasion when Aesha's story is being used as a prop, and it is important to note that Lemmon is not identified as affiliated with this organization.

The view espoused by Lemmon is countered by Kavita Ramdas, former president of the Global Fund for Women, and others. Without using the terminology of super-patriarchy, Ramdas refers to the same social and political mechanism when she writes:

> Aisha's suffering is not simply related to the Taliban. There are women in countries on every continent who have been beaten, sold, raped, and mutilated in the name of honor, religion, and tradition. Aisha's noseless face should not be used as a symbol of Taliban resurgence – instead, it is the face of modern day patriarchy, which continues to dominate social and cultural systems in most parts of the world. It is deeply woven into the fabric of societies that extol violence and patriotism. (Ramdas 2010)

Countering the transnational sexism that has been so prevalent in the readings of this situation in the popular press, Ramdas reminds us that all is not ideal for women in various parts of the world that are believed to be more 'civilized,' more advanced in the treatment of women. Her comments also situate the violence within a longer continuum of violence against women by refusing to exceptionalize this violence or render it more abhorrent than other acts of violence that occur elsewhere in the world.

The controversy about the *Time* cover and the following debate about the role of the US in Afghanistan did not inhibit Women for Afghan Women from carrying out what they believed would be an actual rescue by bringing Aesha to the United States for medical treatment. Diane Sawyer said that Aesha was coming to the US for 'surgery to give her back her face,' giving Western physicians the power to undo that which Afghan men had wrought. Unlike the unspoken suggestion made by the ABC camera crew in the video mentioned earlier, though, simply being in the US did not immediately heal Aesha. The trauma she experienced by living through a lifetime of war, by being so horribly attacked, by having to leave all that was familiar, created deep psychological and emotional issues for Aesha that manifested themselves in a serious way once she arrived in the US.

> But in the weeks that followed, the women in New York say, Aesha fought with families who took her in. She missed the women she'd lived with in the Kabul shelter. She had episodes where she shook, went stiff and her eyes rolled back in her head. She bit herself, screamed and pulled out her hair. She had to be hospitalized. (Ravitz 2012)

Contrary to the expectations of white capitalist patriarchy, Aesha could not be made well by simply rebuilding her nose. Given the emphasis on beauty in Western cultures, the initial focus on repairing Aesha's nose ignored the other aspects of the trauma she experienced in favor of a superficial restoration. The surgeries scheduled to repair her nose and ears had to be postponed so that she could get psychiatric treatment. Women for Afghan Women moved her first to California, then back to New York, in order to find a living situation for her that did not exacerbate Aesha's post-traumatic stress disorder (Gardner 2012; Ravitz 2012). It seems impossibly naive of reporters and news organizations, as well as Women for Afghan Women, to expect Aesha to make an easy transition to a completely new culture. While it is laudable that they recognized that she needed additional time and special care before her surgeries, one wonders how they could believe that Aesha's problems would be solved by just relocating her out of Afghanistan to a country where she would be completely cut off from family, did not speak the language, and was unfamiliar with the culture. Perhaps they too believed she had never known kindness and thought their generosity and good intentions would suffice. She now lives, by her own choice, with a family in Maryland which has helped foster her psychological well-being (Ravtiz 2012), and doctors in Maryland have now agreed to proceed with the surgery to repair her nose. She had the first surgery in mid-June of 2012.

In the time she has lived in the States, she has been economically supported by Women for Afghan Women. It is not clear whether she still is as she no longer lives under their auspices. Either the family with whom she lives or Women for Afghan Women has started a website for Aesha. The website, Aesha's Journey (www.aeshasjourney. com), has an area where one can make donations or purchase some jewelry that Aesha has made. The front page of the site has numerous photos of Aesha in Western dress with the *Time* magazine cover as backdrop. Also on the front page is a section called 'Aesha's Corner' where Aesha herself is supposed to keep the public informed as to her status. It reads: 'This website has been created to give Aesha a voice. Aesha will use this section of the site to personally keep you informed about her new life. Check back often to read her updates.' Weeks after the initial surgery, that area remains unused, Aesha's 'voice' unheard. Since living in Maryland, she has only had ESL training once a week. In New York, it was much more frequent, and she struggled with speaking and writing English (Ravitz 2012). It is unclear, given her level of literacy, how she would keep the public updated on her condition. Who would then serve as 'Aesha's voice'? Two other sections of the site are named 'Aesha's Journey' and 'Aesha's New Life.' In these areas, the site creator describes Aesha's current living situation along with her difficulties and progress in learning English. She is said to require six surgeries on her face and ears. She is described as 'Courageous, Strong. Determined.' She undoubtedly is given all that she has been through at such a young age. She is clearly being marketed, though, perhaps by Women for Afghan Women, or by the family with whom she lives, as the quintessential American success story. Who is measuring her success? Is it Aesha herself? Women for Afghan Women? The family with whom she lives? Has she approved this website? Does she understand its purpose? This website and Aesha's story raise the specter of the history of gender and race discrimination in the US. Removing someone from the viewer's family and all that is familiar is an old colonialist's move based on a belief in white supremacy. Look what happens when Afghan women are distanced from Afghan men, this story seems to be saying, when they are given the opportunities of Western liberation. Well, yes, but like many women who are born in the West, living here can mean that women will require extensive psychological treatment.

The appearance of Aesha Mohammadzai's face on *Time*'s cover had deep implications not only for her and her family, but for all women who experience gendered and sexual violence around the world. Those of us in the West who were traumatized by this image, who walked around for days unable to stop thinking about her and what happened to her, engaged in hot debates about the occupation and the meaning of liberation for women. Some commentators referred to the cover as 'emotional blackmail.' Others called it 'war porn' (Nordland 2010a; Anthony 2010; Woodsome 2010). 'War porn' is an expression used to designate the photographing of all sorts of atrocities, including photos of American soldiers desecrating the bodies of dead Afghans. The use of the term pornography, however, is very complicated here. Does this image of Aesha engender desire? Or does it instead provoke, by means of a belief in Western superiority, a desire to rescue? To make this woman 'like us'? To 'liberate' her? Instead, does it merely evoke Orientalist notions of 'others' who engage in barbaric practices that mark the West as morally superior? Alternatively, if we are using the term pornography to describe a voyeur's obsession – something both fascinating and horrifying, something from which we have difficulty looking away – then perhaps the description of Aesha's image as war porn is an apt one. One could read the appearance of the image as a kind of claiming of Aesha, a marking of her as ours, a desire to possess her, to have her belong to the West. In any case, Aesha's image makes tangible the conundrum of visibility for women in the war on terror. Visibility might mean a kind of safety for a moment, but then the safety dissipates and women trade one heartbreaking, terribly painful situation for another.

If the image of Aesha Mohammadzai is simply about transnational sexism in the form of a Western male patriarchal desire to 'liberate' Aesha and all Afghan women, to make them like Western women, Primavada Gopal urges an examination of the goal and the meaning of 'liberations':

> The mutilated Afghan woman ultimately fills a symbolic void where there should be ideas for real change. The truth is that the US and allied regimes do not have anything substantial to offer Afghanistan beyond feeding the gargantuan war machine they have unleashed. And how could they? In the affluent West itself, modernity is now about dismantling welfare systems, increasing inequality (disproportionately disenfranchising women in the process), and subsidizing corporate profits. Other ideas once associated with modernity – social justice, economic fairness, peace, all of which would enfranchise Afghan women – have been relegated to the past in the name of progress. This bankrupt version of modernity has little to offer Afghans other than bikini waxes and Oprah imitators. (Gopal 2010)

Dismantling the idea of Western supremacy or the West's offer of liberation for women in a single paragraph, Gopal marks the problem alluded to above. If she is right, and ideas about social justice now elude the West, how could the situation for Afghan women involved in domestic violence caused by unequal distribution of power and resources and the proximity to militarized masculinity be untangled at all? Instead we have the scapegoating and fantasy rescue narrative.

Indeed, Aesha's visibility serves many purposes there on the newsstand, legitimizing endless war among the affluent at the Women for Afghan Women benefit and now on the web, where ordinary citizens can send their pennies to hasten her 'liberation.' All of this keeps Westerners from examining their own part in militarism, imperialism, and transnational sexism.

Visibility = liberation?

> The gendered consequences of war go beyond the physical and psychological violence to which women are subjected through rape and terror, extending to insidious practices and invented traditions that further consolidate patriarchy and exacerbate women's social subordination. (Abdi 2007: 183)

One of the consequences of visibility, other than international notoriety as victims, is that women who live under patriarchy – and in the case of women living in Afghanistan and Iraq during occupation under hyper-patriarchy – once they are visible, begin to be identified not as persons but as bodies. Identified as bodies, women can be objectified and sexualized. Women can then become territory and are thus particularly vulnerable to rape. Another aspect of visibility for women in war, one that is particularly important for women in the war on terror given the cultural constraints governing contact between men and women, is sex work. Nonetheless, the lack of options for economic support under hyper-patriarchy along with the new objectification and sexualization that visibility in the form of Western 'liberation' produces also leads to increasing numbers of women participating in sex work.

News sources that are critical of the war focus on the increase in prostitution that the war has wrought in Afghanistan. In *The Nation*, Katrina Vanden Heuvel quotes Kavita Ramdas, who says that all the women's groups with whom she had contact had indicated that

> The presence of foreign troops in Afghanistan in general and in Kabul in particular has highly increased the incidence of both prostitution as well as trafficking. These people are armed – and because war tends to infuse large amounts of testosterone into large groups of men, living and wandering around together this does not create the safest of environments for girls in villages, on girls walking to school, on teachers or other women who are working. So, attacks on women have increased, for all sorts of reasons – the most common one we hear in the West is 'Oh those Islamic fundamentalists don't want women to work or study and so they're attacking them.' But there are plenty of people who don't really care whether it's about Islam or not, they're just interested in showing power by sexually abusing women. (Ramdas, in Vanden Heuvel 2009)

Despite the majority of the Western press's delight in enumerating attacks on schoolgirls in Afghanistan by Afghan men purported to be Taliban, as we have seen a great danger is posed toward Afghan schoolgirls by the presence of Western militaries. What is striking about Ramdas's remarks here is that she makes it clear that the danger posed to Afghan women does not come from Islam; rather the violence is about asserting power and control. This assertion of power and control is especially apparent in light of the rearrangement of hierarchies that occurred because of the occupation. Yet in most press accounts of violence towards women on the streets, the role of the occupation in these attacks is never mentioned. Also scarcely mentioned is the incidence of sexual assault.

In an interview with Amy Goodman on *Democracy Now!*, Yanar Mohammed, director of the Organization of Women's Freedom in Iraq, described the situation for women in Iraq in 2004:

> The story that does not reach this part of the world is how the women are treated in post-war Iraq. What happened to us, how our – let's say destinies were totally devastated by this war. What is told to everybody is that we got rid of a bloody dictator, which is a true story but the part that nobody knows about is that we did have sort of a secure life. We did have our jobs. We did have some stability that we totally lost with the first day of the war. Now, every hour, your everyday life has abductions for women. We cannot go out in the streets safely. We are immediately a moving target on the streets, and we qualify for kidnappings and for rape and for killing, just because we are women. And, on top of all that, what the coalition did was hand over part of the authorities to religious fundamentalists that turned our lives to push us hundreds of years back in time. We are pushed back to the spot where my grandmother was and that's not where we want to be. Women in Iraq have been educated, they have had access to work for more than half a century now. It's the thing that we will not do without anymore. They go into our schools now. They force the women into the veil and, you look at the streets. The women are not safe to be out in the streets. This is our reality in the post-war Iraq. And these are the freedoms and the democracy that we testify now in Baghdad. (Goodman 2004)

The frightening reality for Iraqi women under occupation is that their lives were and are refashioned not only ideologically and through representation but in actuality as they became imprisoned both literally under the rules of detention imposed by the occupiers and in their own homes by local patriarchs. Sharing Al-Ali's suggestion of the establishment of a double patriarchy, Yanar Mohammed places the blame for the change in women's lives in Iraq squarely on the shoulders of the occupying force. Thus she describes new dangers to Iraqi women from *both* the occupying forces *and* local men.

The prevalence of sex work as a means for women in communities that are devastated by war is also not a topic frequently broached by the Western press because to do so would require acknowledging the havoc the war has wreaked on these people, particularly the women in Afghanistan, whom the West was ostensibly trying to rescue. Husbands and fathers who would typically provide for women and their children are now missing, dead, or maimed, and in a culture in which women could not even go to school while the Taliban was in power, women have few options for supporting their families. In *The Nation*, Christian Parenti describes how prostitution works now in Afghanistan:

> Women working in government offices – beyond the control of their husbands but still crushed by poverty – often double and triple their paltry $30 a month salaries through casual prostitution. 'Cellphones make it very easy,' says an Afghan driver. 'The woman I am seeing has just two or three friends. I pay her a month's salary for an hour in the back room of my friends' store.' (Parenti 2006: 13)

It is not clear from Parenti's description whether these are women with men in their lives, though he does mention husbands, who are supplementing the family income, or whether they are actually relying on the poor paying jobs along with the sex work for support. Is this, as we have seen previously described, 'survival sex'? What is clear is that the women are not properly compensated for their employment and that visibility has meant new perilous conumdrums for women in the form of a market in which they can sell their bodies.

Visibility and invisibility problems have begun to affect all women in occupied spaces in negative ways, as is apparent in the strange tale of Dr Aafia Siddiqui.

Aafia Siddiqui

> The seepage of colonial representations of Others is not simply confined to popular media. It also influences the structure of stories covered by the contemporary news media. It is in the latter context that these representations assume a heightened significance – a significance imbued by the aura of the news media as providers of objective, impartial, and balanced public accounts of the world. (Molotch and Lester 1974, in Jiwani 2006: 36)

While visibility has many dangers, invisibility does too in the form of large civilian casualties being ignored by the rest of the world, giving Western militaries the ability to kill with impunity. In addition, as we have seen, invisibility allows media to construct identities for women and other disempowered groups that have little relationship to who they really are. But neither visibility nor invisibility is a static condition, and moving in and out of one or the other is not always voluntary.

One of the most horrifying examples of the flux that occurs between visibility and invisibility is the story of Aafia Siddiqui. Aafia Siddiqui is a

Pakistani woman who, like her brother and sister (Temple-Raston 2008), was educated in the United States, first at Brandeis, and later at MIT, where she earned a PhD in neuroscience. Aafia Siddiqui was recently convicted in a New York court of seven counts of assault, attempted murder, and weapons possession in an incident involving US military officials in an Afghan police station in July 2008 (Hughes 2010). She was subsequently sentenced to eighty-six years in prison for these crimes (United States Attorney's Office Southern District of New York 2010).

It is impossible to discern what actually happened to Aafia Siddiqi and whether she is indeed guilty of a crime. The story, as gathered from various news reports, is as follows: Siddiqui and her husband, Amjad Khan, a physician, lived in the US in the 1990s (Von Mittlestaedt 2008).[4] While living in the Boston area, they founded a 'non-profit Institute of Islamic research and teaching and contributed to Islamic charities that US officials have described as front groups for terrorists' (Branigin 2008).[5] The family returned to Pakistan in 2001. Some time after this, Siddiqui and her husband divorced. None of this is in dispute. What is not clear is what happened next. In March 2003, while in Karachi, Pakistan, Aafia Siddiqui and her three children disappeared. There is speculation, particularly in Pakistan, that she was detained by Pakistani authorities and subsequently handed over to the US military and either held at Bagram Airbase in Afghanistan or moved around from place to place while being held in rendition. This speculation is buttressed by admission by both Pakistani and American officials that they had Dr Siddiqui in custody numerous times, only for them to later back way from those claims (Scroggins 2012: 248, 250). While human rights groups and her mother and sister believe the latter, other relatives, uncles, and her former husband suggest that she simply went underground to avoid arrest.

Her disappearance is described in various news sources, all in the same vein, with great suspicion of her account of what happened:

> Ms. Siddiqi, 36, disappeared with her 3 children while visiting her parents' home in Karachi, Pakistan in March 2003 leading human rights groups and her family to believe she had been secretly detained. But in interviews Monday and in criminal complaint made public later Monday, American officials said they had no knowledge of Ms. Siddiqi's location for the past five years until July 17, when Ms. Siddiqi and a teenage boy were detained in Ghazni, Afghanistan. (Schmitt 2008)

Siddiqui had apparently told her mother that she was going to visit an uncle in Islamabad. A short time later, Pakistan's interior ministry confirmed that she had been picked up. Then they backtracked and said they had been mistaken (Temple-Raston 2008).

In this bizarre articulation of now you see her, now you don't, Aafia Siddiqui, variously known in the Western press as 'the female al Qaeda,' the 'Mata Hari of al Qaida' (Walsh 2009), 'The grey lady of Bagram' (ibid.), and 'Lady Al Qaeda' (Gendar 2010) was being watched by Western intelligence officials while being invisible to Western citizens. News sources seem willing to believe the CIA's claims that they had no knowledge of her whereabouts and were not holding her. The CIA's stance seems particularly remarkable given that in the early days of the war on terror 'John Ashcroft listed her among the 7 "most wanted" al Qaeda fugitives. "Armed and dangerous," he said, describing the Karachi woman as a terrorist "facilitator" who was willing to use her education against America' (Walsh 2009: 6).

Deborah Scroggins, in her book entitled: *Wanted Women. Faith, Lies and the War on Terror: The Lives of Ayaan Hirsi Ali and Aafia Siddiqui*, which she seems to have taken mostly from accounts of Aafia Siddiqui's estranged husband Amjad Khan, describes Aafia Siddiqui as 'a nearly psychotic anti-Semite.' Scroggins further elaborates: 'a gifted speaker, Ms. Siddiqui becomes an important fundraiser for Islamic groups with links to al-Qaeda.' The US government and Ms Scroggins both damn Aafia Siddiqui by association. Scroggins says, 'Her legend seemed to grow and grow' (Scroggins 2012: 273). Scroggins elaborates how dangerous Dr Siddiqui was believed to be:

Former head of the weapons of mass destruction unit at the counterterrorist center at the CIA, Rolf Mowatt-Larssen, told me after he retired that, far from being under arrest, Aafia remained the stuff of nightmares. Mowatt-Larssen had a special deck of fifty-two playing cards made up. Each carried the face of a suspected terrorist he feared might be planning the next big attack. Aafia was the queen of spades, the only woman in the deck. Mowatt-Larssen wouldn't have put her at the top of his list of potential mass murderers, but he couldn't rule her out. She was his wild card. (Ibid.: 327)

It wasn't Aafia's prowess as a scientist that worried Mowatt-Larssen the most. The FBI had gone through her records from MIT and Brandeis. She had not taken any notably advanced biology and chemistry courses, and there was no obvious application to jihad in her neuroscience PhD. What set her apart in his eyes was her combination of high intelligence including general scientific know-how, religious zeal, and years of experience in the United States. 'So far they have very few people who have been able to come to the U.S. and thrive,' he said. 'Aafia is different. She knows about U.S. immigration procedures and visas. She knows how to enroll in American educational institutions. She can open bank accounts and transfer money. She knows how things work here. She could have been very useful to them simply for her understanding of the U.S.' (Ibid.: 328)

'She had the imagination to come up with the next 9/11,' Mowatt-Larssen said. 'The question was whether they would listen to her.' (Ibid.: 328)

Even with the hardest core of al Qaeda operatives, she had a reputation for being headstrong. 'I remember thinking at the time, she must drive them crazy,' Mowatt-Larssen told me. But he couldn't be sure. The CIA had never pinned down her exact role. They just knew that 'she was always in the picture. Connections between her and other people the FBI was looking at surfaced in just about every al Qaeda investigation with a U.S. angle. She was always on our radar.' (Ibid.: 329)

Basic skills required for immigrants to the US to succeed are being perverted here and rendered as potentially sinister and in the service of terrorism. Possession of 'general scientific know-how' makes someone dangerous? Or is it only when a woman has scientific knowledge, like Rihab Taha and Huda Ammash, that it is alarming? Here Mowatt-Larssen is quoted as saying that it was the combination of factors including knowledge of science and 'religious zeal' along with 'years of experience in the United States.' I wonder how many science-y fundamentalist Christians in the US are regarded as dangerous by the CIA, have their image reproduced on decks of playing cards, or disappear for five years. Again, she is damned by association, as are many of the women we have read about who come to the attention of US authorities either inside or outside the US. It is not so much their own actions that bring them this unwanted attention, a stint in prison, or rendition; it is about whom they know, whom they marry, whom they live next door to. Even though she appears on various lists enumerating dangerous terrorists, and she was giving this retired CIA agent 'nightmares,' 'Aafia Siddiqui remained invisible to Western citizens both before and after her disappearance. It was only when she emerges in Ghazni that she begins to be seen and written about as "the most dangerous woman in the world"' (Von Mittlestaedt 2008).

Reporter Yvonne Ridley believes that Aafia Siddiqui was made deeply invisible by being placed in rendition. She and others suggest that

Aafia was seized by Pakistani intelligence, subsequently transferred to US custody and then held for a significant period of time at Bagram Airbase, a notorious prison in Afghanistan. There, Siddiqui would have been one of only two women held in the place and referred to as 'the grey lady of Bagram' or 'Prisoner 650.' So intent was she on finding Aafia and exposing Siddiqui's treatment by the US, Ridley made a film called *In Search of Prisoner 650*. In spite of the danger involved in coming forward, several men who were once held at Bagram have spoken out to attest to Siddiqui's presence there. 'Binyam Mohammed claims that he is totally sure that he saw Aafia Siddiqui being held at Bagram air base while he was being held there prior to 2008' (Mahmood 2009).

In fact, Ridley argues that US officials admitted that Prisoner 650 existed but insisted it was not Aafia Siddiqui. Indeed, at one moment, the Pakistani government acknowledged that they had Aafia in custody, then subsequently denied this:

> Several Pakistani media outlets did report her arrest. A year after her disappearance, *Dawn*, a daily newspaper normally considered to have good sources, quoted a spokesman from the Pakistani interior ministry saying that Siddiqui was arrested in Karachi and later handed to the Americans. Pakistani intelligence sources report that Siddiqui was in Pakistani detention until the end of 2003 and that her son Suleman fell ill and died during that time. It is known that terrorism suspects often spend a period of time in the country before being turned over to the Americans. According to the Asian Human Rights Commission, there are 52 secret prisons in the country, into which thousands of Pakistanis are believed to have disappeared since the beginning of the war on terrorism. (Von Mittlestaedt 2008)

Would Pakistani authorities admit that a child died in their custody if Aafia Siddiqui hadn't been held by them? What possible motivation would they have had to detain her other than at the behest of the American government? If there are fifty-two secret prisons in Pakistan, perhaps it is not only Aafia Siddiqui who has become invisible. Are Westerners to believe that the entire Pakistani government and media are telling falsehoods about the fate of Aafia Siddiqui? Human Rights Watch mentions Aafia's name in a 2007 report as someone believed to have been held as a 'Ghost prisoner.'

Aafia Siddiqui[6] oscillates between states of invisibility and curtailed limited visibility. She goes from being a ghost prisoner – that is, someone held without government acknowledgment, a person detained unofficially, not recorded or registered as a prisoner, and as such visible only to Western intelligence agents and perhaps prison guards – to being suddenly hyper-visible when described as arguably 'the most dangerous woman in the world.' 'Siddiqui's lawyer, Elaine Whitfield Sharp, told NPR that she suspects her client was set up. She suspects Siddiqui was being held captive, was dropped off at the compound and then was immediately picked up again with "conveniently incriminating evidence"' (Temple-Raston 2008).

Five years after her disappearance in Karachi, Siddiqui surfaced in July 2008 at a police station in Ghazni, Afghanistan, a place noted for resistance to the Western military occupation. She and her eldest son were found 'cowering on the ground' (Von Mittlestaedt 2008) after local authorities became suspicious of their 'loitering' outside the provincial governor's compound (Schmitt 2008). The Western media participated in enumerating her possessions at the time of her arrest. She apparently had some version of the following: '... documents describing the creation of explosives as well as excerpts from the "Anarchist's Arsenal." She also carried sealed bottles and glass jars filled with liquids and gels' (ibid.). According to the indictment filed in New York State federal court, she had: 'A witches brew of chemical weapons and glass bottles filled with mysterious liquids in her purse' (Gendar et al. 2008), along with:

> A plastic container filled with white briquettes that the FBI later identified as more than two pounds of sodium cyanide, an extremely toxic industrial chemical. There were writings about a 'mass casualty attack,' maps and diagrams of the Empire State Building, Wall Street, the Brooklyn Bridge, and other famous New York sites, even a discussion of how to build a dirty bomb. (Scroggins 2012: 403)

Handwritten notes referred to a 'mass casualty attack' and listed various locations in the United States, including Plum Island, the Empire State Building, the Statue of Liberty, Wall Street, and the Brooklyn Bridge. Other notes in Siddiqui's possession referred to the construction of 'dirty bombs,' and discussed various ways to attack 'enemies,' including by destroying reconnaissance drones, using underwater bombs, and deploying gliders (Gendar et al. 2008). '"They were here for suicide bombing," an Afghan official in Ghazni told the Globe in a telephone interview last week. Both of them were looking like they were prepared for suicide.' (UPI 2008).

Calling these items 'a witches brew' elicits thoughts of the witch-hunts of early US history. Along with its history, the highly gendered nature of that terminology shows how serious the creators of this narrative about Dr Siddiqui are about convincing the public that she is dangerous. How does one look as if they are prepared for suicide? Most news sources repeat some version of this list of supposed targets. Why Plum Island, which has an 'animal research facility,'[7] would be included on this list is a mystery, it seems, to most US citizens, who have probably never heard of this site. How it would come to the attention of a Pakistani woman beggars the imagination. Gendar et al. in the *New York Daily News*, which has something of a tabloid reputation, also include the threat to 'reconnaissance drones, using underwater bombs, and deploying gliders' in case the reader did not get the message that Siddiqui was dangerous. It's also worth noting that in the *Daily News*'s account, drones are for reconnaissance, not for targeted killing of suspected enemies – and their neighbors, families, and anyone else who gets in the way. How Aafia Siddiqui could have been in Ghazni in preparation for a suicide bombing as the official suggests in the UPI story and in Scroggins (2012: 403) defies the imagination. Why would she bring all these plans to destroy all of these other targets if she was planning to blow up herself and her son at the police station in Ghazni? Wouldn't it have made sense to pass along the bomb-making information and lists to others? Why would the list of targets supposedly in her possession be in New York while she was carrying out a suicide attack in Ghazni? Unsurprisingly, the most outrageous claims were made by Fox News, which reported that:

> Long before Aafia Siddiqui allegedly tried to kill U.S. agents and military officers in Afghanistan, the MIT educated neuroscientist once plotted to assassinate former presidents George H.W. Bush, Jimmy Carter and Bill Clinton, government sources told FOXNews.com. According to sources, Siddiqui was concocting a plan to use biological agents to contaminate former president Carter's water. 'This was very serious, the investigations will go on for some time,' a government source told FOXNews.com. (Winter 2008)

This plot to assassinate certain former presidents was not picked up and reported by any other reputable news sources. Fox chose an interesting combination of presidents, excluding George W. Bush, who was president at the time, but including former Democratic Party presidents as well as Bush's father. Fox's list of the contents of Aafia Siddiqui's purse at the time of her arrest is a little more detailed: 'Authorities found recipes for radioactive, chemical and biological weapons and explosives, documents detailing U.S. military assets, excerpts from Anarchists Arsenal, a bomb-making handbook, and one gigabyte thumb drive, now being analyzed by technology experts' (ibid.).

Intent on exaggerating Aafia Siddiqui's danger to the West, Fox News's account enumerates the various kinds of bomb possibilities she was capable of constructing. Here, they suggest, she could do radioactive, chemical *or* biological explosives. If so, she is self-taught in making radioactive bombs, which seems like quite a feat for someone trained in neuro-cognitive science.

The day after her arrest in Pakistan, a combination of Afghan and US officials came to the police station in Ghazni to question her. Eric Schmitt of the *New York Times* gives this account that is representative of how the incident is most often described in the media:

> An American team including two F.B.I. agents, two American soldiers
> and interpreters went to the police station to talk to her. The F.B.I.
> has wanted her for questioning since May 2004, a Justice Department
> Spokesman said. ... Americans entered a room in the police station,
> unaware that Ms. Siddiqui was being held there, unsecured, behind
> a curtain. One of the soldiers, a warrant officer, sat down and placed
> his M-4 rifle on the floor next to the curtain. Shortly after the meting
> began the other soldier, a captain, heard a woman yelling from the
> curtain. He turned to see Ms. Siddiqui pointing the warrant officer's
> rifle at him. The interpreter sitting closest to Ms. Siddiqui lunged at her
> and pushed the rifle away as she pulled the trigger and shouted, 'God
> is Great.' She fired at least two shots, but no one was hit. The warrant
> officer returned fire with his 9mm pistol, hitting Ms. Siddiqui at least
> once in the torso. Ms. Siddiqui struggled when officers fired to subdue
> her, shouting in English that she wanted to kill Americans. After she
> was subdued, the complaint said, she 'temporarily lost consciousness.'
> (Schmitt 2008)

Maybe she 'lost consciousness' because she had been shot! Deborah Scroggins, though, reports that far from being unconscious, while she was being carried out of the police station on a litter, her hands and feet bound, according to Sergeant Kenneth J. Cook of the US military, she screamed: 'Cover my feet! Cover my fucking feet! Cover my feet you motherfucker!' (Scroggins 2012: 405). Scroggins does not clarify whether Dr Siddiqui cursed her captors in English, Urdu, Pashto or Dari. One should note how accusations of terrorism turn the femininity of this, by all accounts, devout Muslim woman on its head in the Western imagination. These helpless women, desperately in need of rescue, apparently become foul mouthed and shrill the moment they take up jihadist intentions. Despite how dramatically the story of what happened in the police station is told, and it is told with great flourish over and over again in media accounts, Schmitt's above is one of the more measured ones.

In spite of her supposed anti-Western fervor, Aafia Siddiqui did not shoot anyone. She is the only person who was shot that day. 'Left unexplained was how this frail 110 pound woman, confronted by three US Army officers, two FBI agents, and two Army interpreters, inexplicably managed to assault three of them, get one of their rifles, open fire at closer range, hit no one, and only she was severely wounded' (Lendman 2010).

Of course, Stephen Lendman is not a reporter but rather an American, a self-described 'progressive' commentator. Nonetheless, his pointing out the improbabilities in the government's story rings true. Eric Schmitt of the *New York Times* comments on the story in a small way while upholding the basic facts and allowing any skepticism about his story to come from the words of Aafia Siddiqui's attorney:

> The wild scene in the police station is the latest chapter in one of the strangest episodes in the American campaign against terrorism. Human rights groups and a lawyer for Ms. Siddiqui, Elaine Whitfield Sharp, said they believed that Ms. Siddiqui had been secretly detained since 2003, much of the time at Bagram Air Base in Afghanistan. (Schmitt 2008)

In the *New York Daily News*, her arrest was described as follows:

> Law enforcement officials believe they have 'the most significant capture' in the fight against terrorism in five years. The alleged Mata Hari appeared in Manhattan Federal Court in a wheelchair Monday. 'She is a high security risk,' Assistant US Attorney Christopher Lloyd LaVigne told the judge. Some experts believe Siddiqui is much more than that. 'She is the most significant capture in five years,' former CIA agent John Kiriakouy told ABC News. 'To find someone who has such rich information, computer hard drives, emails, that is really a major capture.' (Gendar et al. 2008)

In the *New York Times*: 'United States intelligence agencies have said that Ms Siddiqui has links to at least 2 of the 14 men suspected of being high level members of Al Qaeda who were moved to Guantanamo in Sept 2006' (Schmitt 2008).

Speculation and accusation abound in the news accounts of what Aafia Siddiqui might have done. There are connections between her committing terrorist acts such as helping a man get 'documents to re-enter the US,' so that he could 'conduct research on poisoning reservoirs and blowing up gas stations in the US' (ibid.). How would his intentions be ascertained? 'She was once married to a nephew of 9/11 mastermind Khalid Sheikh Mohammed, who is being held at Guantanamo Bay Detention Center' (ibid.). Her marriage, or at least her supposed association with the family of Khalid Sheikh Moham-med, seems to be the most damning piece of evidence connecting her to terrorist activities. Her family says the marriage never happened (Walsh 2009). Indeed, a major part of her crime seems to be about association. She was initially questioned by the FBI while living in the Boston area; after all, she committed the very suspicious acts of fund-raising for Muslim organizations and had joined a mosque in the area. These threatening actions meant that of course she needed to be investigated by the FBI. During the questioning, she and her then husband, Amjad Khan, were asked whether they knew Osama bin Laden (Scroggins 2012: 187).

At various times in the years since John Ashcroft showed Dr Sid-diqui's picture as one of the seven most wanted terrorists, Aafia Siddiqui has been accused of doing a variety of things, including marrying a terrorist, helping terrorists get into the United States, planning terrorist attacks, and smuggling diamonds.

> And then there is the issue of the blood diamonds. This is the most serious accusation, because it seems to cement the suspicion that Sid-diqui is a terrorist. In June 2001, a few months before the attacks on New York and Washington, Siddiqui is believed by some to have trave-led to the Liberian capital Monrovia, on behalf of al-Qaida's leadership, to buy diamonds worth $19 million (€15 million), which were used to fund al-Qaida operations. (Von Mittlestaedt 2008)

It is interesting that this diamond smuggling accusation is not fre-quently mentioned by other Western news sources given that here it is suggested as the most serious charge against Dr Siddiqui. Appar-ently, in spite of eyewitness testimony that Dr Siddiqui was in Liberia smuggling diamonds, her attorneys were able to produce proof that she was in the US at the same time. As with most of the accusations against her, this too happened to be too difficult to prove, perhaps prompting the set-up in Ghazni.

So many of the accusations against her, dating back to the time she lived in Boston or later when she allegedly traveled back and forth to the United States doing the bidding of a terrorist network, turned out to be false, flimsy, or impossible to prove. In fact, when Aafia Siddiqui went on trial, she was not accused of terrorism at all. 'In 2004, FBI director Robert Mueller called Siddiqui an al-Qaida operative and facilitator. But none of these allegations appear in the charges against her, at least not yet' (Temple-Raston 2008).

In her study of the trials of terrorists inside the United States, Petra Bartosiewicz suggests that the trials are set up in such a way that everyone gets convicted. She cites the Siddiqui case as one such trial (Bartosiewicz 2009). The trial was held in New York City, and even a cursory glance at the reportage reveals some alarming unfairness. Dr Siddiqui was frequently removed from the courtroom. It seems that whenever she articulated something that would call into question the American government's version of the accusations against her, she was removed from the courtroom. When objecting to the account of what happened in the police station by saying about the gun involved: '"I never fired. I never had it" marshals took her away' (Gendar and Kennedy 2010).

> Under cross-examination, she said she was given the bag with incriminating documents, didn't know its contents or whether the handwriting on them was hers. She explained her repeated torture at Bagram, the effects of the strong medication given her, and at one point said, 'If you were in a secret prison or your children were tortured,' after which she was forcibly removed from the court and proceedings continued without her. (Lendman 2010)

Western media chose not to focus on these utterances about what might have happened to her. Rather, they repeated references to her anti-Semitic statements and asserted that her comments were signs of mental illness, though she couldn't be made to seem too mentally ill or she would not have been eligible to go on trial in the US. It was not just her repeated removals from the courtroom, however, that call the trial into question.

There were inconsistencies from the witnesses, and Dr Siddiqui's attorneys point out that the evidence about the shooting was not solid: 'Defense lawyers argued that an absence of bullets, casings or residue from the M4 suggested it had not been shot. They used a video to show that two holes in a wall supposedly caused by the M4 had been there before July 18' (Hughes 2010). Finally, in what can only be described as prejudicial in the extreme, a witness was called who was a military officer who had been present on that day in the police station in Ghazni. The officer had subsequently been wounded in Afghanistan and his physical impairment was not explained to the jury (ibid.): 'The clandestine soldier, whose identity was limited to his rank – chief warrant officer – limped into the courtroom with a cane and a chest-full of medals. He wept when he described the wounds he sustained in an unrelated roadside bombing in September in Afghanistan' (Gendar and Kennedy 2010). Why was he allowed to give this testimony? The account of his wounding had nothing whatsoever to do with what happened in the police station in Ghazni. Watching him weep while giving his account of being injured at the hands of another unspecified enemy could only serve to prejudice the jury against Aafia Siddiqui.

The policies of the court seemed unfair to Dr Siddiqui in terms of allowing press coverage of the trial. During the first day of proceedings, no Pakistani reporters were allowed inside the courtroom. Given the intense media interest in this trial since Dr Siddiqui had become something of a cause célèbre in Pakistan, many Pakistani reporters wanted to cover the trial. With security concerns being cited, however, many reporters from outside the US, including some with press credentials issued by the United Nations or the US State Department, were kept out of the courtroom and allowed access only through closed circuit television (Bartosiewicz 2010). On the trial's first day, only three reporters were inside the courtroom. Those reporters were from the *New York Times*, the *New York Post* and the *New York Daily News*. These exclusions of members of the press from Dr Siddiqui's home country furthers the perception already present that she was not being treated fairly. In addition, hearing the story of the trial from only a few news sources, especially only news sources located in New York, further narrowed and intensified the information the public was given about who Aafia Siddiqui is and what happened to her.

Petra Bartosiewicz describes further discriminatory treatment in the courthouse:

> During lunch break on the first day of the Siddiqui trial a group of Muslim men praying in the waiting areas outside the courtroom were afterwards asked to leave the floor. That prevented them from securing a place in line for the afternoon sessions. Several Muslim women in hijabs were also given similar instructions, but others in the same area, dressed in business attire, including this reporter, were allowed to stay. (Ibid.)

It is difficult to believe, in this time of heightened awareness of racism and of racial profiling, that inside a building owned by the federal government of the United States, where the laws of the land are supposed to be dispensed without prejudice, people could be treated in this fashion without any apparent awareness that they are being discriminated against. Aafia Siddiqui was tried and convicted to eighty-six years in the absence of her peers.

We have at least a limited version of what happened to Aafia Siddiqui inside a Manhattan courtroom, but how do we make sense of what happened to Aafia Siddiqui in what Declan Walsh calls 'one of the most intriguing episodes of America's "war on terror"'? (Walsh 2009). One of her attorneys suggested that she was 'the ultimate victim of the American dark side' (Bartosiewicz 2010). Aafia Siddiqui seems, by all accounts, to have been a smart, religious woman who was interested in promoting Islam and in helping others. So what really happened?

Phyllis Chesler, whose work against Islam we have seen in another chapter, blames Siddiqui's supposed turn to Islamic extremism on, of course, wearing the veil:

> Like a small but increasing number of 'Westernized' Muslim women, Aafia Siddiqui joined her local mosque (in her case, the Roxbury, MA mosque) and started to veil, and as she did, her ambitions became aggressively jihadic. This is not a contradiction. Obediently veiled Muslim women can be very aggressive, murderously so. They certainly police other women in savage and self-righteous ways in Iran and Indonesia. In Iraq, veiled Muslim women have blown up other Muslim female religious pilgrims. And, Muslim women who were normatively spurned by their mothers were manipulated by Samira Jassim, an attentive, 'loving' Iraqi mother-figure, who carefully turned them into suicide killers. Women are very aggressive – but usually towards other women. Traditionally, women do not go up against men whom they view as their potential protectors and as more powerful than they are. Ironically, Islamic jihad wishes to reverse, upend, both Nature and human evolutionary history. Just as normatively degraded mothers are 'turned' into hero-mothers who publicly praise their suicide killer sons – just so, are normatively self-hating women 'turned' into Al-Qaeda heroines who not only directly attack men, but who directly attack infidel male *soldiers*. (Chesler 2010a)

Here Chesler once again blames Islam and just as saliently wearing a veil for ironically freeing women to reveal their formerly hidden natures. It is in women's natures to be violent, she argues here. This violence, however, is mostly exhibited toward other women, but under Islam, which 'reverses, upends Nature and human evolutionary history,' Aafia Siddiqui is allowed to attack all those armed men inside the

Ghazni police station. The same 'Islamic jihad' which Chesler would have enslaving women by forcing them to wear the veil apparently also works toward liberating the hidden killer inside all women. Chesler is not joking here, though it might seem as if she is. This kind of hate-fueled vitriol against Islam and the wearing of the veil has her circling back again and again to blame all of the world's ills on Islam, no matter how convoluted the reasoning.

Deborah Scroggins rather contemptuously calls Dr Siddiqui the 'new symbol of Islamic victimhood' (2012: 427). Stephen Lendman contests such a view when he writes: 'Bogusly charged and convicted, Siddiqui was guilty only of being Muslim in America at the wrong time. She was a pawn in America's "war on terror," used, abused, now convicted, and facing life in prison when sentenced, a victim of gross injustice' (Lendman 2010).

We may never know what actually happened to Aafia Siddiqui. Was there a process of radicalization that culminated in her assisting in jihad? Or were there simply a series of misapprehensions, Dr Siddiqui being a proponent of Islam inside the United States at a time when the nation became collectively mistrustful about the terrorist within, her travel back and forth to Pakistan, her friends, and her donations to certain Muslim charities adding a dose of certainty to the suspicions against her? These impressions of her seem to have been enough to bring her to the attention of US Attorney General John Ashcroft when he showed a photo of her in 2004 and proclaimed her one of the seven terrorists that posed the most danger to the United States (Scroggins 2012: 272).

Were these circumstances enough to cause her to be held in rendition by the US for five years? The CIA denies that she was ever held by the US, but the failure to levy charges against her, including the charges of aiding and abetting terrorists, meant that the rendition program did not come up at the trial (Bartosiewicz 2009). This kept the rendition program from getting much public scrutiny inside the US. Was this the reason she was 'set up' at the police station in Ghazni? Was it done to further screen the rendition program from an already skeptical public in the US, not to mention an angry, distrustful public in Pakistan and Afghanistan? Was Aafia Siddiqui simply an abused woman fleeing her batterer, Amjad Khan, and trying to hide herself and her children from him? Or had she indeed gone underground, fearful of US authorities, somewhere in Pakistan? Were her experiences of being questioned by the FBI so traumatic that she was forced to go underground? If she was the victim of domestic violence, a mother on the run, or a political fugitive, how do we explain her surfacing in Ghazni? What was she doing there? Given her total invisibility in Western media sources following the trial, we will probably never know.

Transnational visibility

Hate rhetoric, the war on terror, the conflicts in Afghanistan, Iraq and the Middle East have generated damaging new media stereotypes. (Shaheen 2008: 7)

In addition to the few images of Afghan and Iraqi women presented on the nightly news or in newspapers and magazines, a handful of fictional representations of them have appeared on American television. Most depictions of Iraqis, Afghans, South Asians, Middle Easterners, or Muslims are of men from that region and that religion. Those men are similarly depicted as all Muslim, and all Muslims are portrayed as vaguely sinister if not downright dangerous. Little attention is paid to nationality, cultural differences, or religious specificity. Even when nationality is specified, certain cultural 'truths' are relied upon to make clear the message that the West is superior and that 'Muslims,' 'Arabs,' or even more specifically Egyptians, Palestinians, or Afghans, are strange, brutal, and impossible to understand.

This practice of othering can be observed in the popular iterations of the long-running American television show *Law and Order*. The original series has had no fewer than seven episodes that featured Muslim criminals or 'terrorists' since 2001. These are augmented by episodes of the associated series, *Law and Order Special Victims Unit (SVU)*, *Law and Order Criminal Intent*, and *Law and Order LA*. Reruns of the original continue to be syndicated, and for years in the US, no matter the time of day or night, one could watch an episode of *Law and Order* on TV. The original series, as well as some of the spin-offs, has now been canceled, but *SVU* is still running. It too is now frequently syndicated on various television stations. So these depictions of Arab or South Asian or Muslim 'evil-doers' are prolific just in *Law and Order* alone, not taking into account the many other representations of Muslims as dangerous that are available.

Women are mostly peripheral in these stories. Women, when they appear at all in episodes, are often victims or dupes. In his study of Arabs on television in the United States, Jack Shaheen tells us that 'no TV series – not one – has ever featured an Arab-American female character' (ibid.: 46). He further asserts that 'Arab-American women remain invisible. They almost never appear on TV, and when they do they are usually silent and submissive' (ibid.: 47). His argument might be extended to include all Muslim women or all women believed to be Muslim from around the world, not just within the United States. When women depicted as, or believed to be, Muslim or from places like Egypt, Iran, Iraq, or Afghanistan appear, their main purpose is to show how imperiled they are, mostly by the actions of men from their cultures. Even when they are victims of crimes that don't involve men from their cultures, the women in these shows make the point that Muslim, Arab, and South Asian women are vulnerable, helpless, and that they require rescue. So even when they are dead and not at the center of the story being told, on television stereotypes about them are being reinforced and propaganda that legitimizes wars on the bodies of women is being spread.

Several episodes are analyzed here to reveal these depictions. *Law and Order* advertises itself and its stories as being 'ripped from the headlines.' In that regard, it makes it easy to observe the cross-over between fiction and reality in both the storylines and the presentation of characters. The first episode examined is called 'Honor.' It appeared on *SVU* prior to the events of September 11th 2001 and seems to have been informed by some US feminists' outrage over the treatment of women by the Taliban. The first post-9/11 episode of the original series aired in May of 2002 when an Arab murder victim turned out to actually be a terrorist. Thirteen months after the attacks, in October 2002, the season opened with an episode entitled 'American Jihad,' which featured an affluent young white man who had converted to Islam and subsequently defended himself against murder charges on the grounds that he was being discriminated against because of his religion. Shortly after the third anniversary of 9/11, 22 September 2004, the episode entitled 'Paradigm' was aired. In 'Paradigm,' the sister of someone who was held at Abu Ghraib prison in Iraq kills one of his former captors in New York City. This episode is very unusual as it features an Iraqi woman killer. It may have been indicative of the negative press surrounding Dr Germ and Mrs Anthrax as dangerous, combined with perceptions of women suicide bombers who are depicted in the Western press as willing to do anything at the behest of men from their culture or religion, or as acting in reaction to losing a brother, father, lover, friend, as the women in this episode did (Naaman 2007). Later that season, in 'Enemy,' an Afghan druglord commits several murders in New York. This druglord, like Hamid Karzai's brother, is actually seen as an ally to the US – but the truth is, according to the story, he is uncivilizable.

The stories are full of Orientalism, and steeped in propaganda that foments fear and supports imperialism. These depictions help create the idea of the evil Muslim man who is full of hatred for the US and US citizens and relentless in carrying out terrorist acts. He is also someone who treats women badly. In the other spin-offs, there are also several episodes in each devoted to the topic of unsavory Arab or South Asian men and the helplessness of the women in their lives. Cast as threats to 'civilization,' these stereotypical representations of the Arab terrorist serve the purpose of demonizing an enemy 'out there' or 'over here' in the nation, and thereby provide ample justification for the invasion of their lands, the passage of draconian laws forbidding their entry, and their criminalization once inside the nation (Jiwani 2006: 36).

As Jiwani suggests, these representations, intentional or not, instill fear of others, and as Sara Ahmed would say 'other others,' both inside and outside the US, prompting wars of annihilation and stricter and stricter immigration laws.

The pre-September 11th 2001 *Special Victims Unit* episode called 'Honor' is about the murder of a young Afghan woman named Nafeesa Amir. Nafeesa was found stabbed, and appeared to have been sexually assaulted, in Central Park in New York City. Immediately the detectives and everyone they encounter – the young woman's friends, her professors – begin to talk about how oppressive Nafeesa's family is, and how the Taliban restricts women's lives in Afghanistan. Her professor tells the detectives: 'She couldn't believe how free the press is here. Over there, the Taliban controls everything. Afghan women can't even leave their homes on their own.' Nafeesa's best friend says her father is 'a control freak. He wouldn't let her go out, made her wear the robes.' When her parents are interviewed, Nafeesa's father says, 'Nafeesa did not understand her place. She chooses a man's work. She is dead to us. She slept with a man who is not her husband.' Nafeesa's mother, Aziza, is silent during this exchange. She is wearing a black niqab. Nafeesa's boyfriend is a naturalized US citizen from Afghanistan. He runs an import-export business (in real life, he would soon become the kind of man viewed with great suspicion by US authorities). He explains to the police that Nafeesa was having a lot of strife with her parents because of her activities in the US – activities that US women her age take for granted – going to college and dating. He says, 'What he [her father] doesn't want is a reputation for letting his women do as they please. He wants every inch of her body covered. The Taliban put women under virtual house arrest. Nafeesa wanted to live as a modern woman, to be more than a factory for producing sons.' Nafeesa was promised, in an arranged marriage, to the son of a cabinet minister. This did not stop her from falling in love with Mr Import-Export Business, which was horrifying to her parents. Nafeesa's father is suspected of her murder but the man has diplomatic immunity as he is described as an attaché for the Afghan embassy. While the detectives are interviewing Nafeesa's father for the second time, Aziza lets her veil fall away from her face in the presence of the police. They have already rescued her.

The detectives arrest Nafeesa's brother for her murder on the airplane as he attempts to flee to Afghanistan, and he smiles when he sees them coming for him and says, 'I am proud that I killed her – she deserved to die.' During the brother's trial, one of Nafeesa's professors testifies that 'Honor killings are part of ancient cultural tradition. For a man honor means controlling his women.' The defense attorney mentions that 'Last year in the West Bank and Gaza three out of four killings were honor killings.' The professor replies, 'Well, the Palestinians ...' He is then interrupted. Here the conflict around the occupation of Palestine by the Israelis gets erased in a similar way to how troubles brought about as a result of the occupations of Afghanistan and Iraq are erased. The suggestion in *Law and Order* is that Palestinians are backward and murderous and outside what one can expect of 'civilized' people. This depiction works to erase Israeli brutality and to absolve Israel of any responsibility for gendered violence within the occupied territories.

Later in the show, Nafeesa's mother Aziza eventually agrees to testify against her son. She testifies with bare face – the American legal system again liberating her. She reveals that Mr Amir exhorted his son to kill Nafeesa to 'prove his manhood.' After the detectives promise Mrs Amir protection in exchange for her testimony, Mr Amir kills her. The ending is a kind of trope for US involvement in Afghanistan, even though this episode was filmed quite a while before the US occupied the country. The US ostensibly invaded Afghanistan to protect Afghan women, and yet so many have died or been otherwise harmed in the process. The *Time* magazine cover caption 'What happens when we leave Afghanistan' might well have been the title of this show. The American police officers look away and Aziza is murdered. Yet it was these same officers who encouraged her to speak out against her husband and her son.

Throughout the show, Afghanistan is referred to as being in the Middle East – a blurring of geographic boundaries that follows the religious and national boundary blurring that the West engages in when it comes to people and spaces that have been Orientalized. In case the audience continues to make distinctions between countries and geographic differences, the defense attorney's tirade against Palestinians at the end of the show, without historical, cultural or political context, paints all Muslim men as, to use the professor's word, 'barbarians.'

The writers of *Law and Order* seemed to become increasingly aware of how these portrayals might be offensive as the war on terror progressed. In the 2004 episode of *SVU* entitled 'Hate,' we once again have a dead Muslim woman. Of course, the detectives suspect a Muslim man, the dead woman's husband, who the viewer gradually finds out is Egyptian, of murdering his wife. Anti-Muslim sentiment is played on when the husband is depicted as the publisher of an 'Arab-American' newspaper and the detectives articulate anti-Muslim opinions related to the attacks of September 11th 2001. Their views, however, are quickly countered by others in the cast. In one scene the captain cautions, 'Let's be careful not to say Muslim men burn their wives.' It is not clear whether the captain wants his detectives not to rush into making assumptions about who committed the crime in this instance or whether he is simply cautioning them against articulating such ideas as a public relations strategy. In another scene the mother of the accused Egyptian man says, 'You just want to make Arabs look like bad people. We are not barbarians.' Years after the episode described above, the word barbarian emerges again, only this time it is used to protest that characterization. Nonetheless, even while trying for fairness, the writers cannot help themselves and revert to the message promoted by the US government when they say of the murder victim whom they discover has been having an affair, 'the lady wanted freedom.' In the end, even though the murderer turns out to be a white guy who is anti-Muslim, there is no real condemnation of the crime as a hate crime and the viewer is left with the idea that all Muslim women, regardless of geographic location or religion or nationality, are imperiled.

In an episode of the original *Law and Order* entitled 'Fear America' (Season 17, 2006), a brown-skinned man is filmed being beheaded. Hooded men spout anti-Arab sentiments while standing in front of an American flag with a sign below it that reads 'Arabs Go Home' while they commit this atrocity. We later discover that the actual perpetrator is Muslim and that he was related to the man's wife. The man was beheaded because it was discovered by a cousin that he was informing on the cousin's terrorist organization. The role of the Muslim woman in this episode is illustrative of Shaheen's argument. Even though all the characters – the victim, his wife and her cousin – are American born, they are represented as primarily Muslim and thus essentially others inside the US. At the end of the hour, the wife, who is not named throughout and who has only been included in shots of grieving and then later in a visit to her cousin once he is arrested, becomes pivotal to convicting the cousin of her husband's murder. She breaks down under the most gentle interrogation by Sam Waterston's character to reveal that, in an attempt to protect her husband, she confessed to her cousin that the husband was informing – setting him up for execution. She is then pressured by her cousin and the imam of her mosque to uphold the cousin's false alibi. She must declare her loyalty to Islam by upholding a lie. She declares that since the death of her husband, 'All I have left is this community. I can't give that up.' First she is depicted as so weak and unsophisticated that she turns for assistance to her cousin, an obvious jihadist. In the end, though, it is her loyalty to her husband and a desire to see his death avenged that wins out. She repudiates her cousin and the imam and by extension Islam in order to support the American justice system. She lives out the fantasy of the colonizer when she allows herself to be taken over by the government, thus rejecting all that she has known before in favor of US laws and customs.

Here's the dilemma

Is it better to remain invisible on American television, as Shaheen suggests Arab-American women have been? I would add to his claim by suggesting that all Muslim women or women believed to be Muslim have similarly been made invisible. For to be made visible in the kinds of depictions we have mentioned above does not help make Arab, South Asian, or Muslim women more sympathetic or more human in the eyes of Western viewers – only more helpless, more foolish, more easily duped. The controversy surrounding a recent reality series on American television called *All-American Muslim*, the series occasioning an excuse for anti-Muslim public rhetoric prompting advertisers to pull ads, might be read as further confirmation that invisibility is the way to go.

Though the case of Aafia Siddiqui carries the conundrum for women in war to the extreme, her story, as well as the story of Aesha Moham-madzai, and the fictionalized stories of the Muslim women depicted on American television, exemplifies how neither visibility nor invisibility promises refuge from the dehumanization, demonization, death, and destruction the war on terror has brought about. My argument in this chapter is twofold. First, Muslim women are hyper-visible in Western media. This hyper-visibility is not, as we might imagine, advantageous to Muslim women as the depictions that are available are inaccurate, extremely limited, and limiting. Secondly, when Muslim women become visible in Western media, it is to decry their terrorist impulses which are inherent and/or to use them as examples of femininity gone wrong. The regime of visibility, invisibility, hyper-visibility works to uphold ideas of Western superiority and the comparative liberation of Western women by allowing over-determined depictions of sinister Muslim women. These representations of dangerous Muslims also help to obscure the workings of hyper-patriarchies that have developed as a result of Western occupation and interference.

4 | We are all soldiers now: deploying Western women

> Western women achieve their own subject status through claims
> that they are the same as, but culturally different from, Muslim
> women, women who have to be rescued. Gender, unmoored from
> class, race, and culture, facilitates this imperialist move, as does
> culture that is equally removed from history and context. (Razack
> 2008: 104)

> ... it falls to the women of the ruling race to police the colour line ...
> They mark the West as a place of values, and the non-West as a place
> of culture, a line in the sand drawn by comparing their own appar-
> ently emancipated status with that of their non-Western sisters.
> (Ibid.: 17)

Prior to the war on Afghanistan, the Bush administration, assisted
notably by the women who surrounded George Bush, including his
wife Laura, counselor Karen Hughes, and Mary Matalin, success-
fully waged a public relations campaign to make the oppression of
women under Taliban rule one of the primary reasons to justify the
invasion of Afghanistan (Lowther 2001; Bumiller 2001; Hall 2001; Pisik
2001; Wallace 2001; Stout 2001; Allen 2001; Whitworth and Webster 2001;
Settle 2001). In the United States, Laura Bush gave the first First Lady's
radio address in place of her husband to push this issue to the fore.
According to CNN, her remarks 'stress that brutal oppression of
women represents the Taliban's and al Qaeda's vision of government
for the world' (Wallace 2001). In her speech, Laura Bush suggested
that for women living under Taliban rule, 'small displays of joy are
outlawed.' And went on to say this oppressive living situation would
soon be exported as it represented 'The world the terrorists would like
to impose on the rest of us' (CNN.com. 2001a). Laura Bush's speech
raises colonial specters of white women historically in Africa and in
Asia working to screen, but also to assist in, their husbands' imperial
desires. Her claims, though, are confusing. Was the war on Afghanistan
about ending the Taliban's oppression of Afghan women, 'rescuing
them from brown men' (Spivak 1988)? Or was it instead an attempt to
forestall any imperialist moves the Taliban and al-Qaeda might make?

Did she mention the Taliban as having imperialist aims as a means to obfuscate Western aspirations? Is the war on terror then really about protecting Western women from Taliban rule? If the US administration went to war to rescue Afghan women *and* protect American women from Taliban imperialism, it would make quite a statement about the supremacy of Western militarized masculinity, while at the same time it would ensure that Western women remain solely at Western men's service when needed.

In this chapter, the deployment of Western women to screen imperial masculine desires, to legitimize war, to recruit other Westerners to support the war, and to win over the hearts and minds of the colonized, is revealed. Some women more directly enact imperialism than the women described above by serving in the US military in what are being called female engagement teams. They reinforce ideas about women's work in wartime while simultaneously breaking gender barriers and ostensibly winning the hearts and minds of the Afghan people. Other women in the US, both fictional like Samantha Jones in *Sex and the City 2*, and Carrie Mathison in *Homeland*, and real women like columnist Maureen Dowd, are all doing their bit to support the empire. This chapter examines how women participate in the logics of empire and play various roles to enable its workings.

The use of women to obfuscate and support imperialist desires in the build-up to the war on Afghanistan was not confined to the United States. Indeed, in Great Britain, Cherie Blair (Evans 2001; Ward 2001; Whitworth and Webster 2001; Settle 2001) was similarly deployed to plead for the rescue of Afghan women as justification for the war. Other British women such as International Development Secretary Clare Short (Ward 2001), and former Labour MP Joan Ruddick (Roberts 2001), were also involved in demanding that women be included in a post-Taliban government and suggesting that emphasis be placed on human rights for women in Afghanistan. Recent revelations in the WikiLeaks scandal suggest that there is a document that verifies that the CIA suggested that Afghan women be used to sell the war to Europeans. 'Afghan women could serve as ideal messengers in humanizing' the war for European audiences (Phalnikar 2010).

Karen Hughes, George Bush's special advisor, is credited with creating the campaign to place Afghan women at the center of the build-up to the war (Bumiller 2001: 2). She served two stints in George Bush's administration and during both she was essential to the task of empire-building. She became a kind of ambassador of transnational sexism in her constant efforts to use Afghan women to justify the war and to point out the unfavorable comparisons between their lives and those of Western women. She left the Bush administration in 2007, after serving as Undersecretary of State. In this position, her job had been to 'Retool the way the United States sells its policies, ideals and views overseas. ... Hughes' focus has been to change the way the United States engages and responds to criticism or misinformation in the Muslim world' (Associated Press 2007). In its description of her job, the AP refers, quite honestly, to the public relations aspect of the Bush administration's policies in the region. The use of the word 'sell' is quite telling here. Also of note are the description of the entire region as 'Muslim' and the combination of the words 'criticism' and 'misinformation,' as if they are one and the same.

As this public relations campaign about the freeing of Afghan women was undertaken, it required, for once, some transnational communication and cooperation. For the campaign to work, Cherie Blair and Laura Bush should seem to represent all Western women and must present a unified front on the desire to liberate Afghan women.

> Cherie Blair and Laura Bush are poised to upstage their husbands on
> the war front next week, albeit briefly. The prime minister's wife will
> spearhead the UK launch of an international campaign to focus public
> attention on the plight of Afghan women under the cruel hand of the
> Taliban. Mrs Blair's initiative will be part of a joint exercise with Laura
> Bush, America's first lady, who will make US history when she delivers
> the usual weekly presidential radio address to launch the international
> campaign for women's rights in Afghanistan. Mrs Blair, known for her
> campaigning zeal on behalf of women's rights, will play host to 'an
> event' at Downing Street – probably on Monday. Also in attendance to
> reinforce the message will be the cabinet's women members: Helen
> Liddell, the Scottish secretary; Estelle Morris, the education secretary;
> Tessa Jowell, culture secretary; Clare Short, the international develop-
> ment secretary, and Hilary Armstrong, chief whip. (Settle 2001: 8)

Women who are highly placed in both governments are undertaking the work of empire-building. All of these 'liberated' Western women end up being little more than hand-servants to their husbands', bosses', or fathers' colonial and militaristic aims. Of course, they are not forced to do this work, and they also benefit from doing it in many ways, not the least of which is they can feel superior to the poor oppressed Afghan women. And, as we shall see below, communication between the actual parties involved – that is, Cherie Blair and Laura Bush – and any Afghan woman at all is not necessary. Because there is nothing actually feminist or sisterly about it, in this version of transnational sisterhood, all the words can and should come from administrative policy-makers.

Across the Atlantic, the women of the Bush administration, including wife Laura, stay 'on message,' as American politicians are encouraged to do. The message gets expanded, though, as perhaps they fear that sisterly concern is not sufficient rationale for the war. In order to whip up enthusiasm for the war, a gullible and mostly uninformed populace is told that it is the Taliban rather than the West that needs to have its imperialist aims curbed. 'A senior White House official said: "The message will be that the Taliban and al Qaeda's oppression of women represents their vision of society that they hope to export to the rest of the world, and that we need to do everything we can to help the Afghan women who have suffered so long"' (ibid.: 8).

Playing on the tragedies that have befallen Afghan women under the Taliban is not enough for the creators of this message. Their further efforts to justify the war and to persuade citizens of various Western nations to participate are designed to instill the fear in Western women, only thirty or so years since being 'liberated' themselves, that their hard-fought-for rights might disappear under Taliban rule outside of Afghanistan.

Western feminism, though, is not all it is advertised to be when Western men – indeed, some thirty years later – continue to attempt to use Western women as tools to further their aims, as the handmaidens of their imperialist actions, and as bolsterers of their belief in their masculine superiority.

Mr Blair's spokesman said: 'We do believe we need to lift the veil and show what has been happening to women in Afghanistan under the Taliban regime. That is something you will see a focus on both on this side of the Atlantic and in the States.' He stressed: 'I don't think you can underline too often the way women's rights have been denied.' The spokesman said he did not know whether the two leaders' wives had spoken to each other about the topic, but added: 'There is a lot of communication going on between us and the Americans on all the different sides of the campaign including communications.' (Settle 2001)

Western men's belief in their right, and moreover their responsibility, to 'lift the veil' and rescue Muslim women is startling here. It shouldn't be all that unexpected, though, since CNN ran the documentary *Beneath the Veil* in very heavy rotation in the build-up to the invasion of Afghanistan and in the early days of the occupation. *Beneath the Veil* was filmed inside Afghanistan prior to the Western invasion and featured the execution of women by the Taliban inside a soccer stadium. The seemingly constant rotation of this film on CNN served as a backdrop to underscore the fears articulated by the women of the Bush and Blair administrations about the brutality of the Taliban (McLarney 2009: 3). The notion of lifting the veil in actuality was taken up by at least one documentary film-maker as *Lifting the Veil* also ran on CNN in 2007. According to the film-maker, this film was made to check on the progress of Afghan women since the occupation (Obaid-Chinoy 2007a). So there is plenty of evidence that the removal of the veil is on the West's agenda and there is historical precedent for that (Kahf 2008: 31). It just seems rather bluntly stated here without a care for religion or cultural sensitivities, but this can be understood in light of the state's attempt to justify the new imperialism.

Blair's spokesman says he doesn't know whether Cherie Blair and Laura Bush had spoken with each other about their shared commitment to supporting the 'liberation' of Afghan women. Apparently, feminist solidarity means simply carrying out the wishes of our respective male-dominated administrations without question or dialogue. It does not mean deliberation or forming views in conversation with others, and it certainly never involves talking to the actual women about whose lives you are speaking and encouraging action to change.

In 2003, Karen Hughes went to Afghanistan to deliver her message about the 'liberation' of Afghanistan to Afghan women in person. She created quite a stir there, and here, with her misunderstanding of the culture and practice of Afghan femininity. She indicated that the wearing of the burqa was a sign of women's ongoing oppression there. Ironically, this woman, who spent a large part of her professional life doing George Bush's bidding, suggested that she was in Afghanistan to set an example of liberation: 'One of the things we heard is that there is still a substantial amount of fear and so I think one of the whole purposes of a delegation of largely women visiting from the United States of America is to maybe provide some small sense of encouragement to the women of Afghanistan' (Kolhatkar 2004: 28). What fear is it that Karen Hughes is trying to dispel? Fear of the West? Of Western women? Of the occupation? How is her presence there going to allay those well-founded fears? Similar questions might be posed about the 'small sense of encouragement' she intends to provide. Should Afghan women welcome occupation with open arms?

One year later, Joyce Rumsfeld, wife of the then Secretary of Defense Donald Rumsfeld, also visited Afghanistan to continue setting an example of women's 'liberation' by carrying out her husband's and the administration's mission (ibid.: 28). Laura Bush then visited Afghanistan for five hours in March of 2005 (Zakaria 2005; Kazem 2005). According to the US State Department, Laura Bush was eager to do this work: 'Mrs. Bush has long been looking forward to visiting Afghanistan. This visit will be an opportunity to highlight the advances made for women in the country and to underscore our long-term commitment to the people of Afghanistan' (Kaufman 2005). By 2005, it was readily apparent in the US that, contrary to initial reports, Afghan women's liberation had not been accomplished. Yet Mrs Bush remains untroubled by facts and undeterred from her colonial mission: 'When I really realized the plight of the women under the Taliban, I also found that American women really stand in solidarity with the women in Afghanistan. I'm delighted to be able to bring that message to Afghanistan' (ibid.). Of course, five hours on the ground in Afghanistan does not represent a huge commitment to either Afghan women or to the imperialist desires of the administration. In those five hours, she was scheduled to meet with Hamid Karzai, have 'a roundtable discussion with teachers and students,' and visit US troops at Bagram Airbase (ibid.). An Associated Press video of her visit shows a bare-headed Laura Bush meeting with women wearing niqabs. She has her scarf tied around her neck. In the photos of her visit that accompany the BBC online version of events, she has changed her clothes but also wears a scarf draped around her neck and no head covering. Perhaps just the sight of her, head uncovered, was presumed to be enough incentive to arouse Afghan women to throw off their burqas. The only women in the video without some sort of head covering are Bush and her staff, and it seems not to have occurred to the Americans that it would be disrespectful to the culture and customs of Afghanistan for Laura Bush to appear without head covering.

In 2003, Karen Hughes invited four Afghan women to her home in Texas to continue to provide an example of Western liberation. Perhaps practicing transnational sexism requires reinforcement in various sites. Hughes explains that: 'Insights into American education and health care will be invaluable to women who for a generation have been excluded from pubic life and whose leadership is so desperately needed' (Lisheron 2003). Will she mention how many Americans remained uninsured and thus without healthcare in her presentation? Karen Hughes' goal in hosting this visit is also to encourage her local church and other private organizations to form partnerships with Afghan groups, schools, etc. At that point she had left the administration, but clearly she was still doing its work. 'I think it is very important that little boys and little girls in Afghanistan don't grow up hating America' (ibid.). Two years of occupation had surely ended any possibility of Afghan children thinking highly of the US. It challenges the imagination to think that one visit to Texas by a very small delegation of Afghan women is going to erase all the harm done by the occupation. The problematic politics of having a Presbyterian church partnering with an Afghan school or at least the potential conflict of religions given the Christian history of religious intolerance is not mentioned in the article. On the other hand, maybe the Taliban is not the only organization with missionary designs. This would not be the first attempt by Western Christians to show the world a 'better way.' What is the nature of this 'partnership'? Who would choose the curriculum? As in earlier colonial missions, white Western women have been deployed to do the work of the Western patriarchs, that is, 'civilizing the natives.' Instead of persuading women to cover their bodies, though, in the new version of empire-building, they are urged to take clothing (burqas) off.

After September 11th 2001, the plight of women in Afghanistan quickly became of great interest to the Bush administration. Suddenly, they were interested in talking with Mavis Leno, who, since 1977, had been the Feminist Majority's Chair of the Campaign to Stop Gender Apartheid in Afghanistan (Wallace 2001; Oskin 2002; Li 2001; Williams 2001). Suddenly, feminist ideas about liberation gain importance. They were important because women who believed themselves to be 'liberated' may more willingly and uncritically participate in the screening of the intentions of 'their' men when justifying war and imperialism. In her work on Muslims in Western societies, Sharene Razack talks about 'feminism used in the service of Empire' (Razack 2008: 148). She explains that: 'Saving Muslim women from the excesses of their society marks Western women as emancipated' (ibid.: 86). This is the foundation of transnational sexism and it is, of course, repeatedly enacted or acted out in the Western press.

Fariba Nawa, in the *Christian Science Monitor*, wrote about Afghan women's reaction to, and differences from, a woman like Nasrine Gross, an Afghan woman who was born and raised in Afghanistan but who married an American man and lived in the US for thirty years. She returned to Afghanistan following the US invasion. Upon her return, she appeared in public without a head covering, smoking cigarettes. Nawa reports that pretty much everyone with whom she came into contact in Afghanistan was appalled. Yet Fariba Nawa seized upon the story as a good example of the contrast between the Americanized, liberated Gross, and women who had spent the last thirty years living in Afghanistan, where they are more conservative and less bold about asserting themselves. After all, Nawa seems to be saying, having lived in a culture that represents the pinnacle of women's liberation around the globe, Nasrine Gross would have some expertise in how to gain liberation. She describes a confrontation between Gross and Rahima Jami, an Afghan woman, at the Loya Jirga held in 2002 that produced the first new government.

'If you're wearing this because you really believe in it then I respect you but if you feel you have to wear it then you should take it off,' Gross told Jami pointing to her head. 'I've chosen to keep my hair visible and I'm sure you respect that too.' Jami nodded but said: '*if* you just put on a small headscarf, it would be much better.' (Nawa 2002: 7)

The contrast in presentation between both women is clear in the interaction above, but while it seems intended to make Gross seem freer, she just seems patronizing, bossy, less polite. Rahima Jami conversely seems much less demanding in her gentle request that Gross 'put on a small headscarf.' Indeed, Gross reveals the ways that her belief system has been influenced by Orientalism and transnational sexism when she makes an assertion for which she has no foundation. She says: 'Most of these women don't believe in wearing the veil, they wear it because they are afraid' (ibid.: 7). Living outside Afghanistan for thirty years does not give you expertise on a culture. In fact, given the shortened life expectancy of women in Afghanistan – forty-five years – this represents a generation. How could Gross possibly know what these women are thinking when it comes to wearing a veil? Might fear be at the heart of all women's adherence to the practice of gender in whatever culture – fear of standing out, fear of rape, fear of lesbian baiting? Gross's experiences in the US and her Western bias are showing here and are further revealed when Nawa writes: 'Gross' argument is that the age of political Islam has manipulated women to believe in their own subjugation' (ibid.: 7). Is such patriarchal manipulation the sole purview of Islam? Don't Christian women believe that their primary purpose in life is to attract a husband? In order to be acceptable/desirable in Western culture, don't US women think that they must fashion their bodies with dieting, cosmetics, and surgical scalpels? Here feminism, or what passes for such in the minds of Nasrine Gross and Fariba Nawa, is about women of the world bowing to Western women's superiority.

Indeed, Hillary Clinton, then a senator from New York State, added her voice to the chorus of other Western women precipitously celebrating the 'liberation' of Afghan women and arguing for a kind of universal liberation that would mimic Western women's rights:

> Critics – some domestic, some in the Islamic world – say that America has no right to impose its values on Afghan society. They argue that to promote equal rights for women and a role for women in Afghan government and society amounts to cultural imperialism, destined to arouse the animosity of Muslims throughout the region. I believe such criticism fails on at least two counts. One, it does not recognize that we, as liberators, have an interest in what follows the Taliban in Afghanistan. We cannot simply drop our bombs and depart with our best wishes, lest we find ourselves returning some years down the road to root out another terrorist regime. Second, the argument that supporting the rights of women will insult the Muslim world is demeaning to women and to Muslims. Women's rights are human rights. They are not simply American, or Western customs. They are universal values which we have a responsibility to promote throughout the world, and especially in a place like Afghanistan. (Clinton 2001)

Paving the way for her future presidential run, and her subsequent appointment as Secretary of State under Barack Obama, Hillary Clinton here justifies the occupation of Afghanistan, then only just begun, in terms of US self-interest. Basically, her argument is that the US has a responsibility to set these folks right and that they, and all Muslims, would be insulted if the US abrogated that responsibility. So Afghans welcome the occupation? Here Hillary Clinton concedes that bombs are being dropped but acknowledges that the bombs need to be followed with 'cultural' work that can help soothe the pain of the occupation, alleviate it, and secure US interests. She frames women's issues through a neoliberal, normative, and global framework of 'rights.' This is what her feminism looks like.

Even though some feminists heaved a sigh of relief when he left office, George W. Bush, former president of the United States, is not finished pushing his imperialist agenda on women around the world. He has established an institute that is affiliated with the School of Education and Human Development at Southern Methodist University (SMU), where part of their goal is to promote literacy for women around the world. The following explanation is from their website:

> The Women's Initiative is a major project of the George W. Bush In-stitute, which since 2010 has conducted several symposia on campus

focusing on economic growth, global health, human freedom, and education, including literacy and economic opportunity for the women of Afghanistan. Future Women's Initiative fellows programs will include women from various areas of the world, with a current concentration on the Middle East. (Tibbetts 2012)

In 2010, Bush and his wife (Laura Bush is an alumna of SMU) both spoke at the opening of a conference focusing on women and girls in Afghanistan (Rado 2010). George Bush talked about the goals of the Institute, saying, 'I really am serious about sending the signal that this institute will be based on principle, not politics. I want our actions to be transformative' (ibid.). There are no politics involved in the US taking the lead in formulating a plan for the education of women and girls around the world? How will Afghan women become literate? How will they learn? What will they read?

Laura Bush focused on the conference that was about to occur when she said, 'Afghan women were denied education and as a teacher and reader myself, I remember my own sadness when I heard that little girls were forbidden from attending school. The stark contrast between their lives and our lives horrified many Americans' (ibid.). While the lack of accessibility to school for girls under the Taliban was certainly a travesty, Laura Bush utilizes transnational sexism in pointing out the horror of Americans when they learned of this practice. The horror is the horror of offending the sensibilities of the superior Western woman. Reaching out to Afghan women and girls, then, is a means to confirm that superiority and, to echo Karen Hughes, to make sure 'they don't grow up hating America.' Mrs Bush also implies that in spite of her husband's denunciation of politics, the politics of imperialism are alive and well in her rhetoric. In February 2012, the Institute brought fourteen Egyptian women to study with SMU faculty. The faculty are mostly from the business school with a few from Law, Sociology, Anthropology, Politics, and Communications (Tibbetts 2012). No faculty is listed as affiliated with Women's and Gender Studies, Post-Colonial Studies or Asian or Middle East studies. What principle that George Bush invokes above dictates excluding any learning that might focus on gender, on race, on the history of colonialism? On the contrary, it is explicitly political to build a curriculum that ensures that these women learn that upholding the status quo is paramount, when these women are taught to take for granted that capitalism is the way to go, and when they are discouraged from asking questions about difference, or imperialism, or gender.

Karen Hughes emerged from obscurity in 2009 to write an editorial which appeared on the Politico website that implored Barack Obama to repudiate the Taliban on behalf of Afghan women (Hughes 2009). Again, in 2011, she and Paula Dobriansky wrote another editorial on the topic, in part to publicize the work of the Bush Institute but also to talk about the possibilities presented by entrepreneurship for the women of Afghanistan. As late as 2011, Laura Bush held to her argument that things had greatly improved for women in Afghanistan. In her speech at the Spirit of Women Spring Event Mrs Bush, in talking about working with the women of Afghanistan, suggested that 'Literacy enables women to ask questions, to understand their rights, to participate in the government' (Clurczak 2011). Is she suggesting that what she did in enacting the policies of her husband's administration was about women asking questions and understanding their rights?

Also in 2010, Mrs Bush wrote an editorial that appeared in the *Washington Post* in which she invoked Aesha Mohammadzai, except she called her Bibi Aisha, as the symbol of all that was once wrong with Afghanistan. She seemed to suggest that both Bibi Aisha and Afghanistan could be corrected by some Western cosmetic surgery. She was gently critical of the Obama administration's plan to work with the Taliban on an exit strategy for Western troops. She lauded the changes that Western occupation has brought for women and girls there, and yet reminded the reader that 'serious challenges remain' (Bush 2010). She went on to say that '... a culture that tolerates injustice against one group of its people ultimately fails to respect and value all its citizens.' This is a pretty startling statement from a woman whose husband presided over a nation tormented by racism, classism, and homophobia for eight years. Yes, this is another example of transnational sexism, but perhaps we might develop a similar concept around racism to analyze her remarks here since during her husband's administration there were copious examples of racial injustice, and yet looking at Afghanistan allows Laura Bush to lead the cheers of 'United we stand.' Mrs Bush ends by saying, 'Now is a moment of decision. It is incumbent upon the Afghan people to make the most of this moment in their history' (ibid.). The people of Afghanistan might argue that it has always been up to them to determine their way forward and yet, most recently, they have had ten-plus years of Western occupation.

Female engagement teams

The deployment of Karen Hughes, Cherie Blair and others is not the only example of the way Western women serve to screen and enact

Western men's imperialist desires. Following in the footsteps of women like Nasrine Gross, women in Western militaries are being deployed in a similar fashion. Two hundred and thirty thousand US women have served in Iraq and Afghanistan as of spring 2010 (McCartney 2010). Of course, serving in militaries is, for women, a complicated business. Because militaries are structured in masculinist ways with masculinist rules, women do not easily fit there and they are used by militaries, at least the American military, as a last resort. For the war on terror, the all-volunteer force in the US coupled with the failure of the rhetoric surrounding that war on terror to attract the large numbers of recruits that the military had hoped for and that are required in order to wage two wars at once created a personnel crisis. There were not enough bodies to fill the ranks. First, the US military lowered its recruiting standards. They raised the enlistment age, offered signing bonuses, extended tours, established lower scores on psychological and aptitude tests (Toronto Star 2006; Alvarez 2007), accepted recruits with 'criminal pasts' (Alvarez 2007) and offered expedited citizenship (Echegaray 2007; Boot and O'Hanlon 2006). Along with changing recruiting requirements, the US military, as it has done ever since it was changed to an all-volunteer force in 1973, immediately following the very unpopular Vietnam war, continued to reach out to women.

The result is that women have entered the military in increasing numbers since the end of the draft and now make up 14 percent of the US forces (Black 2012). 'Though men continue to make up the bulk of the fighting force, the proportion of women in the military is soaring, says the Pew Research Study, which also found a greater share of women than men in the military are African American' (ibid.). In the UK women make up 10 percent of the military (Hopkins 2012), in Canada 15 percent (CBC News 2006), and in Australia 18.5 percent (Topping 2011). Women now make up 15 percent of the military worldwide (Corbett 2007). As of 2009, 'More than a dozen countries allow women in some or all ground combat occupations. Among those pushing boundaries most aggressively is Canada, which has recruited women for the infantry and sent them to Afghanistan.' In fact, in 2006, Canadian Nichola Goddard became the 'first battlefield death of a combat-certified (Canadian) female soldier' (Fortney 2012).

So dependent is the US military on women that for a moment it seemed that the unlikely hero of the war on Iraq would turn out to be a small blond woman from rural, impoverished West Virginia, who had, the story went initially, fiercely fought off the Iraqis. The notion of young women as fierce warriors, however, is also one that a nation which went to war in the name of security – to protect women – could not endure. Militarized masculinity is founded on the idea that women like diminutive, blond Jessica Lynch require protecting. Thus, in order for the story to be fully realized, Jessica Lynch herself required 'rescuing' by male soldiers.[1]

As of 2006, Sara Corbett tells us, the numbers of US women serving in the war on terror are quite astonishing: 'So far, more than 160,000 female soldiers have been deployed to Iraq and Afghanistan, as compared with the 7,500 who served in Vietnam and the 41,000 who were dispatched to the gulf war in the early '90s. Today one of every 10 U.S. soldiers in Iraq is female' (Corbett 2007: 53).

One in every ten US soldiers is a woman. That is a pretty startling statistic and one that calls into question the notion that wars are fought to protect women. This number indicates that women are, in fact, fighting the wars.

Because militaries are founded on certain ideas about gender, in particular the supremacy of masculinity, they have historically been organized in such a way to segregate women into positions that are more associated with their work outside the military. In the military, women have done clerical, cooking, and nursing work. The infantry and other roles that have traditionally been associated with combat have been open only to men (Alvarez 2009). These roles have been the surest route to promotion within the military and to the best jobs once one is discharged. The exclusion of women from these posts has obviously had a deleterious effect on their economic circumstances, but it has also helped keep in place notions of women's weakness and helplessness in international affairs, and particularly in matters of war.

The combination of lower numbers of enlisted men, particularly with the US fighting wars in both Afghanistan and Iraq simultaneously, along with women agitating for equality, has led to renewed discussion on ending the combat bans. In addition, the way that these wars are being fought means that this notion that there is a front line from which women in the military can be kept away is increasingly ludicrous. As a result women serving in militaries in the war on terror have been placed in harm's way to a greater degree than ever before, even before the renewed discussions on women's relationship to combat (ibid.).

Women can lead some male troops into combat as officers, but they cannot serve with them in battle. Yet, over and over, in Iraq and Afghanistan, Army commanders have resorted to bureaucratic trickery when they needed more soldiers for crucial jobs, like bomb disposal and intelligence. On paper, for instance, women have been 'attached' to a combat unit rather than 'assigned.' (Ibid.)

In addition to 'bureaucratic trickery,' simply serving in jobs that were once considered safe behind the lines of combat has become much more dangerous with new methods of warfare and the insurgency. Women who drive supply trucks, for example, long believed to be a relatively safe role, have experienced large casualties and loss of life. 'One of the most dangerous things you can do in Iraq is drive a truck, and that's considered a combat support role. You've got women that are in harm's way right up there with the men' (Corbett 2007: 42).

> Nonetheless, as soldiers in the Iraq and Afghanistan wars, women have done nearly as much in battle as their male counterparts: patrolled streets with machine guns, served as gunners on vehicles, disposed of explosives, and driven trucks down bomb-ridden roads. They have proved indispensable in their ability to interact with and search Iraqi and Afghan women for weapons, a job men cannot do for cultural reasons. The Marine Corps has created revolving units – 'lionesses' – dedicated to just this task. A small number of women have even conducted raids, engaging the enemy directly in total disregard of existing policies. (Alvarez 2009)

For these women, serving their country means assisting in the occupations of Iraq and Afghanistan by ignoring long-held prohibitions that mean women are fit only for certain duties. One Canadian woman who is not restricted by the ban against combat in her country's military said: '"Someone once asked me if I could shoot somebody, and my answer was, in a split second," says Robinson [co-founder of the Association for Women's Equity in Canadian Forces] who lives in Ottawa. "We're not a humanitarian force, we exist to protect Canada"' (Fortney 2012).

Robinson's comments here deviate from the script in Canada that positions the Canadian forces as peacekeepers and not an actual military force. The very effective recruiting discourse that suggests that one is protecting Canada or the US by invading another country is one that helps soldiers remain engaged in their work, work that often must seem unrewarding but that also might involve killing. And women as well as men believe themselves fully capable of doing this work.

In Australia, the debate about women in combat positions within the Australian military was complicated by what seems like the necessity of having Western women in Afghanistan to 'civilize' Afghan men. The

Two female US Army soldiers search two Iraqi women before allowing them to enter the Kardum Shihan School in Bassam, Iraq, during a medical civic action program on 17 March 2006. The soldiers are from Bravo Company, 2nd Battalion, 22nd Infantry Regiment (DoD photo by Staff Sgt Kevin L. Moses Sr, US Army).

headline of Australian journalist Sally Sara's article tell us just that 'Female soldiers could "civilise" Afghan men' (Sara 2011). In the article, Sara tells us that there is strong opposition within Afghanistan to the presence of women soldiers but that certain Afghan women approve the plan. She quotes a woman named Shinkai Karokhail, who is a member of the Afghan parliament, as suggesting that the presence of more women soldiers would 'set a good example to Afghan men who are not pulling their weight in the development of the country' (ibid.). She then directly attributes the 'civilizing' comment to Karokhail:

'To change the mentality of some Afghan men, we can make them more civilized,' she said. 'They always think women are only a cleaner or a cook or a person who can produce kids and raise them. But they will understand if they give a chance to their own daughter and women of Afghanistan, they could do a lot the way women of other countries do for their own countries and even other countries.' (Ibid.)

Such a fascinating connection is made between Western women's willingness to be in combat – to kill or be killed – and their presence, these newly trained killers, as civilizers. How is it civilized to be prepared to kill someone that you have never met and about whom you know almost nothing? Conversely, in the paradigm, Afghan men's willingness to kill is a sign of their barbarity.

This is what 'liberation' looks like

While honoring local customs cannot be lauded enough, under the guise of doing so the US military is using women to search other women, asking them to perform a violation of someone else's body simply because they might share similar anatomies. The women are furthermore doing this at the behest of men. For these women, becoming 'lionesses' is deeply troubling and has far-reaching consequences for the possibility of feminist struggle. This small gesture toward recognizing the violation of men touching women's bodies in searches was the beginning of an effort to 'win the hearts and minds' (Kovach 2010) of the Afghan people. In early 2010, the first 'female engagement teams' (FETs) (an extension of the Lioness program in Iraq) were deployed to Afghanistan (Bumiller 2010a). Forty female Marines were in the first training class. Their job is to accompany male infantry units on patrol so that they can engage with Afghan women. Sound familiar? This deployment is reminiscent of colonial wives in Asia and Africa in the 1800s.

> The Marines in a recent 'cultural awareness' class scribbled careful notes as the instructor coached them on do's and don't's when talking to villagers in Afghanistan: Don't start by firing off questions, do break the ice by playing with the children, don't let your interpreter hijack the conversation. And one more thing: 'If you have a pony tail,' said Marina Kielpinski, the instructor, 'let it go out the back of your helmet so people can see you're a woman.' These are not your mother's Marines here in the rugged California chaparral of Camp Pendleton, where 40 young women are preparing to deploy to Afghanistan in one of the more forward-leaning experiments of the American military. (Ibid.)

Despite echoes of imperial women from the past, Elisabeth Bumiller describes the training of these young women as a 'forward-leaning experiment.' What is forward about it? American women are being asked to reinscribe the gendered division of labor by doing in a war zone what is traditionally women's work – engaging in social duties and interacting with children, while they are being protected by other male soldiers with guns. In the gendered arrangements in this war, even though they have extensive combat refresher courses before being sent into the field, women soldiers cannot be trusted to defend themselves. The program also relies on the belief that women, despite all the vast differences between them that citizens of the West have been told about over and over again, can communicate simply by virtue of possession of a certain anatomy.

Later in the story, Bumiller adds that the Americans 'arrive in a village, get permission from the male elder to speak with the women, settle into a compound, hand out school supplies and medicine, drink tea, make conversation and, ideally, get information about the village, local grievances and the Taliban' (ibid.). These soldiers' female bodies are being used to turn a social interaction into the work of empire – assistance in colonization. The reference to intelligence gathering makes the female engagement teams seem more interested in gathering information about the Taliban than in interacting with the local women and ensuring, as Karen Hughes would have it, that the Afghan children don't hate us (the US). The FETs might as well be CIA agents, as they may well be suspected of being.

In a Department of Defense story about the FETs, the women soldiers sound a bit more benevolent. Whether this attempt at sounding harmless is a ploy to screen the true intent of the teams or whether it is an artifact of gender is hard to determine.

> With help from male Marines and members of the Afghan National Army, female Marines moved from compound to compound, hoping to speak to Afghan women to ascertain their medical and humanitarian assistance requirements. 'This is extremely important,' said Marine 2nd Lt. Carly E. Towers, the officer in charge of the engagement team. 'Our mission out here is to talk to and work with the locals to build cooperation and security.' 'We just try to sit down, talk to them, and get to know them a bit,' said Towers, a Naval Academy graduate. 'We ask them if they have any questions for us. We're trying to build rapport.' In deference to Afghan culture, Towers and her team members remove their helmets and don head scarves to cover their hair whenever they enter a compound. Relationships established through these interactions, Towers said, help to build bonds of trust between the Afghans and the Marines. (Henderson 2009)

Ideas about gender mean that the women, even though they are US sailors and Marines presumably trained to defend themselves, still require protection by male soldiers while they go about 'building bonds of trust.' I imagine it would take more than a few visits by female Marines to erase the distrust that has built up through the years of occupation, but this is the task that has been set before these women.

Also, this approach is indicative of the US military's belief in the power of the women in Afghan families to decide whether the Americans are acceptable or not – a power denied them by years of rhetoric about these women's helplessness in the face of the oppression imposed by male relatives and husbands. Contrary to all the Western media has said before about Afghan women, Elisabeth Bumiller writes about their knowledge and power.

> Marines who have worked with the ad hoc teams in Afghanistan said that rural Afghan women, rarely seen by outsiders, had more influence in their villages than male commanders might think, and that the Afghan women's good will could make Afghans, both men and women, less suspicious of American troops. (Bumiller 2010a)

> Rural Afghan women, who meet at wells and pass news about the village, are often repositories of information about a district's social fabric, power brokers and militants, all crucial data for American forces. On some occasions, Captain Pottinger said in an e-mail message, women have provided information about specific insurgents and the makers of bombs (ibid.).

Here, an intelligence officer reveals the belief underlying the FETs of women holding power and knowledge in rural Afghanistan. He suggests that Afghan women's 'good will' is a way to make all Afghans 'less suspicious' of the US military. Yet in the second quote Captain Pottinger seems to have no hesitation about revealing that important intelligence has been gained from the FETs' talks with these women. How would that make Afghans 'less suspicious'? In another US Department of Defense release, intelligence gathering is clearly marked as one of the goals of the FET:

> 'The team provides us access to half of the population that we normally do not have access to,' Hoffman said. 'They did extremely well interacting with the female villagers.' Marine Corps 2nd Lt. Johanna Shaffer, the team leader, said their first mission, a cordon-and-search operation in support of Operation Pathfinder, was very successful. 'We were accepted by both the men and women villagers and were able to obtain valuable information about the way they lived and what they thought about the Marine Corps operating in the area,' Shaffer said. (Burton 2009)

It is not only what the locals think about the Marines operating in that area, however, that they are after.

Capt. Matt Pottinger, an intelligence officer based in the capital, Kabul, who helped create and train the first engagement team in Afghanistan, recently wrote that when one of the teams visited a village in southern Afghanistan, a gray-bearded man opened his home to the women by saying, 'Your men come to fight, but we know the women are here to help.' The man also sheepishly admitted, Captain Pottinger wrote in Small Wars Journal, an online publication, that the women were 'good for my old eyes.' (Bumiller 2010a)

Here Captain Pottinger further undermines the women in his charge by suggesting, or allowing the Afghan man to suggest, that women don't fight, they help. Is this the gendered thinking of this Afghan man? Or is this idea imposed on him by Captain Pottinger? Is Captain Pottinger afraid to put too much emphasis on the effectiveness of the women for fear it would further undermine the masculinity of a military floundering after years in Afghanistan? In addition, this unnamed – but sage in the eyes of Captain Pottinger and the reporter – old man sexualizes these women soldiers. Are we to believe that women who are wearing camouflage and many pounds of equipment including body armor and helmets, who are carrying M4 rifles (ibid.), are still sexy? On the other hand, do such assertions compel us to see the Afghan man as lecherous, confirming the worst fears of Laura Bush and Karen Hughes as to Afghan men's intent? In either case, this rhetorical move demeans the women's effectiveness by making them just another collection of body parts to be lusted after by men all over the world.

In the news coverage of the FETs the question of culture comes up again and again. While military leaders claim to be using the FETs as a way to honor Afghan culture, their presence flies in the face of contemporary Afghan culture in the sense that women there are not expected to run around the countryside in camouflage and body armor carrying guns.

The concept employed by her team varies greatly from the program in Iraq because of differences in Afghan culture, Shaffer said. 'The cultural background here is completely different than that of Iraq,' Shaffer said. 'Women here are more timid than in Iraq. There is less of a chance that an Afghan woman would try to harm us, because they understand that we are here to help them.' 'We also do not know much about the daily life of Afghan women,' she continued. 'This provides us not only the opportunity to learn about the women, but also to build and maintain faith and trust of the Afghan women.' (Burton 2009)

Not knowing much about the daily life of Afghan women does not stop Ms Shaffer from assuming that she knows what Afghan women think about the presence of the occupying troops or from making sweeping statements about them in comparison to Iraqi women. The differences in representation of women from Iraq and Afghanistan discussed in an earlier chapter are borne out here where she suggests that Iraqi women are dangerous.

> During the mission, the female Marines donned brightly colored head and neck scarves as a sign of cultural respect to the Afghan women. 'The scarves showed the Afghan women that we were women too, and we respect their culture,' Shaffer said. 'They automatically felt more comfortable with us. They showed us their homes, and even though they didn't have much, they were still very generous to us. They accepted us as sisters, and we're glad that we were here to help them.' (Ibid.)

There is a contradiction in the matter of the headscarf, the helmet and the ponytail. Although I am not an expert on headwear of any kind, it seems impossible to me that one could wear a headscarf and still have one's ponytail hanging out the back of one's helmet as the training officer suggested above. And isn't the whole idea of wearing a veil to cover your hair? How is it culturally sensitive, then, to reveal your ponytail? The soldier above suggests that Afghan women accepted an occupying force coming into their homes with guns as 'sisters.' Either common anatomy is a much stronger bond than anyone could imagine, or notions of 'sisterhood' differ enormously among female members of the US military.

> Although Afghan women tend to be more reserved than Afghan men, they still have a large influence on their children, Shaffer said, so en-gaging with them is important. 'If the women know we are here to help them, they will likely pass that on to their children,' she said. 'If the chil-dren have a positive perspective of alliance forces, they will be less likely to join insurgent groups or participate in insurgent activities.' (Ibid.)

Like Karen Hughes and Laura Bush, this soldier is expressing a desire to influence the views of Afghan children. None of these women seems able to acknowledge the harm the occupation would be having on the children – for ten years.

These military women are being deployed – literally, in several ways. They provide an example of what Western 'liberated' women look like, they engage the people and gain access to their homes (a difficult feat for male military personnel unless they raid compounds), they acquire strategic military information, and they insure against future terrorist attacks. This is one enormous task.

The enemy is us

Once the gender lines are crossed in the military, once women step outside their prescribed roles as caregivers and helpmeets, trouble begins. As Dorit Naaman has noted, 'When women opt to fight alongside men, they challenge the dichotomy of woman as victim/man as defender' (2007: 935). Sheila Jeffreys explains:

> Male soldiers are trained to kill on the basis that they are men and that women are the 'other' against whom they can recognize themselves. Women are also offered as the 'other' that male soldiers are to defend and die for … Masculinity in the military is not then just a historical hangover, but fundamental to what militaries are for and necessary for their operation. This masculinity is deliberately created by militaries through the provision of prostitution and pornography, which enable men to 'other' women and understand themselves as masculine. (2007: 6)

This gender confusion whereby women need protecting but fight alongside men, whereby they are comrades but not equal comrades, whereby they want to be treated equally but are not expected to achieve equal standards, leads to what Sheila Jeffreys calls 'double jeopardy,' when women in the military, who are hyper-visible within the ranks, are in danger from both the external enemy and their own colleagues (ibid.: 1). This does not mean that these women do not have power or that they are not participating in the disempowerment of many. Yet that men have trouble adjusting to the presence of women in the ranks – are women compatriots or prostitutes? – is evidenced by the high number of rapes and incidents of sexual harassment reported by women soldiers about their male colleagues (Riley 2008: 1202).

While reports of rape and sexual harassment within the ranks have recently begun to appear in US publications, the increased incidence of such cases is not often associated with the shifting of gender roles. In the *New York Times*, Lizette Alvarez does make the connection: 'This quiet change has not come seamlessly – and it has altered military culture on the battlefield in ways large and small. Women need separate bunks and bathrooms. They face sexual discrimination and rape, and counselors and rape kits are now common in war zones' (Alvarez 2009).

> Counselors and rape kits may be available in the war zones now as Alvarez suggests, but women are still loathe to use them for many

reasons ... Many of the women I spoke with said they felt the burden of having to represent themselves – to defy stereotypes about women being too weak for military duty in a war zone by displaying more resiliency and showing less emotion than they otherwise might. There appears to have been little, too, in the way of female bonding in the war zone. Most reported that they avoided friendships with other women during the deployment, in part because of the fact that there were fewer women to choose from and in part because of the ridicule that came with having a close friend. 'You're one of three things in the military – a bitch, a whore, or a dyke,' says Abbie Pickett, who is 24 and a combat support specialist with the Wisconsin Army National guard. 'As a female, you get classified pretty quickly.' (Corbett 2007: 55–6)

The bitch, whore, dyke conundrum categorizes women who have reached beyond their accepted roles under militarized masculinity of being either silent and passive or a cheerleader. Doing the empire's bidding is one thing, but when women think they can participate in battles as men do, they need to be slapped down either through being presented with demeaning categories, or by being sexually harassed or raped.

Congresswoman Jane Harman, in speaking out about the problem of enlisted women being raped and sexually harassed in the US military, famously said:

Women serving in the US military are more likely to be raped by a fellow soldier than killed by enemy fire in Iraq. In the case of sexual assault and rape, the enemy eats across the table at the mess hall, shares a vehicle on patrol, and bandages wounds inflicted on the battle-field. As the old Pogo cartoon says, 'We have met the enemy and he is us.' (Harman 2008)

Well, not 'us' women – but certainly 'us' American men. But then who can be surprised at this? It is worth repeating that the perpetrators of these sexual assaults and rapes are not the brown-skinned men that so much time and energy have gone into demonizing and saving brown-skinned women from; no, it is the women's military colleagues, their brothers-at-arms, who are harming them in these ways.[2]

Last year 3,158 sexual crimes were reported within the US military. Of those cases, only 529 reached a courtroom, and only 104 convictions were made, according to a 2010 report from SAPRO [Sexual Assault Prevention and Response Office, a division of the Department of Defense]. But these figures are only a fraction of the reality. Sexual assaults are notoriously under-reported. The same report estimated that there were a further 19,000 unreported cases of sexual assault last year. The Department of Veterans Affairs, meanwhile, released an independent study estimating that one in three women had experience of military sexual trauma while on active service. That is double the rate for civilians, which is one in six, according to the US Department of Justice. (Broadbent 2011)

The majority of sexual abuse allegations end with no prosecution at all. Of 2,171 suspects of investigations that were completed during the fiscal year that ended in September 2008, only 317 faced a court-martial. Another 515 faced administrative punishments or discharges. Nearly half of the completed investigations lacked evidence or were 'unsubstantiated or unfounded.' (Myers 2009a)

These are the US Defense Department's own statistics and they are startling. If one in three women in the military is raped or sexually assaulted, how many perpetrators does that add up to? In other words, what sort of force would it take to rescue not only Afghan and Iraqi women but also American women from the rescuers? That is a lot of rape and sexual assault. It is also a lot of rape and sexual assault to ignore, as seems clear from the low rates of prosecution. Of course, as we now know courtesy of hundreds of photos from Abu Ghraib prison, US women soldiers too are guilty of rape and sexual assault. Where are those statistics kept?

Throughout history every single instance of women breaking barriers into occupations once held solely by men will have stories such as these to tell. Yet this particular story comes from the institution that is charged with bringing freedom around the world. These perpetrators are supposed to be the liberators. These narratives signal men's resistance to giving up (what they believe is) privilege. While these positions within the military have been a certain route to promotion, they are also dangerous and leave soldiers in torment. Doing the work of a US soldier also means participating in the oppression of others. While clearly some women don't really understand what they are up against, others do and still they seek to share this work.

The consequences of enacting imperialism and in the process breaking gender barriers have far-reaching and long-term effects on the lives of the women doing that work, as well as on the lives of the women being rescued. The women who do the work of colonialism often return to civilian life with lifelong reminders of their service. These souvenirs come in the form of injuries both physical and psychological.

The researchers who carried out this study also looked at the prevalence of PTSD symptoms – including flashbacks, nightmares, emotional numbing and round-the-clock anxiety – and found that women who endured sexual assault [in the military] were more likely to develop PTSD than those who were exposed to combat. (Corbett 2007: 55)

Suicide and homelessness are common outcomes for sufferers of MST (military sexual trauma). Forty percent of homeless women veterans have reported experiences of sexual assault in the military, according to the Service Women's Action Network. 'Other common effects of MST are feelings of isolation, sleeping problems, hyper-vigilance, depression, and substance abuse,' explains Dr Amy Street, a clinical psychologist at the VA Hospital in Boston who works with victims (VA hospitals are run by the Veterans Affairs Department). 'Victims talk about feeling numb, being cut off from emotions, unable to function. The best treatments are therapies, which require sufferers to talk about their attacks. This is very uncomfortable for them, but they are effective' (Broadbent 2011).

So while women are more and more at the service of empire, that service is often repaid by death, injury, rape, sexual assault or harassment, and post-traumatic stress disorder. Service in the US military for women is the gift that keeps on giving.

The media, in reporting in detail these stories of rape and sexual assault, though perhaps with the best intentions of making these incidents visible while the military attempts to cover them up, also has the effect of seeming to caution women against what happens when you get too carried away and try to do men's work. Staying home does not seem to be an option, however, as nearly everyone who studies the military agrees that women are now essential to any mission. John A. Nagl, 'a retired lieutenant colonel who helped write the Army's new counterinsurgency field manual,' and now 'president of the Center for a New American Security, a military research institution in Washington,' said, 'We literally could not have fought this war without women' (Alvarez 2009). In addition, John McHugh, Congressional representative from upstate New York, said about women in the military, 'Women in uniform today are not just invaluable, they're irreplaceable.' This is what liberation has achieved for US women.

Doing the empire's work on page and screen

In the last chapter we saw some examples in US popular culture of how Arab, South Asian or Muslim women are depicted or not on

American television. In this chapter, I present some examples of American women acting in the service of empire. Columnist Maureen Dowd has written about a trip to Saudi Arabia that upholds Western ideas about primitive, brutal, Muslim men. *Sex and the City 2* furthers that narrative when the women from the popular television show travel to Abu Dhabi in the United Arab Emirates. And finally, the Showtime series *Homeland*, in which white, blond Carrie Mathison attempts to save the US from further terrorist attacks by quite specifically Muslim men who are responsible for committing all the atrocities of the war, is analyzed.

Two of the most egregious examples of Islamaphobic, Orientalist journalism were published in August 2010. Along with the infamous, previously discussed *Time* cover, that same month *Vanity Fair* magazine published Maureen Dowd's account of a trip she took to Saudi Arabia. Her description is rife with all sorts of negative stereotypes and ridicule of the region, its cultures and traditions, and the men who live there. In her introduction, she refers to Saudi Arabia as: 'the most bewitching, bewildering, beheading vacation spot you never vacation in' (Dowd 2010: 124). In Dowd's Saudi Arabia the men are either brutes who would deny women their freedom or 'boyish looking' and soft – not really men in the Western construct of masculinity. Dowd seems not to be conscious of her own gender practices, her privilege or her transnational sexism in drawing comparisons between Saudi women and US women.

It is true that women in Saudi Arabia live lives full of restrictions: they can't drive, for example, and must cover their bodies in public, and, according to Dowd, they cannot go to cemeteries (ibid.: 124). Even though change is slowly happening there, Dowd describes it as 'the hardest place on earth for a woman to negotiate' (ibid.: 124). Changes for women occasion only ridicule from Dowd, who disparages the prohibitions listed above while never mentioning the religious mandates for them. In fact, she flaunts her disregard for the religion and the rules by appearing one day in the hotel lobby in a 'hot pink skirt with fringe' (ibid.: 128). She relates what happened next as: 'The men in the lobby glared at me with such hostility that I thought they would pelt me to death with their dates' (ibid.: 128). Even as she relates her fear of these men, she suggests they are not manly men in the Western definition because they eat dates – not something a real man eats. Despite her ridicule of the men for not being manly enough, she relates that her 'minder' had no illusions about the danger she was in from these men. 'Go get your abaya,' he told her, 'they'll kill you' (ibid.: 128). Here Muslim men are not quite men but they are also dangerous and a threat to women. In Dowd's version of the world, their primary danger is to Western women – or more directly to her.

While she gestures to the oppression of women in Saudi Arabia, she also depicts the women who live there as consuming maniacs. She says that when the men leave the shopping malls for prayers, 'the women wander zombie-like among the shuttered storefronts' (ibid.: 170). In writing about the shopping possibilities and practices in Saudi Arabia, Dowd says: 'At the ubiquitous malls, women covered in black robes and gloves, with only their eyes showing, shop for LaPerla lingerie, Versace gowns, Dior handbags, and Bulgari jewelry' (ibid.: 170). While all of these stores have their origins in the West, where Western women's purchases made them famous and rich, Dowd writes as if these stores don't exist outside of Saudi women's interest in them. She goes on to say of Saudi women: 'Beauty is a drug for Saudi women, even though they're stuck at home most of the time – or maybe because of that' (ibid.: 170). Beauty is a drug for Saudi women? As previously noted, they are shopping there mostly for items produced in the West. In the West, even in a less than ideal economy, Western women continue to support clothing designers, cosmetic makers, an entire diet industry, along with thousands of plastic surgeons, hairdressers, make-up artists, nail salons and spas, and it is the Saudi women who are hooked on beauty? In Dowd's version of transnational sexism:

> The media link women's emancipation to the emancipation of consumer wants, needs, desires. This kind of liberation facilitates participation in the free market, the free exchange of goods, and free access to products. Bodies must be freely available to engage in this consumption and hungry for the fruits of the consumer economy. (McLarney 2009: 8)

And yet, like Saddam Hussein's daughters, the Saudi women must not exhibit too much interest in shopping, in caring for their bodies, in cosmetic surgery, for that is the sole purview of Western women.

Dowd ends her article by describing a yachting trip she is taken on where she can wear her bikini and drink sparkling pomegranate juice. This voyage so soothes her that 'my thoughts drifted to the silent movie *The Sheik*.' She is clearly influenced in her depiction of the Saudi people by a 1926 US-produced film, yet it is the Saudis she points to as backward. Maureen Dowd, who has written columns critical of US involvement in Afghanistan,[3] here only joins in on the Orientalism, demonization, and transnational sexism.

No sex in the desert

Speaking of being 'addicted to beauty,' in what is yet another offensive example of racist, Orientalist depictions of an Arab country and of Islam, an American major motion picture, New Line Cinema's *Sex and the City 2*, further trivializes Arab culture and Islam, and demonizes Islamic men. The film opened in May of 2010 and it features a trip to Abu Dhabi, capital of the United Arab Emirates, for Carrie, Samantha, Miranda and Charlotte. While there, the four women dress and act as if there are no religious or cultural standards that might be considered, let alone adhered to. Once again, transnational sexism means that these US women are put forward as the standard of women's liberation. These four women spent several years of a TV series and two films obsessing about men, they tried to figure out how to get men, then how to keep them, how to have sex with them, when to have sex with them, or how to get rid of them. They spent much of their energy and conversation on the topic of men, sometimes to the detriment of careers, children, their relationships with each other and emotional well-being, and transnational sexism has them being the examples of what it means for women to be free.

Given their affection for patriarchy, it is no surprise that the women travel to Abu Dhabi thanks to the largesse of a sheikh to whom Samantha is pitching public relations services. The women take this all-expenses-paid trip to what they think of as 'the new Middle East.' What constitutes this new Middle East is never clearly defined, but the expression occurs again when Samantha, who has railed against the restrictions in Abu Dhabi and pretty much flagrantly ignored all of them, finally gets into trouble for kissing a man on the beach and shouts, 'New Middle East, my ass.'

Even though they are in the 'new Middle East,' the women go shopping in a souk in spite of the fact that Abu Dhabi is the site of many modern shopping opportunities and tourist attractions, described in the *New York Times* travel section in 2011:

> A five-star shopping list. Top-notch museums? New branches of the Louvre and Guggenheim are rising from the sands. High-profile events? The Abu Dhabi Grand Prix, Abu Dhabi Film Festival and Gourmet Abu Dhabi have made their debuts in recent years. Toss in a multibillion-dollar hotel project and a stunning new mosque and you have one of the world's most ambitious new destinations. (Sherwood 2011)

The film was made in 2009 but certainly Abu Dhabi did not transform itself in two years. The film-makers, however, probably would not know much about Abu Dhabi and could not show the women shopping in their opulent malls and taking in their elegant museums because the film was not actually made in Abu Dhabi. It was made in Morocco.[4] Apparently the new Middle East is interchangeable, with one locale standing in for any other. And even with all of the sights to be seen and explored in Abu Dhabi, the preferred activity for the women is, of course, shopping.

This entire section of the film is simply an exercise in transnational sexism in which the freedoms allotted to Western women are lauded while the local women's customs are looked upon with disfavor. In a restaurant in the hotel, Carrie watches an Arab woman with a heavily made-up face who wears a black niqab that is edged in white. Carrie points the woman out to the others and Miranda says: 'Younger Muslim women are embracing old traditions in new and personal ways.' Carrie replies: 'I could get into the head wrap but the veil across the mouth freaks me out. It's like they don't want them to have a voice.' Of course, the American women in the film use their voices to repeatedly scream out the car windows at strangers about having fun, to obsess, in one case, about their husband having an affair with the children's nanny, and to scream, as Samantha does, 'Condoms, condoms, yes, I have sex. Bite me!' to horrified Arab men in the souk when she drops her bag and condoms roll out. It is not as if Western women are using their voices to discuss weighty matters such as endless war or the new imperialism.

Samantha remarks that the 'niqab certainly cuts back on the botox bill.' Unlike Maureen Dowd above, Samantha acknowledges that women in the West have cosmetic surgery, and she assumes that it is also a practice in Abu Dhabi. There is one moment that challenges the transnational sexism that prevails throughout the rest of the film, however, when Carrie asserts, about men in the West: 'Men in the US pretend they're comfortable with strong women while a lot of them would be more comfortable with us eating French fries behind the veil.'

The film seems to be one very long commercial for designer clothes. Until the last scene of the film, it is the American women and not the local women who possess obscene amounts of clothes. Carrie wears at least two turbans, Samantha also wears one, and Miranda and Samantha both wear some version of safari gear. In one scene Carrie says, 'I knew I should have packed my burka,' and one of the other women replies: 'How about a burkini?' The 'new Middle East' seems an awful lot like the old colonial state, particularly in one scene, where Carrie walks along the beach while her South Asian manservant – domesticated by the presence of all this Western liberation of women – walks beside her holding an umbrella over her head to block the sun.

The Arab men in the film are all depicted as prudish brutes, or as feminized – maybe gay – non-men. There is an unfavorable comparison of men as well when a British businessman rides up to the women in the middle of the desert, showing off his body and his masculinity by driving in a fast car. Towards the end of the film, a false transnational sisterhood occurs when Samantha, Carrie, Charlotte, and Miranda require rescue from brown men. Who provides this rescue? Brown women, who are at least 'civilized' enough to recognize a fellow lover of designer goods, which the Arab women wear under their abayas, which they throw off in joy, saying, 'We love the fashion,' once they bring the American women under their protection. Carrie, in her narration of the film, notes that the women are wearing that season's designer clothes 'underneath hundreds of years of tradition.' 'These products signal women as active participants in the market, not as passively cut off from the global culture of exchange. Participation in this consumer culture gives them their humanity' (McLarney 2009: 5).

Ellen McLarney, a Middle Eastern Studies scholar, describes how the removal of the burqa was a way of bringing Afghan women into consumer culture in what she calls the 'aestheticization of women's bodies as liberation' (ibid.: 3–4). It is difficult to think of capitalism, however, as the great uniter of women.

Another blond hero

The real-life chosen hero of the war on terror, Jessica Lynch, refused that veneration by telling the truth about the incident that led to her capture – the convoy got lost and she was terrified. She revealed that she never fired a shot at the enemy. Her rescue was revealed to be a ruse, staged and filmed for the admiration of Western audiences. She was actually 'rescued' from people who had tried to return her to US troops. Back in the US, she basically said in the media, I'm not going to be used for recruiting purposes (Riley 2006). It was necessary for Hollywood then to come up with a totally fictionalized version of a blond woman hero of the war on terror. The American television show *Homeland* was actually adapted from an earlier Israeli television show called *Prisoners of War* (Franklin 2011). Its protagonist is a young woman called Carrie Mathison. Unfortunately, she is not a perfect hero. She has mostly untreated manic-depressive illness, but the advantage of Carrie as a hero is that, unlike Jessica Lynch, she can't resist the heroic designation.

This Showtime series premiered in the fall of 2011. The US version features Claire Danes in the role of Carrie Mathison, a CIA officer whose sole reason for living seems to be to prevent another terrorist attack on the US. She is haunted by the events of September 11th 2001, to such a degree that she risks her career and physical safety in order to get information about, and then watch over, a returned American Marine POW named Nicholas Brody who she believes has been 'turned' by his captors. Both of these characters are white, both live middle-class or upper-middle-class lives in spite of the fact that the Marine has been imprisoned in Afghanistan – or Iraq – for eight years. They portray the Afghans or Iraqis, they never specify, as torturing Nicholas Brody while he is imprisoned in order to get information. Carrie learns of this while in Iraq, so perhaps the audience is meant to assume that Nicholas was held by the Iraqis. The writers of this series play with the facts to great advantage to Americans. They make the Iraqis the torturers. In the show, they attribute all the horrible things that US soldiers have been caught doing to Iraqi or Afghan prisoners to the Iraqi jailers. For example, they depict the Iraqis as conducting night raids, and Brody is held for long periods of time in solitary confinement, in painful positions, and at one point he is forced to murder his colleague with whom he was being held. All of this torture is alternated, the writers suggest, with kindness from one of the Iraqi leaders. When the leader's son is killed in an American bombing, Brody converts to Islam. His practice of Islam, though unknown to the other characters in the show, is what keeps the viewer suspicious of him.

Carrie is suspicious of him from the start. Without evidence, she is convinced that he has been 'turned' by his captors. She is the only character in the show not implicitly worthy of suspicion of collaboration with the enemy. She is intent on proving Brody's duplicity, and she breaks every rule in order to do so. In this not-quite-all-right white woman's hands rests the well-being of the nation. Lest we think that her portrayal is promising for women in the US, the gender dynamics in the show will quickly disabuse one of that notion. In the midst of Carrie's obsession with Brody, she has sex with him and then she becomes something of a stalker. Her concerns about Brody are routinely dismissed by everyone around her as a function of her mental illness. Even though she is struggling with an actual mental illness, the way Carrie is seen by everyone with whom she works is as difficult, stubborn, and out of control. She is still a subject of patriarchy too, though, as she is mentored by an older man played by Mandy Patinkin, and he is depicted as the only one who can truly control her with his fathering approach. For Carrie, as for many Western women, sexuality and acting on her desires are complicated. Her reputation at work is damaged by her relationship with her married boss, who is also African-American. He seems to now regard her as dangerous to his career and to his family. Carrie's sexual relationship with Brody is portrayed in the first season as a means to gather information against him, so we have the old inference about women using their bodies in unscrupulous ways.

Carrie Mathison seems an unlikely hero in the war on terror though in many ways she is perfect. She is the embodiment of what transnational sexism suggests is the superior woman; she is white, blond, and sexually available to men. Even though she struggles with psychiatric problems, she exhibits her superiority by constantly outsmarting what are depicted as very devious Muslim men. Her superiority over Muslim women is present too, since they are completely invisible in the show so far – outside the circle of international intrigue. And Carrie's single-minded focus on preventing terror – in this series terror comes only from Muslims, not from homegrown racist white men – means that no questions have to be asked about what kind of damage has been done to Carrie by Western patriarchy. It's all the fault of the Iraqis.

In this chapter, we have seen the variety of ways in which Western women are deployed to fight both literally and not so literally in the war on terror. Whether in military supply trucks or luxury hotels, in Afghan villages or the beaches of Abu Dhabi/Morocco, in gathering military intelligence or reproducing patriarchal ideas about the proper practice of femininity, many Western women are soldiers now.

5 | This is what liberation looks like

> Destruction of honest inquiry, the notion that one fact is as good as the next, is one of the most disturbing consequences of war. The prosecution of war entails lying, often on a massive scale – something most governments engage in but especially when under the duress of war. (Hedges 2003: 149–50)

Transnational sexism is used in the Western media – both fact-based and fictional – to depict Iraqi and Afghan women, indeed all women believed to be Muslim, as in need of rescue, and as creators of mass destruction either as the mothers of jihad, as unwitting dupes of male manipulation, or as killers driven mad by grief. Even their most earnest efforts to become like Western women through participation in capitalism by purchase of certain shoes, clothing, and beauty services does not lift the mantle of inferiority tinged with danger imposed by transnational sexism on these women. At the same time, transnational sexism allows Western women to be held up as the standard of liberation to which women around the world must aspire, while they, we, are expected to embrace objectification, to accept being subjugated, while carrying out our work as handmaidens of Western militaries and in some cases as fierce fighters against Muslim terrorists, as in Showtime's *Homeland*, described in the previous chapter, or in Kathryn Bigelow's film *Zero Dark Thirty*. Western women are expected to fulfill these roles without being depicted as dangerous or as shaped by male influence and masculine desires.

How might we prevent further misapprehensions about Muslim women, their liberation, and the role of Western women in the oppression of women around the world? How can we learn to read propaganda in a way that allows us to understand how ideas about women's roles and men's propensity for evil are being manipulated? In January 2013, the US ended a combat ban for women serving in the US military (Bumiller and Shanker 2013). This decision will surely have ramifications for civilian women in terms of increased opportunity in government, business, and the public sector. How will women who do not wish to participate in war applaud increased roles for women in war while refusing the accompanying insult to Muslim masculinity that might be involved?

One last look at the depictions of men and women in Afghanistan and Iraq as Western troops leave or prepare to leave these formerly occupied states prompts some additional closing questions about how we might think about Iraqi and Afghan women in the years to come. Finally, I offer some suggestions about how to undo this unholy alliance between government, media and citizenry in the West that facilitates war by prohibiting alliances among women around the world.

Leaving Afghanistan and Iraq

As this book goes to press, Western forces have left Iraq. Plans were made by Barack Obama and NATO representatives, when they met in Chicago in May of 2012, for the withdrawal of Western troops from Afghanistan. Rather than cooling the rhetoric around the war on terror, however, these events seem to have occasioned a wider media assault, and misleading ideas about gender and Islam and Afghan and Iraqi women continue to be propagated. The results of this rhetoric can be observed in the behavior of US troops in relation to both Afghan and Iraqi civilians. In recent months, new photos taken by US soldiers posing with body parts of Afghan insurgents have been published by the *Los Angeles Times* (Zucchino 2012). The publication of these photos, against the wishes of the US military, comes within a few months of the surfacing of a videotape of US Marines urinating on the bodies of deceased Afghans (Whitlock 2010: A01), after the 'inadvertent' Qur'an burnings (Cloud and King 2012), after stories of multiple murders of Afghan and Iraqi civilians by members of the US military, and after the 2004 scandal at Abu Ghraib. US soldiers, steeped in the enemy-creating discourse that surrounds them inside and outside the military, are still taking pictures of themselves with tortured, maimed, or lifeless bodies of these 'enemies,' many of whom are Afghan or Iraqi civilians.

Afghan civilians require rescuing from the rescuers, suggesting that perhaps it is not Afghan men who need civilizing. There have been many complaints about civilian deaths in Afghanistan as a result of the presence of Western troops. There are inadvertent civilian deaths as a result of skirmishes with resisters and inaccurate drone attacks, as well as soldiers being too quick to respond to a perceived threat or too emotional to stand down after an attack (Savage 2010; Cole et al. 2011). But in May of 2010, CBS news reported that some US soldiers might be responsible for the intentional deaths of Afghan civilians:

> Members of a squad of about 10 American soldiers are under investiga-
> tion for murdering at least 3 local villagers who had angered them.

According to the allegations, this is not a case of civilians being mistaken for Taliban fighters and not a one-time moment of rage. Instead it happened on different occasions over the past several months.

Not until the following fall was the story taken up by other media sources. In September, the *Washington Post* reported that 'members of the platoon have been charged with dismembering and photographing corpses, as well as hoarding a skull and other human bones' (Whitlock 2010). In what is reminiscent of events in Abu Ghraib in Iraq, soldiers also took and distributed to others, including family members, photos of themselves with the corpses of Afghan civilians they had murdered (Fallon 2010; Rubin 2011b; Cole et al. 2011). These photos were not widely published in the United States. They were, however, published by the German newspaper *Der Spiegel* (Cole et al. 2011). There are two photos of different grinning soldiers standing over the bloody body of an Afghan man. According to the military, there are more photos that remain unpublished (ibid.). Civilized indeed.

Question to Western media: Are we at war?

From reading this book, one might get the impression that the Western press is full of stories about the war. That simply is not the case. In fact, the war gets so little attention in Western media that the soldiers have to prove to themselves that they were there, that they did something, whether it is torture, killing, or desecrating dead Iraqis or Afghans and photographing themselves doing it.

The discourse around the notion of an Islamic or Arab enemy has been effective to the point that members of the government continue to see Islam as a threat to the continued well-being of the US, with Representative Peter King of the House Homeland Security Committee, for example, holding hearings on 'the radicalization of Muslims' in the US (Carnia 2011). In addition, in 2012 former presidential candidate and current Congresswoman Michele Bachmann, in conjunction with the Center for Security Policy – an anti-Muslim organization that, according to its website, gave its 2012 'Keeper of the Flame Award' to Peter King – sent a letter to the State Department's Inspector General's office accusing Huma Abedin, a long-time aide to former Secretary of State Hillary Clinton, of posing an Islamist threat to the government by influencing policies. Bachmann was widely denounced for writing this letter, but how many people heard or read about her censure? How many simply believe that anyone who is Muslim is somehow a threat? And that Muslims in the US government pose a particular danger to the US nation-state? In responding to depictions of Muslims and Arabs in US media, Arab-American political pollster James Zogby (2012) admonishes Michelle Bachmann and all politicians – and his critique might be extended to all Western media: 'We must commit to changing the way we talk about Islam and the Arab World, and our nation's Muslim and Arab communities.'

While things inside the United States continue to be worrisome in terms of the treatment of Arabs, South Asians, and Muslims who are struggling to be recognized as US citizens and part of the fabric of the culture, and trying to avoid discrimination and violence,[1] the flux that has come about as a result of Western occupation in Afghanistan, Iraq, and now increasingly in Pakistan continues unabated. Furthermore, the deployment of women by Western media sources infused with Orientalism, and transnational sexism, continues to serve nationalistic, militaristic, and imperial ends.

In early July 2012, the Taliban made public a film about an Afghan woman being shot for committing adultery in front of cheering villagers. Undeterred from the goal of withdrawing US troops from Afghanistan by 2014, the Obama administration continued to attempt to talk with the Taliban about the future of Afghanistan while these kinds of atrocities were occurring. An administration official explains:

'Gender issues are going to have to take a back seat to other priori-ties,' said the senior official, who spoke on the condition of anonym-ity to discuss internal policy deliberations. 'There's no way we can be successful if we maintain every special interest and pet project. All those pet rocks in our rucksack were taking us down.' (Chan-drasekaran 2011)

So much for the rescue narrative that helped sanction the war. In the *Time* magazine article accompanying the infamous cover photo of Aesha Mohammadzai, Fawzia Koofi, former deputy speaker of Afghan-istan's parliament, says, 'Women's rights must not be the sacrifice by which peace is achieved' (p. 22). Yet here, the Obama administration official not only indulges in some transnational sexism by likening Afghan women to pet rocks, but also demeans the Western women who were and are sincerely concerned about the well-being of Afghan women by suggesting that for these women their political commit-ment to the cause of Afghan women's liberation is a 'pet project.' Perhaps they are right about this. A more sincere commitment to Afghan women and their interests might occasion a hue and cry in the United States about the possibility of US forces leaving Afghanistan.

Other than the controversy about the *Time* cover, however, which soon faded away, like all news of the war on terror, none has been heard.

Hugh Hefner as liberator

Transnational sexism allows Western troops, the Western media, and those Westerners who took up the cause of liberation for Muslim women to walk away, first from Iraq and soon from Afghanistan. In this paradigm, women in Afghanistan are not fully human, they are not grateful for the attention of the West, and most troublingly they persist in having relationships with Afghan men, subscribing to and participating in Afghan patriarchy, rather than recognizing Western male supremacy.

> No amount of foreign troops can change the status of Afghan women. An enormous amount of work must be done to shift culturally and religiously sanctioned codes of behavior, and then to raise life expectations. But it is hard to imagine that such efforts could be waged without the protection of the NATO troops. Even then, many Afghan women may still see security in tradition, no matter how unkind it has been to them. (Anthony 2010)

What remains for women in Afghanistan is hyper-patriarchy, a partial and perhaps temporary liberation, and false notions about their agency in terms of making choices about how they live. Who asked Afghan women whether they wished to be rescued by the West? Who asked Aesha Mohammadzai whether she wanted to become the symbol for continued Western occupation of Afghanistan? Who asked Afghan women whether negotiating with the Taliban was a good idea or a bad idea? If they say something, would it be heard in the West? If they say nothing, does that mean they are choosing tradition over 'liberation'?

In May of 2011, Sila Sahin, a Turkish actress of Muslim descent, posed nude for German *Playboy*. In several of the photos she is depicted as partially veiled with her breasts exposed. In a few of them, she poses underneath a tent on sand – though a body of water is visible near by. In another photo she is posed wearing a transparent full body veil. Though her head and face are veiled, again her breasts are exposed. While this depiction of a Muslim woman in what are euphemistically called 'lads' mags' is surprising, she is not the first. In January 2006, Wafah Dufour, who is purportedly Osama bin Laden's niece, daughter of his half-brother, appeared partially clothed in *GQ* magazine. The appearance of these two women might be heralded by George Bush's 'Mission Accomplished' banner.[2] This is liberation. The right of Muslim women to bare themselves is, in part, what Western troops have been fighting for. Now Muslim women can appear in Western popular culture in the fashion that makes Western patriarchy most comfortable – objectified, dehumanized, sexualized.

Where do we go from here?

Outside Afghanistan Western media has propagated and enhanced negative ideas about Muslims, Arabs, and South Asians, has circulated ideas that malign Muslim, Arab, and South Asian women in particular. Women from those communities living in the West have to grapple with transnational sexism, Orientalism unchecked, and eruptions of Islamophobia.[3] How can we make sense of what Western media has wrought? Does the media share a mission with state governments? Are they instead blinded by government propaganda and misogyny, and handcuffed by budgetary constraints? Has their mission been a colonial one – the Westernization of Afghanistan and Iraq? Or has their goal been to continue to maintain the boundaries between 'us' and 'them,' boundaries that are necessary for transnational sexism?

In his book about why wars are fought, Chris Hedges, long-time war correspondent, talks about the ways in which the government and media work together to create an atmosphere in which questions are not welcomed and in which the populace must be persuaded that the government's actions are justified. That is the situation described in this book. He writes:

> Before conflicts begin, the first people silenced – often with violence – are not the nationalist leaders of the opposing ethnic or religious group, who are useful in that they serve to dump gasoline on the evolving conflict. Those voices within the ethnic group or the nation that question the state's lust and need for war are targeted. These dissidents are the most dangerous. They give us an alternative language, one that refuses to define the other as 'barbarian' or 'evil,' one that recognizes the humanity of the enemy, one that does not condone violence as a form of communication. Such voices are rarely heeded. And until we learn once again to speak in our own voice and reject that handed to us by the state in times of war, we flirt with our own destruction. (Hedges 2003: 16)

In the context of the war on terror the anti-war silences are created by heated rhetoric about men who commited the acts perpetrated on September 11th 2001, and assisted when that rhetoric gets extended to create loathing about how men who look a certain way, who live in a certain geographic space, and who practice a particular religion, treat women. The creation of the rescue narrative along with the fear and rage directed at Muslim men have allowed for ten-plus years of war, invasion of states that had little to do with the events of September 11th 2001, the deaths and maiming of untold numbers of civilians and soldiers from both sides. It feels unstoppable and yet stop it we must.

In the opening quote in this chapter, Chris Hedges calls for 'honest inquiry' in wartime. Honest inquiry in the case of the women of Afghanistan and Iraq and indeed of all Muslim women would mean a more accurate portrait of their lives that included tradition, religion, and ritual in place of ideas about them that are now infused with transnational sexism and Orientalist representations about how 'those people' over there live. More in-depth education in the West about people around the world might dissipate some of the mystery that currently exists around Islam, and around Arabs and South Asians. Honest inquiry would reveal that, as Hedges points out (ibid.: 8), the attacks on the World Trade Center and the Pentagon were not perpetrated by cave-dwelling maniacs but rather men steeped in Western knowledge and technology who knew precisely how to use the technology against the West and where to attack the enemy at his most vulnerable. Honest inquiry might make clear the ways in which the West, but more particularly the US, uses a history of colonialism and militarized influence to create cultures that we now describe as bloodthirsty or primitive.

Honest inquiry could lead to an analysis that places gender politics and analysis at its heart, that exposes Western masculinity for the fallacy it really is, and that promotes Western femininity, not because women's bodies are more readily available for male recreation but because those bodies are tough and formidable on their own. Honest inquiry might reveal the need for gender analysis that will make clear the lie of Western women's liberation present in the wearing of a bikini, in posing in *Playboy*, in multiple plastic surgeries. It might make visible the machinations of gender necessary to make war be about men only while increasingly, in the West, women are fighting these wars. It might show the ways in which belief in the supremacy of white masculinity is demonstrated when blond white women are recruited, even if only fictionally, to be the defeaters of brown-skinned enemies. Because transnational sexism is not only about women; Muslim men are feminized in the Western imagination so that they can be both hated and feared and demeaned as not fully masculine.

Honest inquiry might point to a need for greater media literacy so that future generations do not take everything they read or see as truth but rather are able to ask questions about the sources of this information that circulates around us, with those questions leading to an analysis of how these stories are told – looking especially at how gender is being used and manipulated.

An honest inquiry can help us unravel the secrets, humanize the enemy, form alliances across state borders, interrupt imperialism, stop killing.

Notes

Introduction

1 I understand that using the term 'the West' is problematic in that it assumes a false homogenization of all who live in that geographic and ideological space. For purposes of this research, however, I am using the term 'the West' to mark a particular power relation and ideological stance in relation to 'other' peoples whose lives occur geographically outside the space known as 'the West' but not outside its imperialist influence, either at the literal level through occupation or the ideological in terms of the imposition of certain ideas.

2 My intention is not to contribute to the prevalent fetishization of September 11th 2001, particularly in the US. I intend only to mark a time when US and indeed world attention shifted to persons from a particular geographic region associated in the Western imagination with certain people of color who may or may not practice a religion that is believed to pose a threat to Western well-being. In addition, I do want to acknowledge that the events of that day continue to have material consequences on people of color, particularly those having contact in various ways with the US.

3 In this particular war, women have visibility/invisibility problems (Riley 2008).

4 See Jack Shaheen's work (2008) on how Arabs are equated with being Muslim on television and in films in the US.

5 Arundahati Roy's 'Do turkeys enjoy Thanksgiving?', www. hindu. com/2004/01/18/stories/2004011800 181400.htm, served as the initial inspiration for this idea as she described what she called 'the new racism.' I began to use her idea about the new sexism as a model for how contemporary sexism was being practiced without knowing exactly what to call it. My thanks to Chandra Talpade Mohanty for her suggestion of the term transnational sexism.

6 Several feminists have written about this unfair and unfavorable contrast, most notably Chandra Talpade Mohanty (1991), Sherene Razack (2008), Yasmin Jiwani (2006), and Sunera Thobani (2007).

7 Of course, one might justifiably ask, if Western women are so liberated, why such high rates of rape and sexual assault? Why does a gendered wage and labor gap still exist? Why is it still surprising when women hold political office, run major corporations, drive a race-car, or play a sport well? In the West, liberation for women is still measured in terms of sexual availability for men, in the accessibility of women's bodies.

8 Some might argue that this is true given that some high-profile US feminists supported the invasion of Afghanistan to the horror of other feminists around the world.

9 Cynthia Enloe, feminist international relations scholar, has

long posed this vitally important question to remind us that states are not made up of entirely masculine citizens and that the decisions and actions taken by these states have lasting repercussions on women's lives.

10 When I use the term 'Western,' I am referring to the United States, Canada, Great Britain, Ireland, and Australia. I understand that this terminology is inexact, that most of Europe is being excluded when it should be included, and that ideas of Western origin creep into publications from areas and authors outside these geographic confines. I try to be as specific as possible in noting the origins of the data I am dealing with and am careful to note when the source is either from outside what is traditionally considered to be the West either geographically or ideologically. All data used for this project was written originally in English.

11 Prior to television, radio was often used as the primary means of communicating enemy-creating propaganda (Horten 2002).

12 See, for example: *True Lies*, *Delta Force*, *The Siege*, or *Rules of Engagement*. And many more.

13 See, for example: *Black Hawk Down*, *Collateral Damage*, *Hart's War*, *Gods and Generals*.

14 The *South Park* episode was critical of US policy in the region. Nonetheless, Osama bin Laden was depicted as having a penis so small that it required a microscope to see it. *Law and Order*, as I shall show later, has featured numerous episodes that include a Muslim man who requires 'civilizing' or a Muslim woman who needs rescuing.

15 'Saddam Hussein has agreed to let UN weapons inspectors in Iraq. But he also said under no circumstances will Geraldo be let back in the country' (Conan O'Brien, politicalhumor.about.com/od/osamabinladen/a/Osama-Bin-Laden-Jokes.htm).

16 Doris Graber, Professor of Political Scientist and Communication, calls what the media does 'political socialization' (2010: 163). She also refers to it as 'shared values' (ibid.: 166). It seems clear she is talking about ideology and the construction and dissemination of uniform interpretations and viewpoints.

17 Women of color, other than the token elites, are absent in considerations of the proper practice of gender. To the creators of these representations the practice of white femininity is the only legitimate one.

1 Rescuing Afghan women

1 There are three acceptable spellings of the word burqa. I use burqa, but other spellings will appear as the source has used them and I simply repeat that use here.

2 See for example Carlotta Gall, 'Long in dark, Afghan women say to read is finally to see,' *New York Times*, 22 September 2002, or John F. Burns, 'Relishing beautiful new freedoms in Kabul,' *New York Times*, 15 September 2002, and many others.

3 The number of civilian deaths caused by US drone strikes is hotly debated. CIA use of drones further complicates accurate reporting. See, for example, Gregg Carlstrom, 'How accurate are US drones?,' Al Jazeera, www.aljazeera.com/focus/2010/05/2010530134138783448.html.

4 Like other ignorant Westerners, I too tend to conflate the words veil and burqa (see Scott 2007: 16),

though I try to make an effort to be explicit. The BBC published a useful graphic to help Westerners and non-Muslims differentiate between varieties of veils. It can be found here: www.bbc.co.uk/news/world-europe-11305033.

5 The *Vancouver Sun* is noted for being a Conservative-leaning newspaper in Canada.

6 Sima Simar is identified in the article as 'chairwoman of the Afghan Independent Human Rights Commission,' a United Nations Organization established to monitor human rights in Afghanistan (Crawford 2010).

7 There are debates in several countries in Europe about Muslim women wearing veils in public. Some countries have banned it. For information on the banning of the veil in France, see Chrisafis (2011), Erlanger (2011), BBC News (2010) and others. For a feminist analysis of this issue see Scott (2007).

8 *Front Page Magazine* was created by right-wing polemicist David Horowitz.

9 Anyone who has watched a few episodes of *Law and Order* would know that having weapons within easy reach of prisoners is not advisable and thus not acceptable procedure with prisoners. Though this is not the only time we are challenged to believe this. See the section on the arrest of Aafia Siddiqui.

10 Of course, I suppose I am now counted as a page viewer even though I spent my time viewing his webpage with my mouth open at the obvious distortion and hatred that seem to drive his content.

11 For more analysis of Chesler's anti-Islam activities as they relate to so-called honor killings in the US

and Canada, see Dana Olwan's work, e.g. 'Bodies that matter in death: honour killings and Canadian racial logics,' *Canadian Journal of Sociology*, special issue: 'Race,' ed. A. Park and M. Santos (forthcoming).

12 Anna Maria Cardinalli is a flamenco guitarist who got a PhD in the tradition of flamenco from Notre Dame. What qualifies her to study Afghan men and sexual practices is unknown.

13 In December 2010, the *Washington Examiner* ran the story by Sara A. Carter attributing the report to a joint effort between US and British forces. She also quotes a Wikileaks document.

14 The *Guardian* ran a story (Boone 2010c) about a Wikileaks embassy cable that revealed that Western contractors had hired 'dancing boys' for their own entertainment and that there was a government effort to squash this story.

15 For an examination of the coverage of Bibi Aisha, see Chapter 4.

2 'Real housewives'

1 There were also numerous stories detailing the glee of citizens and government officials in the United States at the killing of bin Laden.

2 Of course, those US dollars she is reportedly using probably have been in the hands of the family since the time of the Iran–Iraq war when the US government considered Saddam Hussein a valued friend in the region.

3 Huda Ammash is also referred to in the British press as Chemical Sally (Roberts 2003).

4 Of course, the failure of the weapons inspectors to find any

evidence of this biological weapons program did not prompt US officials to release Ammash from custody for quite some time.

5 This seems like scant evidence on which to base an assessment of her importance to Saddam Hussein's administration, and yet the absence of WMDs may indicate that scant evidence was frequently used as intelligence on Iraq. Is it not possible that Ammash sat in the only seat left at the table? As the lone woman at these functions, she probably didn't get the choice seat at any table.

6 Stephan Faris in the *New York Daily News* of 17 April 2003 reported that she and Rashid were separated but none of the other sources reports this.

7 Of course, the failure on the part of weapons inspectors to turn up any of these weapons did not prompt the press to take back any of this heated rhetoric about Taha.

8 Even though women in the US, both women of color and white women, participate in the production of weapons, the culture, the industry and the women themselves all act as if they don't. See, for example, Riley (2010).

9 It never seems to occur to either US intelligence, military or the Western press that perhaps Huda Ammash was coerced into Saddam Hussein's administration and that her father's death served as impetus to keep her in line.

10 Of course, recruiting for state-sponsored militaries always has a degree of brainwashing or intense persuasion involved but it is never talked about in the same way.

11 Blackwater is a corporation that has been quite controversial since its founding in 1998. It has strong ties to the US government, as notably former vice-president Dick Cheney was a shareholder. Known to work closely with the CIA, Blackwater has been a subcontractor to the military in both Afghanistan and Iraq. There have been numerous accusations of bad behavior by Blackwater operatives, including the killing of seventeen Afghan civilians. For more on Blackwater see: topics.nytimes.com/top/news/business/companies/blackwater_usa/index.html.

3 'Where are the women?'

1 Bibi is an honorific which was used in order to protect her identity. Recntly, Aesha, who objected to its use as she says it is for old women, has begun using Mohammadzai as her surname. It is not clear whether that is a family name or simply a name she chose.

2 Of course, the use of drone warfare means that human beings are less and less seen and are more invisible than ever in this war. This is evidenced in the use of the appalling term 'bug splat' to describe civilian casualties from either conventional or drone bombings. For more on the history of the use of this term, see Jennifer Robinson's '"Bugsplat": The ugly U.S. drone war in Pakistan,' Al Jazeeera, 29 November 2001, www.aljazeera.com/indepth/opinion/2011/11/201111278839153400.html.

3 abcnews.go.com/International/image-mutilated-afghan-woman-ayesha-wins-world-press/story?id=12893437#.T_QDd65q_PY.

4 Juliane von Mittlestaedt's article in *Der Spiegel* about Aafia Siddiqui, 'The most dangerous woman in the world,' was originally published in German. It was translated by Christopher Sultan.

5 Aafia Siddiqui is now divorced

from Amjad Khan. He has lately been quoted in the Pakistani press as affirming the charges against her, saying that she had extremist views on Islam as well as violent tendencies in general.

6 Her youngest child Suleman is believed to have died while she was being held in Pakistan. The *Daily Times*, a Pakistani newspaper, reported in 2010 that they discovered 'nearly a dozen juvenile girls (between 11 and 12) who have been languishing in several Afghan jails ... Not much is known about these girls, and most are referred to by the numbers allotted to them, just like Dr. Aafia was' (Minhas 2010). Deborah Scroggins reports that shortly thereafter, Dr Siddiqui's daughter Maryam appeared at the gate of her sister's home in Karachi. She had been missing for seven years.

7 There is some mystery and controversy surrounding this facility and what is done there. The facility has recently been taken over by the Department of Homeland Security, which makes one wonder what exactly is being researched there. There are also accusations that diseases have been leaked from Plum Island that have infected animal and eventually human populations on the mainland with Lyme disease or West Nile virus. For a full exploration of the debate, see Michael C. Carroll's *Lab 257: The Disturbing Story of the Government's Secret Germ Laboratory*, William Morrow, New York, 2005.

4 We are all soldiers now

1 There was a lot written about the capture of Jessica Lynch and what it meant for the US military. There was a racial disparity in the attention paid to Lynch as opposed to the lack of attention paid to two other women, both captured or killed on that same day in that same incident. Panamanian-American Shoshanna Johnson was taken prisoner and Native American Lori Piestewa died in that same incident. See Riley (2006).

2 There are also instances of men being raped inside the military but the incidence is much lower than that for women and of course, owing to fear of stigma, the reporting of such assaults is most likely extremely low. See, for example, Myers (2009a) and Broadbent (2011).

3 See, for example, 'Heart of darkness,' *New York Times*, 21 March 2012, p. A23, www.nytimes.com/2012/03/21/opinion/dowd-heart-of-darkness.html, 'The Great Game imposter,' *New York Times*, 24 November 2010, p. A27, www.nytimes.com/2010/11/24/opinion/24dowd.html, 'Doubts about certitude,' *New York Times*, 16 December 2009, p. A43, www.nytimes.com/2009/12/16/opinion/16dowd.html?_r=1, and in the *Pittsburgh Post Gazette*, 'Playing the Afghan game,' 2011, www.post-gazette.com/stories/opinion/perspectives/maureen-dowd-playing-the-afghan-game-285098/?p=2.

4 In the following season of *The Real Housewives of New York City*, the women travel to Morocco, in part mimicking the women from *Sex and the City 2* only with lower budgets, less opulence. *Real Housewives* acknowledged, however, that they are in Morocco. There is no bonding, real or pretend, between the housewives and the local women. They are quite openly disgusted at the accommodations in Morocco and there are almost no local women included in the filming.

5 This is what liberation looks like

1 In August 2012, a white supremacist shot several people at a Sikh temple in Wisconsin.

2 George W. Bush appeared on the USS *Abraham Lincoln* in May of 2003 in a flight suit in front of a huge banner that declared, very precipitously, 'Mission Accomplished.'

3 In an attempt to interrupt this circulation of Orientalist and transnational sexist representations, women like Yasmin Jiwani, Dana Olwan and Evelyn Alsultany write critically of such media representations.

Bibliography

Abawi, A. (2009a) 'Afghan widows struggle for survival,' CNN.com, 8 December, afghanistan.blogs.cnn.com/2009/12/08/afghan-widows-struggle-for-survival/.

— (2009b) 'Ignored by society, Afghan dancing boys suffer centuries old tradition,' CNN.com, 26 October, articles.cnn.com/2009-10-26/world/ctw.afghanistan.sex.trade_1_boys-afghan-dance?_s=PM:WORLD.

ABC News (2003) '"Dr. Germ": Iraqi bio-weapons scientist says her country wants only peace,' abcnews.go.com/GMA/story?id=125371&p.=1#.T8Sgd-67j3eY.

Abdi, C. (2007) 'Convergence of civil war and the religious right: re-imagining Somali women,' *Signs: Journal of Women in Culture and Society*, 33: 183–207.

Abdul-Ahad, G. (2009) 'The dancing boys of Afghanistan,' *Guardian*, 11 September, p. 26.

Addario, L. (2001) 'Jihad's women,' *New York Times Magazine*, 21 October, pp. 38–41.

Ahmed, C. (2009) 'The new face of plastic surgery in Iraq,' *Los Angeles Times*, 12 July, articles.latimes.com/2009/jul/12/world/fg-iraq-plastic-surgery12.

Ahmed, S. (2000) *Strange Encounters: Embodied Others in Post-Coloniality*, London: Routledge.

Aho, J. A. (1994) *This Thing of Darkness: A Sociology of the Enemy*, University of Washington Press.

Al-Ali, N. and N. Pratt (2009) *What Kind of Liberation? Women and the Occupation of Iraq*, Berkeley: University of California Press.

Aleccia, J. (2011) 'What was in medicine chests at bin Laden compound,' MSNBC, 6 May, www.msnbc.msn.com/id/42934673/ns/world_news-death_of_bin_laden/t/what-was-medicine-chests-bin-laden-compound/#.UCvBTq7j3PY.

Allen, M. (2001) 'Laura Bush gives radio address,' *Washington Post*, 18 November, p. A14.

Alvarez, L. (2007) 'Army giving more waivers in recruiting,' *New York Times*, 14 February, p. 1.

— (2009) 'G.I. Jane breaks the combat barrier,' *New York Times*, 15 August, p. A1.

Amiri, R. (2002) 'The fear beneath the burka,' *New York Times*, 20 March, p. A29.

Anthony, A. (2010) 'Afghanistan's propaganda war takes a new twist,' *Guardian*, 4 December, www.guardian.co.uk/world/2010/dec/05/bibi-aisha-afghanistan-disfigured-Taliban.

Arraf, J. and M. Al-Dulaimy (2010) 'Witness: secret Iraq prison for women and children,' *Christian Science Monitor*, 20 May.

Ashton, C. (2011) 'Iraqi women: winners or losers in war-torn society?' BBC News, www.bbc.co.uk/news/world-middle-east-15743078.

Associated Press (2003) 'On the trail of Dr. Germ,' 18 April,

www.smh.com.au/articles/
2003/04/17/1050172711365.html.

— (2007) 'Karen Hughes to leave
State Department,' 31 October,
www.msnbc.msn.com/id/
21560044/ns/politics-white_house/
t/karen-hughes-leave-state-
department/#.TmsyYa7j3PY.

— (2010) 'Number of C-sections
rising in Iraq, officials
worry about health effects in
women,' *Washington Post Online*,
16 August, www.washington
post.com/world/middle-east/
number-of-c-sections-rising-in-
iraq-officials-worry-about-health-
effects-on-women/2011/08/16/
gIQAHt5XIJ_story.html.

Ayotte, K. and M. Husian (2005)
'Securing Afghan women: neo-
colonialism, epistemic violence
and the rhetoric of the veil,'
NWSA Journal, 17(3): 112–33.

Badkhen, A. (2008) 'Rape's vast
toll in Iraq War remains
largely ignored,' *Christian Science
Monitor*, 24 November, www.
csmonitor.com/World/Middle-
East/2008/1124/p07s01-wome.html.

Bahadur, G. (2008) 'Survival sex,'
Ms magazine, Summer, www.
msmagazine.com/Summer2008/
SurvivalSex.asp.

Baker, A. (2010) 'Afghan women and
the return of the Taliban,' *Time*, 9
August, pp. 24–8.

Banerjee, N. (2004) 'Iraqi women's
window of opportunity for political gains is closing,' *New York
Times*, 26 February, p. 13.

Bartosiewicz, P. (2009) 'Terrorism
trial in New York carries few risks
for government,' Opinion, *LA
Times*, articles.latimes.com/2009/
nov/29/opinion/la-oe-petra29-
2009nov29.

— (2010) 'A Pakistani on trial – with
no Pakistani reporters,' *Time*,

23 January, www.time.com/time/
nation/article/0,8599,1956197,00.
html?xid=rsstopstories#ixzz0dcb
SICFx.

Basu, M. (2003) 'Luxury gone,
Saddam's kin lie low in Iraq,'
Atlanta Journal and Constitution,
26 July, p. 5A.

Batal al-Shishani, M. (2010) 'Is the
role of women in al-Qaeda increasing?' BBC News, 7 October,
www.bbc.co.uk/news/world-
middle-east-11484672.

Bates, D. (2011) 'Osama bin Lothario:
terror chief "was a sex machine
who would vanish into the
bedroom with his wife for days,"'
Mail Online, 10 June, www.daily-
mail.co.uk/news/article-2002152/
Osama-bin-Laden-sex-machine-
vanish-bedroom-wife-days.html.

Bazzi, M. (2003) 'U.S. arrests family
of a top Hussein official,' *Newsday*, 8 December, p. A02.

BBC News (2005a) 'US sets Saddam's
scientists free,' 19 December,
news.bbc.co.uk/2/hi/middle_
east/4542084.stm.

— (2005b) 'Iraq's jailed Mrs Anthrax
"dying,"' 1 January, news.bbc.
co.uk/2/hi/middle_east/4138767.
stm.

— (2010) 'French Senate votes to
ban Islamic full veil in public,'
14 September, www.bbc.co.uk/
news/world-europe-11305033.

Begley, S. (2005) 'People believe "a
fact" that fits their views even
if it's false,' *Wall Street Journal*,
4 February, online.wsj.com/article/
0,,SB110746526775045356,00.html.

Bergen, P. (2012) 'A visit to bin
Laden's lair,' CNN, 3 May, www.
cnn.com/2012/05/03/opinion/
bergen-bin-laden-lair/index.html.

Bjorken, J., C. Bencomo and
J. Horowitz (2003) 'Climate of fear:
sexual violence and abduction

of women and girls in Baghdad,' *Human Rights Watch*, 15(8), 16 July.

Black, J. (2012) 'Report: Growing number of military women see combat, serve in leadership roles,' MSNBC, 4 April, usnews.msnbc.msn.com/_news/2011/12/22/9613645-report-growing-number-of-military-women-see-combat-serve-in-leadership-roles?lite.

Blackburn, B. (2010) 'Portrait of mutilated Afghan woman Ayesha wins World Press Photo Award,' ABC News, 11 February, abcnews.go.com/International/image-mutilated-afghan-woman-ayesha-wins-world-press/story?id=12893437#.T_QDd65q_PY.

Boone, J. (2010a) 'Afghan elections: record number of women stand for Parliament. Despite everyday prejudice and Taliban death threats a record number of female candidates are standing in September polls,' *Guardian*, 24 August, p. 18.

— (2010b) 'Afghanistan election five campaigners for female candidate shot dead,' *Guardian*, 29 August, p. 13.

— (2010c) 'Foreign contractors hired Afghan "dancing boys," Wiki Leaks cable reveals,' *Guardian*, 2 December, www.guardian.co.uk/world/2010/dec/02/foreign-contractors-hired-dancing-boys?INTCMP=SRCH.

Boot, M. and M. O'Hanlon (2006) 'A military path to citizenship,' *Washington Post*, 19 October, p. A29.

Borger, J. (2003) 'Iraq's Dr. Germ surrenders to coalition forces,' *Guardian*, 13 May, p. 13.

— (2005) 'US gives up search for Saddam's WMD,' *Guardian*, 13 January.

Bradley, P. (1998) *Slavery, Propaganda, and the American Revolution*, Jackson: University of Mississippi Press.

Branigin, W. (2008) 'Pakistani woman faces assault charges,' *Washington Post*, 6 August, p. A14.

Broadbent, L. (2011) 'Rape in the U.S. military: America's dirty little secret,' *Guardian*, 9 December, www.guardian.co.uk/society/2011/dec/09/rape-us-military.

Bruce, A. (2008) 'A Baghdad trailer park for widows and children,' *Washington Post.com*, 15 September, blog.washingtonpost.com/unseen-iraq/.

Brunstrom, D. (2005) 'Afghans vote in landmark elections,' *Toronto Star*, 19 September, p. A10.

Bumiller, E. (2001) 'A nation challenged: shaping opinion; First Lady to speak about Afghan women,' *New York Times*, 16 November, p. B2.

— (2010a) 'Letting women reach women in Afghan war,' *New York Times*, 7 March, p. A1.

— (2010b) 'In camouflague or veil, a fragile bond,' *New York Times*, 29 May, p. A1.

Bumiller, E. and R. Norland (2010) 'Light turnout in Afghan parliamenty election as violence deters voters,' *New York Times*, 19 September.

Bumiller, E. and T. Shanker (2013) 'Equality at the front line: Pentagon is set to lift ban on women's combat roles,' *New York Times*, 24 January, p. A1.

Burke, J. (2011) 'Osama bin Laden's wives told they are free to leave Pakistan,' *Guardian*, 8 December, p. 32.

Burton, M. (2009) 'All-female Marine team conducts first mission in southern Afghanistan,' States

News Service, US Department of Defense, 10 March, www. defense.gov/news/newsarticle. aspx?id=53416.

Bush, L. (2010) 'Afghanistan must embrace women's rights,' *Washington Post*, 10 October, p. A19.

Carnia, C. (2011) 'Emotions run high at Congressional hearings on Muslims,' *USA Today*, 10 March, content.usatoday. com/communities/onpolitics/ post/2011/03/peter-king-radical-muslim-hearings-congress-/1#. UC_MHK7j3PY.

Cavendish, J. (2010) 'In Afghan election corruption colors aims of many female candidates,' *Christian Science Monitor*, 17 September, www.csmonitor.com/World/ Asia-South-Central/2010/0917/ In-Afghan-election-corruption-colors-aims-of-many-female-candidates.

CBC News (2006) 'Women in the Canadian military,' CBC News, 30 May, www.cbc.ca/news/ background/cdnmilitary/women-cdnmilitary.html.

— (2010) 'U.S. soldiers accused in Afghan civilian murders,' 20 May, www.cbsnews.com/ stories/2010/05/20/eveningnews/ main6504056.shtml.

Chandrasekaran, R. (2011) 'In Afghanistan U.S. shifts strategy on women's right,' *Washington Post*, 6 March, www. washington post.com/wp-dyn/ content/article/2011/03/05/ AR2011030504233.html.

Chesler, P. (2010a) 'How a "nice American girl" became a jihadist,' *Frontp.mag.com*, 5 February, frontp.mag.com/2010/phyllis-chesler/how-a-'nice-american-girl'-became-a-jihadist/.

— (2010b) 'Islamic homosexual

pederasty and Afghanistan's "dancing boys,"' Chesler Chronicles, *Pajamas Media*, 21 April, pajamasmedia.com/ phyllischesler/2010/04/21/islamic-homosexual-pederasty-and-afghanistan's-'dancing-boys-'/.

— (2011) 'Terrorists in drag: bombs beneath the burqa,' *Frontp. mag.com*, 6 July, frontp.mag. com/2011/07/06/terrorists-in-drag-bombs-beneath-the-burqa/.

Chisea, A. (2004) 'Women become Iraqi terror targets,' *Glasgow Herald*, 23 January, p. 16.

Chrisafis, A. (2011) 'French veil ban: first woman fined for wearing niqab,' *Guardian*, 12 April, p. 19.

Clinton, H. (2001) 'New hope for Afghanistan's women,' *Time*, 24 November, www.time. com/time/nation/article/0, 8599,185643,00.html.

Cloud, D. and L. King (2012) 'Probe finds troops who burned Korans misinterpreted orders; U.S. officials say several could face discipline. Some Afghans want trial,' *Los Angeles Times*, 3 March, Part AA, p. 2.

Clurczak, E. (2011) 'Bush shares tales of dual role as First Lady, global advocate,' *Hattiesburg American*, 29 April, www.zirana. com/MS_hattiesburg/scraped/ bush_shares_tales_of_dual_role_ as_first_lady_global_advocate. html.

CNN.com. (2001a) 'First Lady blasts Taliban treatment of women,' 17 November, archives.cnn. com/2001/ALLPOLITICS/11/17/ bush.radio/index.html.

— (2001b) 'Mavis Leno: lives of Afghan women,' 9 November, archives.cnn.com/2001/ COMMUNITY/11/09/leno.cnna/ index.html.

Coker, M. (2002) 'Afghan women: burqa-free is still only for the brave,' *New York Times*, p. A19.

Cole, M., B. Ross, A. M. Hill and L. Ferran (2011) 'Repugnant photos emerge of U.S. soldiers accused of sport killings,' ABC World News with Diane Sawyer, 21 March, abcnews.go.com/ Blotter/repugnant-pictures-emerge-us-soldiers-accused-sport-killings/story?id=13183933.

Cole, S. and J. Cole (2004) 'Veil of anxiety over women's rights,' *Los Angeles Times*, 7 March, articles. latimes.com/2004/mar/07/ opinion/op-cole7.

Colson, M. (2003) 'Iraqi women have lost the post-war: rapes, sequestrations and a return to the veil develop,' *La Liberación*, 2 September, www.casi.org.uk/ discuss/2003/msg04234.html.

Cooke, M. (2002) 'Gender and September 11: saving brown women,' *Signs: Journal of Women in Culture and Society*, 28(1): 468–70.

Cooper, M. (2001) 'Lights! Cameras! Attack! Hollywood enlists,' *The Nation*, 10 December, www.the nation.com/article/lights-cameras-attack-hollywood-enlists.

Corbett, S. (2007) 'The women's war,' *New York Times Magazine*, 18 March, p. 42.

Crawford, T. (2010) 'Afghan women face health risks wearing burkas, activist says,' *Vancouver Sun*, 20 October, www. canada.com/vancouversun/ news/westcoastnews/story.html? id=c6a6e9b0-67b6-4701-954c-167ad2d6fb71.

Cubilié, A. (2005) *Women Witnessing Terror: Testimony and the Cultural Politics of Human Rights*, New York: Fordham University Press.

Daily Mail (2011) '"I want to be martyred with you"; Bin Laden's young wife's suicide pledge to terror mastermind,' *Mail Online*, 12 May, www.dailymail.co.uk/ news/article-1386158/Osama-Bin-Laden-wife-Amal-al-Sadas-suicide-pledge-terror-mastermind.html.

Dickey, C. and G. Kovach (2002) 'Revered – and yet repressed,' *Newsweek*, 14 January, p. 48.

Dickey, C. and C. Soloway (2002) 'The secrets of Dr. Germ,' *Newsweek*, 9 December, p. 40.

Douglas, H. (2010) 'Threats and rockets don't stop Afghan women running in election,' *Sunday Express*, 19 September, pp. 42–3.

Dowd, M. (2010) 'A girl's guide to Saudi Arabia,' *Vanity Fair*, August, pp. 122–71.

Doyle, J. (2010) 'The taboo topic our Afghan mission ignores,' *Globe and Mail*, 20 April, p. R3.

Echegaray, C. (2007) 'Service before citizenship,' *Tampa Tribune*, 6 February, p. 1.

Ehrenreich, B. (2001) 'Veiled threat: to fully grasp the dangers of the post-Sept. 11 world, we have to examine the Taliban's hatred of women,' *Los Angeles Times*, 4 November, www.commondreams.org/ views01/1104-02.htm.

Eisenstein, Z. (2006) 'Afterword: Newly seeing,' in R. Riley and N. Inayatullah (eds), *Interrogating Imperialism: Conversations on Gender, Race, and War*, New York: Palgrave Macmillan.

— (2007) *Sexual Decoys: Gender, Race, and War in Imperial Democracy*, London: Zed Books.

Enloe, C. (2000) *Maneuvers: The International Politics of Militarizing Women's Lives*, Berkeley: University of California Press.

— (2004) 'Crucial reporting: human rights reports and why we should be reading them,' *Women's Review of Books*, February, p. 21.

Erlanger, S. (2011) 'France enforces ban on full face veils in public,' *New York Times*, 11 April, p. A4.

Evans, D. (2001) 'Cherie Blair takes her turn at Tali-bashing,' *Vancouver Sun*, 20 November, p. A5.

Fallon, A. (2010) 'US soldier jailed for seven years over murders of Afghan civilians,' *Guardian*, 23 September, www.guardian.co.uk/world/2011/sep/24/us-soldier-jailed-afghan-civilians.

Fanon, F. (1965) 'Algeria unveiled,' in *New Left Reader*, New York: Monthly Review Press, pp. 161–85.

Faris, S. (2003) 'Dr. Germ off and running,' *Daily News*, New York, 17 April, p. 8.

Farmer, B. (2010) 'Paedophilia culturally accepted in South Afghanistan,' *Daily Telegraph*, 13 January, www.telegraph.co.uk/news/world news/asia/afghanistan/8257943/Paedophilia-culturally-accepted-in-south-Afghanistan.html.

Farrell, S. (2007) 'Warrant seeks Hussein's wife and daughter,' *New York Times*, 18 August, p. A5.

Filkins, D. (2004a) 'The struggle for Iraq: reconstruction,' *New York Times*, 17 February, p. A1.

— (2004b) 'Iraqi women 1, Islamists 0,' *New York Times*, 28 February, p. 6.

— (2009) 'Afghan girls scarred by acid defy terror, embracing school,' *New York Times*, 14 January, p. A1.

Finch, L. (2000) 'Psychological propaganda: the war of ideas on ideas during the first half of the twentieth century,' *Armed Forces and Society: An Interdisciplinary Journal*, 26: 367–91.

Forman, T. (2011) 'US wants access to bin Laden's family,' CNN, 10 May, ibnlive.in.com/news/us-wants-access-to-bin-ladens-family/151681-2.html.

Fortney, V. (2012) 'In Afghanistan, Canada's female soldiers earned the right to fight, and die as equals,' *Calgary Herald*, 28 February, www.canada.com/news/Afghanistan+Canada+female+soldiers+earned+right+fight+equals/6191423/story.html.

Fox News (2010) 'Afghan men struggle with sexual identity, study shows,' 28 January, www.foxnews.com/politics/2010/01/28/afghan-men-struggle-sexual-identity-study-finds/.

Franklin, N. (2011) 'National insecurity,' *New Yorker*, 11 October, pp. 84–5.

Freedman, D. (2004) 'Misreporting war has a long history,' in D. Miller, *Tell Me Lies: Propaganda and Media Distortion in the Attack on Iraq*, London: Pluto Press.

Gall, C. (2005) 'Afghan living standards among the lowest, U.N. finds,' *New York Times*, 12 February, www.nytimes.com/2005/02/22/international/asia/22 afghanistan.html.

Gallagher, I. (2007) 'Relaxing in the Dazzle beauty salon, Saddam's daughter took the call: her father was to hang – death of a tyrant,' *Daily Telegraph* (Australia), 1 January, p. 69.

Garcia, M. (2003) 'Burqa no longer law, but women remain oppressed in Afghanistan,' Knight Ridder, 8 March, www.highbeam.com/doc/1G1-98497553.html.

Gardner, T. (2012) 'The women who dared defy the Taliban,' *Mail Online*, 12 May, www.dailymail.co.uk/news/article-2147275/Aesha-Mohammadzai-Afghan-

22-rebuilding-life-US-having-nose-hacked-off.html.

Gendar, A. (2010) '"Lady Al Qaeda" Aafia Siddiqui convicted of attempted murder,' *Daily News*, New York, 3 February, articles.ny dailynews.com/2010-02-03/news/27055245_1_afghan-police-station-aafia-siddiqui-defense-lawyer.

Gendar, A. and H. Kennedy (2010) 'Two jurors released from "Lady al Qaeda" Aafia Siddiqui trial; wounded soldier relives day of attack,' *Daily News*, New York, 25 January, articles.nydailynews.com/2010-01-25/news/17945199_1_two-jurors-afghan-soldier.

Gendar, A., J. Martinez and S. Gaskell (2008) 'Pakistani scientist busted, called most significant terror capture in five years,' *Daily News*, New York, 12 August.

Gertz, B. (2010) 'Inside the ring: gay Afghans,' *Washington Times*, 8 September, www.washington times.com/news/2010/sep/8/inside-the-ring-181646287/.

Giordono, J. (2008) '10 female detainees given to Iraq,' *Stars and Stripes*, 17 December, www.stripes.com/news/10-female-detainees-given-to-iraq-1.86264.

Goodman, A. (2004) 'This war has unleashed the political freedom to oppress women,' *Democracy Now!*, 5 January.

Goodwin, J. and J. Neuwirth (2001) 'The rifle and the veil,' *New York Times*, 19 October, p. A19.

Gopal, P. (2010) 'Burqas and bikinis: *Time* Magazine's cover is the latest cynical attempt to oversimplify the reality of Afghan lives,' *Guardian*, 3 August.

Graber, D. (2010) *Mass Media and American Politics*, Washington, DC: CQ Press.

Granger, K., J. Kline, J. Gerlach,

G. Davis and T. Poe (2005) 'Battling against terror: Afghan democracy on the move,' *Washington Times*, 26 September, p. A21.

Grigsby Bates, K. (2010) 'Bibi Aisha, disfigured Afghan woman featured on *Time* cover visits the United States,' NPR, 13 October, www.npr.org/blogs/thetwo-way/2010/10/13/130527903/bibi-aisha-disfigured-afghan-woman-featured-on-time-cover-visits-u-s.

Hairan, A. (2010) 'Is *Time*'s Aisha story fake?' RAWA, 29 August, www.rawa.org/temp/runews/2010/08/29/is-time-s-aisha-story-fake.html.

Hall, M. (2001) 'First Lady turns gaze to Afghan women,' *USA Today*, 16 November, p. 13A.

Harding, L. (2004) 'The other prisoners,' *Guardian*, 19 May, Section G2, p. 10, www.guardian.co.uk/world/2004/may/20/iraq.gender?INTCMP=SRCH.

Harman, J. (2008) 'Finally some progress in combating rape and assault in the military,' *Huffington Post*, 10 September, www.huffingtonpost.com/rep-jane-harman/finally-some-progress-in_b_125504.htmlz.

Harvey, O. (2006) 'Devil's daughter,' *Sun* (London), 13 March.

Hassan, N. (2007) '50,000 Iraqi refugees forced into prostitution,' *Independent*, 24 June, www.independent.co.uk/news/world/middle-east/50000-iraqi-refugees-forced-into-prostitution-454424.html.

Hauslohner, A. (2010) 'When women set themselves on fire,' *Time*, 7 July, www.time.com/time/world/article/0,8599,2002340-1,00.html.

Healy, J. (2011) 'Making themselves heard in a changed Iraq,' *New York Times*, 27 December, p. A8.

Hedges, C. (2003) *War Is a Force that Gives Us Meaning*, New York: Anchor Books.

Heffernan, V. (2005) 'What to expect when expecting heaven,' *New York Times*, 20 December, p. E1.

Hemmer, B. and M. Boettcher (2003) 'Look at documents of Iraq's Dr. Rihab Taha,' CNN, 28 January.

Hendawi, H. (2010) 'Iraq's widows: a grim legacy for postwar Iraq,' AP, www.indianexpress.com/news/iraqs-widows-a-grim-legacy-for-postwar-iraq/642851/.

Henderson, D. (2009) 'Female Marines, sailors assist Afghan women,' *Defense Department Documents and Publications*, 29 December, www.defense.gov/news/newsarticle.aspx?id=57295.

Hendren, J. (2003) 'Turn up heat on Iraqi fugitive: US troops are holding Izzat Ibrahim's wife and daughter,' *Los Angeles Times*, 27 November, p. 9.

Herman, E. (2004) 'Normalising godfatherly aggression,' in D. Miller, *Tell Me Lies: Propaganda and Media Distortion in the Attack on Iraq*, London: Pluto Press.

Heyzer, N. (2003) 'Making a nation more equal,' *New York Times*, 3 December, p. A31.

Hiro, D. (2002) *Iraq: In the Eye of the Storm*, New York: Thunder's Mouth Press.

Hoffman, L. (2002a) 'Meet Dr. Germ: she built Iraq's deadly stockpile,' Scripps Howard Inc., 1 December, www.ph.ucla.edu/epi/bioter/meetdrgerm.html.

— (2002b) 'Meet Dr. Germ: mother of Iraqi bio-weapons may have answers,' *The Sun-Herald*, 2 December.

hooks, b. (2005) *Bell Hooks: Cultural Criticism and Transformation*, Media Education Foundation, www.mediaed.org/assets/products/402/transcript_402.pdf.

Hopkins, N. (2012) 'Meet Nicky Moffat, the highest ranked woman in the British Army,' *Guardian*, 11 January, www.guardian.co.uk/uk/2012/jan/11/nicky-moffat-highest-ranking-woman-army.

Horten, G. (2002) *Radio Goes to War: The Cultural Politics of Propaganda During World War II*, Berkeley: University of California Press.

Hosenball, M. and T. Zakaria (2011) 'Pornography found in bin Laden's hideout,' Reuters, 13 May, www.reuters.com/article/2011/05/13/us-binladen-porn-idUSTRE74C4RK20110513.

Hughes, C. J. (2010) 'Pakistani scientist found guilty of shootings,' *New York Times*, 4 February, p. A21.

Hughes, K. (2009) 'Don't forget Afghanistan's women,' *Politico*, 23 October, www.politico.com/news/stories/1009/28619.html.

Hughes, K. and P. Dobriansky (2011) 'Don't forget Afghanistan's women,' *Daily Beast*, 10 April, www.thedailybeast.com/articles/2011/04/10/karen-hughes-and-paula-dobriansky-dont-forget-afghanistans-women.html.

Human Rights Watch (2007) 'Ghost prisoner: two years in secret CIA detention,' *Human Rights Watch*, 19(1G), www.hrw.org/sites/default/files/reports/us0207webwcover.pdf.

Hunter, K. (2010) 'Afghan women join fight for election,' Channel Four News, 15 September, www.channel4.com/news/articles/politics/international_politics/afghan%2Bwomen%2Bjoin%2Bfight%2Bfor%2Belection/3767282.html.

Iltis, T. (2010) '*Time* exploits victim to promote war,' RAWA,

15 August, www.rawa.org/temp/runews/2010/08/15/time-exploits-victim-to-promote-war.html.

Jaber, H. (2007) 'Saddam was my father,' *Sunday Times* (London), 7 January, p. 1.

Jamjoom, M. (2009) 'War forces Iraqi mom into prostitution,' CNN.com, 2 November, articles. cnn.com/2009-11-02/world/iraq. prostitute_1_yanar-mohammed-prostitute-iraq?_s=PM:WORLD.

— (2010) 'Buying beauty in Baghdad,' CNN.com, 13 April, articles.cnn.com/2010-04-13/world/iraq.cosmetic_1_cosmetic-surgery-beauty-salons-iraqi-women?_s=PM:WORLD.

Jeffreys, S. (2007) 'Double jeopardy: women, the U.S. Military and the war in Iraq,' *Women's Studies International Forum*, 30: 16–25.

Jelinek, P. (2003a) 'Top Iraqi scientist captured,' news.com.au, 6 May.

— (2003b) 'Captured Iraqi scientist may know about bio weapons,' *Boston Globe*, 13 May, p. A13.

Jiwani, Y. (2006) *Discourses of Denial: Mediations of Race, Gender, and Violence*, Vancouver: University of British Columbia Press.

Jones, D. (2007) 'Vengance of Little Saddam; she's as ruthless as her father and didn't shed a tear as she watched his TV execution,' *Daily Mail* (London), 6 January, p. 18.

Kahf, M. (2008) 'From her royal body the robe was removed: the blessings of the veil and the trauma of forced unveiling in the Middle East,' in J. Heath (ed.), *The Veil: Women Writers on Its History, Lore and Politics*, Berkeley: University of California Press, pp. 27–43.

Kami, A. (2011) 'The daily struggle of Iraq's widows of war,' Reuters, 9 November, www.reuters.com/article/2011/11/09/us-iraq-widows-idUSTRE7A841T20111109.

Kasperowicz, P. (2012) 'GOP, Dems come together to fight human trafficking by contractors in Iraq, Afghanistan,' *The Hill*, 27 March, thehill.com/blogs/floor-action/house/218353-gop-dems-come-together-to-fight-human-trafficking-by-contractors-in-iraq-afghanistan.

Kaufman, S. (2005) 'Laura Bush in Kabul to promote Afghan women's education: First Lady to announce $21 million in education grants during visit,' *Federal Information and News Dispatch*, 29 March.

Kazem, H. (2005) 'In Afghanistan, Laura Bush focuses on the roles of women,' *Christian Science Monitor*, 31 March, www.cs monitor.com/2005/0331/p07s01-wosc.html.

Kelley, J. and C. Soriano (2003) '"Dr. Germ" military chief of staff in custody,' *USA Today*, 13 May, p. 11A.

Kellner, D. (2004) '9/11, spectacles of terror, and media manipulation,' in D. Miller, *Tell Me Lies: Propaganda and Media Distortion in the Attack on Iraq*, London: Pluto Press.

Kennedy, H. (2011) 'Osama bin Laden wasn't on kidney dialysis, took herbal Viagra,' *Daily News*, New York, 8 May, articles. nydailynews.com/2011-05-08/news/29541926_1_kidney-dialysis-drone-strike-kidney-failure.

Khaleeli, H. (2011) 'Afghan women fear for the future: life for many Afghan women improved dramatically with the fall of the Taliban but as the West prepares to pull out fears are growing for the future,' *Guardian*, 3 February, Section G2, p. 16.

Khalil, A. (2004) 'What Iraqi women want,' *Buffalo News*, 22 February, p. F1.

Khpalwak, A. (2010) 'Taliban not responsible for cutting Aisha's nose, ears: AIHRC,' RAWA, 6 December, www.rawa.org/temp/ runews/2010/12/06/taliban-not-responsible-for-cutting- aisha-s-nose-ears-aihrc.html.

King, L. (2010) 'Women running for Afghanistan parliament now have tougher time,' *Los Angeles Times*, 6 September, articles. latimes.com/2010/sep/06/world/ la-fg-afghanistan-campaign-danger-20100907.

Kolhatkar, S. (2004) 'Afghan women continue to fend for themselves,' *Znet*, 9 March.

Koppes, C. and D. Black (1990) *Hollywood Goes to War: How Politics, Profits and Propaganda Shaped World War II Movies*, University of California Press.

Kovach, G. (2010) 'Reaching out to Afghan women,' *San Diego Union Tribune*, 24 February, www.utsandiego.com/news/2010/feb/24/ reaching-out-to-afghan-women/.

Lamb, C. (2011a) 'Talk of who betrayed Osama bin Laden sparks a harem scuffle,' *The Australian*, 23 May, www.the australian.com.au/news/world/ talk-of-who-betrayed-osama-bin-laden-sparks-a-harem-scuffle/ story-e6frg6so-1226060643865.

— (2011b) 'Afghan women still battling for rights,' *Courant.com*, 4 April, articles. courant.com/2011-04-04/ news/c-op-lamb-afghanistan-women-0405-20110404_1_taliban-attacks-herat-equal-rights.

Lawrence, Q. (2011) 'Kabul seeks control of women's shelters,' NPR, 21 February, www.npr. org/2011/02/21/133865996/kabul-seeks-control-of-womens-shelters.

Lee, A. (2003) 'Saddam's wife joins daughters in British asylum bid,' *Straits Times*, 6 June, 209.157.64.200/focus/f-news/923976/posts.

Leeder, J. (2009) 'Behind the veil: women in Kandahar,' *Globe and Mail*, 16 September, www. theglobeandmail.com/news/ world/behind-the-veil----women-in-afghanistan/article1288709/.

Leiby, R. (2012) 'Bin Laden roamed Pakistan for 9 years his widow says,' *Washington Post*, 3 March, www.washingtonpost.com/world/ asia_pacific/bin-laden-roamed-pakistan-for-9-years-his-widow-says/2012/03/30/gIQAYQAylS_story. html.

Leinwand, D. and L. Parker (2003) 'Troops raid house of "Dr. Germ,"' *USA Today*, 16 April, p. 4A.

Lemmon, G. (2010) 'Maimed Afghan woman a reminder of what's at stake,' CNN.com, 17 August, www. cnn.com/2010/OPINION/08/16/ lemmon.mutilated.woman.pic/ index.html?iref=allsearch.

Lendman, S. (2010) 'Aafia Siddiqui: victimized by American depravity,' *Baltimore Chronicle and Sentinel*, 31 March, sjlendman. blogspot.com/2010/03/aafia-siddiqui-victimized-by-american. html.

Lewis, J. and R. Brookes (2004) 'Reporting the war on British television,' in D. Miller, *Tell Me Lies: Propaganda and Media Distortion in the Attack on Iraq*, London: Pluto Press.

Li, D. (2001) 'Lifting a veil of tears,' *New York Post*, 29 September, p. 59.

Lisheron, M. (2003) 'Showing Afghan women the way; Karen Hughes hopes guests glean insights on education, health,' *Austin American Statesman*, 17 July, p. B1.

Lister, S. (2003) 'Muslim cleric pledged "virgins,"' *The Times* (London), 24 January, p. 13.

Loewen, J. (2012 [1995]) *Lies My Teacher Told Me: Everything Your American History Textbook Got Wrong*, New Press.

Londoño, E. and J. Hamdard (2011) 'Afghan militants dressed as women to smuggle weapons for Kabul attack,' *Washington Post*, 14 September, www. washingtonpost.com/world/asia-pacific/suicide-bombers-gunmen-launch-coordinated-attack-in-kabul/2011/09/13/gIQAsHu1OK_story.html.

Lowther, W. (2001) 'Fight for your rights, Laura Bush ...' *Mail on Sunday*, 18 November, p. 10.

— (2003) 'Weapons hunt breakthrough as Chemical Sally is seized,' *Daily Mail* (London), 6 May, www.highbeam.com/doc/1G1-101282755.html.

Lutz, C. and J. Collins (1993) *Reading National Geographic*, Chicago, IL: University of Chicago Press.

Mackey, S. (2002) *The Reckoning: Iraq and the Legacy of Saddam Hussein*, New York: Norton.

Mahmood, A. (2009) 'Prisoner 650 was indeed Dr. Aafia,' *The Nation* (Pakistan), 2 April, www.nation.com.pk/pakistan-news-newspaper-daily-english-online/Politics/02-Apr-2009/Prisoner-650-was-indeed-Dr-Aafia.

Mahmood, S. and C. Hirschkind (2002) 'Feminism, the Taliban and the politics of counter-insurgency,' *Anthropological Quarterly*, 75(2): 339–54.

Mamdani, M. (2005) *Good Muslim, Bad Muslim: America, the Cold War, and the Roots of Terror*, New York: Pantheon Books.

Mansour, E. (2009) 'Fundamental injustice,' *Edinburgh Journal*, 16, www.journal-online.co.uk/article/5258-fundamental-injustice.

Marks, P. (2001) 'Adept in politics and advertising, 4 women shape a campaign,' *New York Times*, 11 November, www.nytimes.com/2001/11/11/us/nation-challenged-gatekeepers-adept-politics-advertising-4-women-shape-campaign.html.

Masood, S. (2012) 'Pakistan court orders deportation of Bin Laden's wives,' *New York Times*, www.nytimes.com/2012/04/03/world/asia/pakistan-court-orders-deportation-of-bin-ladens-wives.html.

McCarthy, R. (2001) 'Burkas stay on as women of Kabul wait for their liberation: rout of Taliban fails to improve the female lot,' *Guardian*, 28 November, p. 5.

McCarthy, R. and B. Julian (2003) 'Americans arrest wife, daughter of Saddam deputy,' *Guardian*, 27 November, www.guardian.co.uk/world/2003/nov/27/iraq.rorymccarthy?INTCMP=SRCH.

McCartney, R. (2010) 'Women have equal opportunity to serve in military – and to sacrifice their lives,' *Washington Post*, 30 May, www.washingtonpost.com/wpdyn/content/article/2010/05/29/AR2010052903618.html.

McChesney, R. (2008) *The Political Economy of Media: Enduring Issue, Emerging Dilemmas*, New York: Monthly Review Press.

McElroy, W. (2003) 'Iraq war may kill feminism as we know it,' Fox News, www.foxnews.com/story/0,2933,81318,00.html.

McKelvey, T. (2005) 'Unusual suspects: what happened to the women held at Abu Ghraib? The government isn't talking, but some women are,' *American Prospect*, 14 January.

McLarney, E. (2009) 'The burqa in vogue: fashioning Afghanistan,' *Journal of Middle East Women's Studies*, 5(1): 1–23.

McNamara, M. (2009) 'Iraqi refugees turn to prostitution,' CBS Evening News, 11 February, www.cbsnews.com/2100-18563_162-2445663.html.

McNutt, K. (2005) 'Sexualized violence against Iraqi women by US occupying forces: a briefing paper of International Educational Development,' Presented to the United Nations Commission on Human rights, 2005 Session, Geneva, Switzerland.

Medica Mondiale (2010) 'We were full of hope for a better future,' Position Paper, www.medicamondiale.org/fileadmin/content/07_Infothek/Positionspapiere/Position_paper_Afghanistan_-_medica_mondiale_-_English_-_J-205.pdf.

Miller, D. (2004a) *Tell Me Lies: Propaganda and Media Distortion in the Attack on Iraq*, London: Pluto Press.

— (2004b) 'The propaganda machine,' in D. Miller, *Tell Me Lies: Propaganda and Media Distortion in the Attack on Iraq*, London: Pluto Press.

Miller, L., J. Stauber and S. Rampton (2004) 'War is sell,' in D. Miller, *Tell Me Lies: Propaganda and Media Distortion in the Attack on Iraq*, London: Pluto Press.

Minhas, S. (2010) 'Search for Dr. Aafia's daughter yields startling results,' *Daily Times*, 3 March, www.dailytimes.com.pk/default.

asp?p.=2010%5C03%5C03%5Cstory_3-3-2010_pg1_9.

Mohanty, C. (1991) 'Cartographies of struggle: Third World Women and the politics of feminism,' in C. Mohanty, A. Russo and L. Torres (eds), *Third World Women and the Politics of Feminism*, Bloomington: University of Indiana Press.

Myers, S. (2009a) 'A peril in war zones: sexual abuse by fellow GI's,' *New York Times*, 27 December, p. A1.

— (2009b) 'Iraq arrests woman tied to bombings,' *New York Times*, 4 February, p. A12.

Naaman, D. (2007) 'Brides of Palestine/angels of death: media, gender and performance in the case of the Palestinian female suicide bombers,' *Signs: A Journal of Women in Culture and Society*, 32: 933–45.

Nairn, A. (2010) 'Obama has kept the machine set on kill,' *Democracy Now!*, 6 January, www.democracynow.org/2010/1/6/obama_has_kept_the_machine_set.

Nasrawi, S. (2003) 'Ammash Was foe's daughter before becoming Saddam's velvet glove,' Associated Press Worldstream, 5 May, www.highbeam.com/doc/1P1-73715107.html.

Nawa, F. (2002) 'U.S. grown feminist's pace of reform riles Afghan women,' *Christian Science Monitor*, 31 July, p. 7.

Nicholson, B. (2011) 'Fog of war becomes murkier,' *The Australian*, 20 July, www.theaustralian.com.au/national-affairs/defence/fog-of-war-becomes-murkier/story-e6frg8yo-1226097837074.

Nordberg, J. (2010) 'Where boys are prized girls live the part,' *New York Times*, 21 September, p. A1.

Nordland, R. (2010a) 'Portrait of pain ignites debate over Afghan war,' *New York Times*, 5 August, p. A6.

— (2010b) 'Working to help a haven for Afghan women blossom,' *New York Times*, 21 June, p. A4.

— (2011) 'For soldiers, death sees no gender lines,' *New York Times*, 22 June, p. A4.

Obaid-Chinoy, S. (2007a) 'Afghanistan: lifting the veil,' CNN, 15 September, transcripts.cnn.com/TRANSCRIPTS/0709/15/siu.02.html.

— (2007b) 'Forgotten women turn Kabul into widow's capital,' *Independent on Sunday*, 17 May, www.independent.co.uk/news/world/asia/forgotten-women-turn-kabul-into-widows-capital-449137.html.

Osborn, K. (2003) '"Dr. Germ" being held by US forces,' CNN.com, 13 May, www.cnn.com/2003/US/05/13/hln.terror.dr.germ.

Oskin, B. (2002) 'Taliban's fall brings closure to Mavis Leno,' *Pasadena Star News*, 25 February, news.google.com/newspapers?nid=1907&dat=20020228&id=tjhHAAAAIBAJ&sjid=0_0MAAAAIBAJ&pg=4492,3678972.

Our Foreign Staff (2011) 'Osama bin Laden was a user of herbal Viagra,' *Daily Telegraph*, 9 May, www.telegraph.co.uk/news/worldnews/al-qaeda/8502363/Osama-bin-Laden-was-a-user-of-herbal-viagra.html.

Page, C. (1996) *U.S. Official Propaganda during the Vietnam War 1965–1973: The Limits of Persuasion*, London: Leicester University Press.

Parenti, C. (2006) 'Taliban rising,' *The Nation*, 30 October, pp. 11–16.

Partlow, J. (2011) 'Afghan widows form community on Kabul Hill,' *Washington Post*, 14 August, www.washingtonpost.com/world/asia-pacific/afghan-widows-form-community-onkabulhill/2011/08/02/gIQA35KtFJ_story.html.

Peltz, J. (2010) 'On *Time* cover, Afghan woman symbolizes war stakes,' AP, 4 August, thegreatone22.wordpress.com/2010/08/04/on-time-cover-afghan-woman-symbolizes-war-stakes/.

Phalnikar, S. (2010) 'Report says Afghan women can help sell war to Europeans,' *Deutsche Welle*, 27 March, www.dw-world.de/dw/article/0,,5404617,00.html.

Pharr, S. (1988) *Homophobia: A Weapon of Sexism*, Women's Project.

Pipes, D. (2006) 'Niqabs and burqas as security threats,' Lion's Den Daniel Pipes blog, 4 November, updated July 2011, www.danielpipes.org/blog/2006/11/niqabs-and-burqas-as-security-threats.

Pisik, B. (2001) 'First Lady presses Afghan women's rights,' *Washington Times*, 20 November, p. A9.

Prince, S. (1993) 'Celluloid heroes and smart bombs: Hollywood at war in the Middle East,' in Robert E. Denton (ed.), *The Media and the Persian Gulf War*, Westport, CT: Praeger Press.

Puar, J. (2007) *Terrorist Assemblages: Homonationalism in Queer Times*, Duke University Press.

Puar, J. and A. Rai (2002) 'Monster terrorist fag: the war on terrorism and the production of docile patriots,' *Social Text*, 20(3): 117–48.

Qobil, R. (2010) 'The sexually abused dancing boys of Afghanistan,' BBC News, 7 September, www.bbc.co.uk/news/world-south-asia-11217772.

Rado, D. (2010) 'At SMU Institute, Bushes put attention on

Afghan women's plight,' *Dallas Morning News*, 20 March, www.dallasnews.com/news/education/headlines/20100320-At-SMU-institute-Bushes-put-3717.ece.

Raghavan, S. (2003) 'Troops detain wife of No. 2 Most Wanted,' *Montreal Gazette*, 27 November, p. A25.

— (2008) 'Female suicide bombers are latest war tactic,' *Washington Post*, 17 September, p. A01.

Ramdas, K. (2010) 'Violence against women is no rationale for military violence,' *Huffington Post*, 5 August, www.huffingtonpost.com/kavita-n-ramdas/violence-against-women-is_b_672387.html.

Rather, D. (2009) 'Afghanistan's veil of oppression,' CBS News, 11 February, www.cbsnews.com/stories/2000/10/23/eveningnews/main243429.shtml.

Ravitz, J. (2012) 'Saving Aesha,' CNN.com, edition.cnn.com/interactive/2012/05/world/saving.aesha/?hpt=hp_c1.

Raymond, B. (2001) 'What drives the terrorist willing to die for a cause?' *The Express*, 15 September, p. 27.

Razack, S. (2008) *Casting Out: The Eviction of Muslims from Western Law and Politics*, Toronto: University of Toronto Press.

Reid, R. (2009) 'We have the promises of the world,' *Human Rights Watch Report on Women in Afghanistan*, www.hrw.org/node/86805/section/3.

Rennie, D. (2003) 'Saddam's daughters given royal asylum in Jordan,' *Daily Telegraph*, 1 August, p. 16.

Reuters (2011) 'Lifting the veil in Afghanistan,' in.reuters.com/news/pictures/slideshow?articleId=INRTR2NNVW#a=14.

Riley, R. (2006) 'Valiant, vicious, or virtuous? Representation and the problem of women warriors,' in R. Riley and N. Inayatullah, *Interrogating Imperialism: Conversations on Gender, Race, and War*, New York: Palgrave Macmillan, pp. 183–206.

— (2008) 'Women and war: militarism, bodies, and the practice of gender,' *Sociology Compass*, 4 February, pp. 1192–1208.

— (2010) 'Hidden soldiers: working for the "national defense,"' in M. Hohn and S. Moon (eds), *Over There: Living with the U.S. Military Empire from World War Two to the Present*, Durham, NC: Duke University Press.

Roberts, B. (2001) 'War on terror: "women must get key role,"' *Daily Mirror*, 14 November, p. 10.

— (2003) 'Gulf War 2 deck of death,' *Daily Mirror*, 29 March, www.the freelibrary.com/GULF+WAR+2:+DECK+OF+DEATH;+Cards+show+wanted+tyrants.-a09994 0118'>GULF WAR 2: DECK OF DEATH.

Robertson, N. (2010) 'Burn victims find help amid Afghan misery: female self-immolation cases had doubled in past year,' CNN, 24 November, articles.cnn.com/2010-11-24/world/afghanistan.immolation_1_afghan-refugees-burns-victims-herat?_s=PM: WORLD.

Rose, D. (2003) 'Doctor Germ,' *Evening Standard*, 29 January.

Rosen, N. (2010) *Aftermath Following the Bloodshed of America's Wars in the Muslim World*, New York: Nation Books.

Ross, B. (2011) 'The young wife who defended Osama bin Laden,' *ABC World News with Diane Sawyer*, abcnews.go.com/Blotter/young-wife-defended-osama-bin-laden-

navy-seals/story?id=13525087#.
T8TvIa7j3eY.

— (2012) 'Osama Bin Laden: keeping up with the Kardashians?' ABC News, 30 March, abcnews. go.com/Blotter/osama-bin-laden-keeping-kardashians/story? id=16041453#.T6T7jK5q_PY.

Ross, B., A. Patel and D. Adib (2011) 'Osama bin Laden's matchmaker: the real housewives of Abbottabad,' ABC News, 10 May, abcnews.go.com/Blotter/osama-bin-laden-matchmaker-real-housewives-abbottabad/story?id=13564832#.T8Tvfq7j3eY.

Roy, A. (2004) 'The new American century,' The Nation, 9 February, www.thenation.com/article/new-american-century.

Rubin, A. (2004) 'Fighting for their future,' Los Angeles Times.

— (2009) 'How Baida wanted to die,' New York Times, 16 August, p. MM38.

— (2010a) 'Why did you burn yourself?' New York Times blog, 8 November, atwar.blogs.nytimes. com/2010/11/08/why-did-you-burn-yourself/?ref=asia.

— (2010b) 'For Afghan wives, a desperate, fiery way out,' New York Times, 8 November, p. A1.

— (2011a) 'Afghan proposal would clamp down on women's shelters,' New York Times, 11 February, p. A1.

— (2011b) 'Photos stoke tension over Afghan civilian deaths,' New York Times, 21 March, www. nytimes.com/2011/03/22/world/asia/22afghanistan.html.

— (2011c) 'Growing violence clouds Afghanistan's future,' Fresh Air, 8 September.

— (2011d) 'My first Afghan burqa,' New York Times, 5 May, atwar. blogs.nytimes.com/2011/05/05/my-first-afghan-burqa/.

Rubin, E. (2005) 'Women's work,' New York Times Magazine, 25 January, Section 6, p. 53.

Russo, A. (2006) 'The Feminist Majority Foundation's campaign to stop gender apartheid,' International Feminist Journal of Politics, 8: 557–80.

Said, E. (1979) Orientalism, New York: Vintage Books.

— (1981) Covering Islam: How the Media and the Experts Determine How We See the Rest of the World, New York: Vintage Books.

Saletan, W. (2011) 'Is bin Laden's porn more damning than his terrorism?' Slate.com, 17 May, www. msnbc.msn.com/id/43065572/ns/slate_com/t/bin-ladens-porn-more-damning-his-terrorism/#. UC1acK7j3PY.

Salome, L. (2002) 'Springtime may liberate some Afghan women from their burqas,' Cox News Service, 19 March.

Sandler, L. (2003a) 'Women under siege,' The Nation, 29 December.

— (2003b) 'Iraq's women: occupied territory,' Amnesty Now, 29(4).

Sara, S. (2011) 'Female soldiers could civilize Afghan men,' Australian Broadcast News, 13 April, www. abc.net.au/news/2011-04-13/female-soldiers-could-civilise-afghan-men/2616680.

Sasson, J., O. bin Laden and N. bin Laden (2009) Growing Up bin Laden: Osama's Wife and Son Take Us Inside Their Secret World, New York: St Martin's Press.

Savage, C. (2010) 'Case of accused soldiers may be worst of 2 wars,' New York Times, 3 October, www.nytimes.com/2010/10/04/us/04soldiers.html.

Sawyer, D. (2003) 'Dr. Germ: interview with Dr. Rihab Taha, female bio-weapons scientist for

Iraq,' ABC News, 10 February, www.politicsandthelifesciences.org/Biosecurity_course_folder/readings/drgerm.pdf.

Schmitt, E. (2004) 'Rapes reported by servicewomen in the Persian Gulf and elsewhere,' *New York Times*, 26 February, p. 1.

— (2008) 'Pakistani suspected of Qaeda ties is held,' *New York Times*, www.nytimes.com/2008/08/05/world/asia/05detain.html.

Schwellenbach, N. and C. Leonnig (2010) 'U.S. policy a paper tiger against sex trade in war zones,' *Washington Post*, 18 July, www.washingtonpost.com/wp-dyn/content/article/2010/07/17/AR2010071701401.html?sid=ST2010071802771.

Scott, J. W. (2007) *The Politics of the Veil*, Princeton, NJ: Princeton University Press.

Scroggins, D. (2012) *Wanted Women. Faith, Lies and the War on Terror: The Lives of Ayaan Hirsi Ali and Aafia Siddiqui*, New York: HarperCollins.

Sengupta, K. (2007) 'What happened to the Husseins? Death of a dynasty,' *Independent* (London), 21 August, p. 24.

— (2009) 'The burqa-clad bombers who terrorise Afghanistan,' *Independent on Sunday*, 22 July, www.independent.co.uk/news/world/asia/the-burqaclad-bombers-who-terrorise-afghanistan-1755887.html.

Seper, J. (2003) 'US forces detain "Mrs. Anthrax": scientist specialized in germ warfare,' *Washington Times*, 6 May, www.highbeam.com/doc/1G1-101263260.html.

Settle, M. (2001) 'First Ladies head campaign to free Afghan women,' *The Herald* (Glasgow), 17 November, p. 8.

Shah, S. (2012) 'Investigator tells of Osama Bin Laden household rift as wives face charges,' *Guardian*, 8 March, www.guardian.co.uk/world/2012/mar/08/osama-bin-laden-household-rift?INTCMP=SRCH.

Shaheen, J. (2008) *Guilty: Hollywood's Verdict on Arabs after 9/11*, Northanpton, MA: Olive Branch Press.

Shane, S. (2011) 'Pornography is found in Bin Laden compound files, U.S. officials say,' *New York Times*, 14 May, p. A7.

Sharma, G. (2003) 'Afghan women fear fallout of Iraq war,' *oneWorld.net*, www.commondreams.org/headlines03/0403-02.htm.

Sherwell, P. (2004) 'Saddam's eldest daughter is making the most of her life in exile,' *Sunday Telegraph* (London), 6 June, p. 28.

Sherwood, S. (2011) '36 hours in Abu Dhabi,' *New York Times*, 10 April, p. TR11.

Shimizu, C. (2007) *The Hypersexuality of Race: Performing Asian American Women on Screen and Scene*, Durham, NC: Duke University Press.

Sidner, S. and M. Moshaberat (2012) 'Saving face: the struggle and survival of Afghan women,' MSNBC, 18 May, www.cnn.com/2012/05/18/world/asia/afghanistan-domestic-violence/?hpt=wo_t2.

Simonovic, I. (2011) 'Afghan women are still at risk,' *Guardian*, 27 March, www.guardian.co.uk/commentisfree/2011/mar/27/afghan-women-rights-afghanistan-peace.

Sisk, R. (2004) 'Vow to Iraq women U.S. would veto any move to limit their rights,' *Daily News*, 17 February, p. 20.

Skoch, I. (2012) 'Slut and traitor. Otherwise known as Osama's widows,' *Global Post.com*, 20

March, www.globalpost.com/ dispatches/globalpost-blogs/ wanderlust/osama-bin-laden-sluts-wives.

Smith A. (2005) *Conquest: Sexual Violence and American Indian Genocide*, Boston, MA: South End Press.

— (2012) 'Did the U.S. leave behind a civil war in Iraq?' *Socialist Worker*, 17 January, socialistworker. org/2012/01/17/civil-war-the-us-left-behind.

Smith, G. (2012) 'Osama's feuding wives: how widows of Bin Laden were pulled apart by troops after fight over deadly "betrayal" of Al-Qaeda leader,' *Mail Online*, 16 March.

Smith-Spark, L. (2011) 'Silent victims: Iraqi women trafficked for sex', CNN, 10 November, www.cnn. com/2011/11/09/world/meast/iraq-freedom-project.

Somerville, Q. (2010) 'Risky climate for women candidates in Afghan election,' BBC online, 16 September, www.bbc.co.uk/news/ world-south-asia-11334475.

Soquel, D. (2010) 'Iraqi refugee urged to trade sex for food, cash,' *Women's Enews*, womensenews. org/story/war/101116/iraqi-refugee-urged- trade-sex-food-cash.

Spivak, G. (1988) 'Can the subaltern speak?' in C. Nelson and L. Grossberg (eds), *Marxism and Interpretation of Culture*, Chicago: University of Illinois Press, pp. 271–313.

Stabile, C. and D. Kumar (2005) 'Unveiling imperialism: media, gender, and the war on Afghanistan,' *Media, Culture and Society*, 27(5): 765–82.

Starkey, J. (2010) 'The woman running for her life,' *The Times*, 18 September, p. 41.

Steele, J. (2005) 'Alawi trails in third place in poll update,' *Guardian*, 19 December, www.guardian. co.uk/world/2005/dec/20/iraq. jonathansteele?INTCMP=SRCH.

Storey, J. (2006) *Cultural Theory and Popular Culture*, University of Georgia Press.

Stout, D. (2001) 'Mrs. Bush cites women's plight under the Taliban,' *New York Times*, 18 November, Section 1B, p. 4.

Suncer, M. (2004) 'The new Afghanistan constitution: will it respect women's rights?' *FindLaw's Writ*, 15 January, writ.findlaw.com/ commentary/20040116_sunder. html.

Swanson, S. (2003) 'Iraq's Mrs. Anthrax is key figure in weapons program,' *Chicago Tribune*, 11 April, articles.chicago tribune.com/2003-04-11/news/ 0304110247_1_biological-weapons-mrs-anthrax-baath-party.

Tavernise, S. (2008) 'Fear keeps Iraqis out of their Baghdad homes,' *New York Times*, 24 August, p. A1.

Tavernise, S., Q. Mizher and K. AlAnsary (2005) 'Rising civilian toll is the Iraq war's silent, sinister pulse,' *New York Times*, 26 October, www.nytimes. com/2005/10/26/international/ middleeast/26civilians. html?_r=1&p.wanted.

Tayler, L. (2004) 'Rights movement taking flight,' *Newsday*, 27 February, p. A28.

Temple-Raston, D. (2008) 'Pakistani woman's arrest prompts questions,' National Public Radio, 14 August.

Thobani, S. (2007) 'White wars: Western feminisms and the war on terror,' *Feminist Theory*, London: Sage, pp. 169–85.

Tibbetts, K. (2012) 'SMU faculty members mentor first Women's Initiative Fellows,' 22 May, blog. smu.edu/forum/2012/05/22/smu-faculty-mentor-first-class-of-womens-initiative-fellows/.

Todd, B. and T. Lister (2011) 'Bin laden's wives – and daughter who would "kill enemies of Islam,"' CNN, 5 May, articles.cnn.com/2011-05-05/world/osama.many.wives_1_qaeda-s-leader-bin-laden-abu-jandal?_s=PM:WORLD.

Topping, A. (2011) 'Australian military lets women into frontline roles,' *Guardian*, 27 September, www.guardian.co.uk/world/2011/sep/27/australian-military-women-frontline-roles.

Toronto Star (2006) 'How military is keeping numbers up,' *Toronto Star*, 29 September, p. A12.

Turse, N. (2010) 'Is this what success looks like in Afghanistan?' CBS News, 13 September, www.cbsnews.com/stories/2010/09/12/opinion/main6860126.shtml.

UNAMA (2009) 'Silence is violence. End the abuse of women in Afghanistan,' 8 July, unama.unmissions.org/Portals/UNAMA/vaw-english.pdf.

United States Attorney's Office Southern District of New York (2010) 'Aafia Siddiqui sentenced in Manhattan federal court to 86 years for attempting to murder U.S. nationals in Afghanistan and six additional crimes,' 23 September, www.fbi.gov/newyork/press-releases/2010/nyfo092310.htm.

UPI (United Press International) (2008) 'Activist charged with being al Qaida,' 12 August, www.upi.com/Top_News/2008/08/12/Activist-charged-with-being-with-al-Qaida/UPI-42871218568354/.

Valdmanis, T. (2001) 'Women hope rights will be unveiled,' *USA Today*, 27 November, p. 10A.

Vanden Heuvel, K. (2009) 'Helping Afghan women and girls,' *The Nation* blog, 2 February, www.thenation.com/blog/helping-afghan-women-and-girls.

Vidal, J. (2010) 'A planet at war with itself,' *Guardian*, 14 September, www.guardian.co.uk/global-development/2010/sep/14/mdg7-afghanistan-health-environment.

VOA News (2011) 'Afghan, NATO forces capture militant dressed as woman,' www.voanews.com/english/asia/Afghan-NATO-Forces-Capture-Militant-Dressed-as-Woman-12651084.html.

Von Mittlestaedt, J. (2008) 'The most dangerous woman in the world,' *Der Spiegel*, 27 November, www.spiegel.de/international/world/america-s-most-wanted-the-most-dangerous-woman-in-the-world-a-593195.html.

Wallace, K. (2001) 'White House to highlight Taliban treatment of women,' CNN.com, 16 November, www.cnn.com/2001/US/11/15/ret.wh.taliban.women/index.html.

Walsh, D. (2009) 'The mystery of Dr. Aafia Siddiqui,' *Guardian*, 23 November, G2, p. 6.

Walter, N. (2002) 'How we forgot about the women of Afghanistan,' *Independent*, 19 December, www.commondreams.org/views02/1219-02.htm.

Ward, L. (2001) 'Beyond the burqa: Cherie joins campaign for Afghan women,' *Guardian*, 20 November, p. 4.

Watt, N. (2003) 'Raid on laboratory of Dr. Germ fails to turn up the smoking gun,' *Guardian*, 17 April, p. 4.

Whitlock, C. (2010) 'Members

of Stryker Combat Brigade in Afghanistan accused of killing civilians for sport,' *Washington Post*, 18 September, www. washington post.com/ wp-dyn/content/article/2010/ 09/18/AR2010091803935. html?sid=ST2010091803942.

Whitlock, C. and G. Jaffe (2012) 'Panetta decries Afghan video,' *Washington Post*, 13 January, p. A01.

Whitworth, D. and P. Webster (2001) 'Laura Bush campaigns for rights of Afghan women ...' *Vancouver Sun*, 17 November, p. A8.

Williams, E. (2011) 'The ghosts of Baghdad: one British woman and the agonizing search for the missing millions in Iraq,' *Mail Online*, 6 July, www.dailymail.co.uk/home/ moslive/article-2009451/Iraq-The-British-woman-agonising-search-missing-millions-html.

Williams, J. (2001) 'Mavis Leno speaks up for Afghan women,' *USA Today*, 27 September, p. 2D.

Williams, T. (2010) 'Wanted: jihadists to marry widows,' *New York Times*, 9 July.

Winter, J. (2008) 'MIT grad with links to Al Qaeda plotted to kill former U.S. presidents, authorities say,' Fox News, 14 August, www.foxnews.com/ story/0,2933,404164,00.html.

Woodcock, A. (2001) 'Cherie Blair backs Afghan women,' *Western Mail*, 20 November, p. 5.

Woodsome, K. (2010) 'Plight of maimed Afghan woman stirs war debate,' Voice of America, 12 August, www.voanews.com/ content/plight-of-maimed-afghan-women-stirs-war-debate-100621714/123766.html.

Yasin, S. (2011) 'Bin Laden's wife and the stereotyping of Muslim women,' *Guardian*, 13 May, www. guardian.co.uk/commentisfree/ 2011/may/13/bin-laden-wife-muslim-women?INTCMP=SRCH.

Yegenoglu, M. (1998) *Colonial Fantasies: Towards a Feminist Reading of Orientalism*, New York: Cambridge University Press.

Zakaria, T. (2005) 'Laura Bush in Afghanistan to back women's education,' *Washington Post.com*, 30 March.

Zeiger, D. (2008) 'That (Afghan) girl! Ideology unveiled in *National Geographic*,' in J. Heath (ed.), *The Veil: Women Writers on Its History, Lore and Politics*, Berkeley: University of California Press.

Zogby, J. (2012) 'Beyond Bachmann: a challenge for the GOP,' *Huffington Post*, 21 July, www.huffingtonpost. com/james-zogby/beyond-bachmann-a-challen_1_b_1691689. html.

Zoroya, G. (2004) 'In Afghanistan, a historic moment; pride, jitters as people prepare for first vote,' *USA Today*, 7 October, p. 1A.

Zucchino, D. (2012) 'U.S. troops posed with body parts of Afghan bombers,' *Los Angeles Times*, 18 April, p. A1.

Index